USING COLLECTIVE IMPACT TO BRING COMMUNITY CHANGE

Collective Impact as a tool to bring about community change has seen remarkable growth in usage since 2011. Collective Impact has been used successfully with a variety of local issues and has raised the consciousness of how community groups interact as well as the approaches that can lead to long-term innovations.

This edited volume sets forth conceptual foundations for using Collective Impact as well as sharing basic approaches that have succeeded in projects under diverse circumstances. It will be useful for both academics and practitioners as Collective Impact continues to undergo substantial changes in focus and direction. Building on Kania and Kramer's influential work, it provides readers with detailed insights not only into how the Collective Impact system works but also innovative applications to issues facing community developers. The diverse topics shared by the contributing authors make this volume especially important for practitioners designing programs to bring about long-term changes in their communities.

Including discussion about how Collective Impact has succeeded in different governmental settings, this book demonstrates how Collective Impact has been modified to accommodate the associated cultural differences with 10 chapters written by experienced on-the-ground community development experts.

Norman Walzer, PhD, is Senior Research Scholar in the Center for Governmental Studies at Northern Illinois University, DeKalb, Illinois. He co-edited a previous research volume on Collective Impact and community development issues. He also has actively researched local economic development issues including community supported enterprises as well as the impact of governmental structure on local public finance.

Liz Weaver, BA, MM, is Co-CEO with Tamarack Institute. Liz provides strategic direction to the organization and leads many of its key learning activities including capacity building services for the Ontario Trillium Foundation. She is a nonprofit organizational professional with experience in leading cross-sector, place-based collaborations on poverty at local and national levels.

The Community Development Research and Practice Series
Volume 9

As the series continues to grow, it is our intent to continue to serve scholars, community developers, planners, public administrators, and others involved in research, practice, and policymaking in the realm of community development. The series strives to provide both timely and applied information for researchers, students, and practitioners. Building on a long history since 1970 of publishing the Community Development Society's journal, *Community Development* (www.comm-dev.org), the book series contributes to a growing and rapidly changing knowledge base as a resource for practitioners and researchers alike. For additional information please see the series page at http://www.routledge.com/books/series/CDRP/.

The Community Development Society, a nonprofit association of those interested in pushing the discipline forward, is delighted to offer this book series in partnership with Routledge. The series is designed to integrate innovative thinking on tools, strategies, and experiences as a resource especially well-suited for bridging the gaps between theory, research, and practice. The Community Development Society actively promotes continued advancement of the discipline and practice. Fundamental to this mission is adherence to its core Principles of Good Practice.

We invite you to explore the series, and continue to do so as new volumes are added. We hope you will find it a valuable resource for supporting community development research and practice.

USING COLLECTIVE IMPACT TO BRING COMMUNITY CHANGE

Edited by
Norman Walzer and Liz Weaver

Routledge
Taylor & Francis Group

NEW YORK AND LONDON

First published 2019
by Routledge
711 Third Avenue, New York, NY 10017

and by Routledge
2 Park Square, Milton Park, Abingdon, Oxon, OX14 4RN

Routledge is an imprint of the Taylor & Francis Group, an informa business

© 2019 Taylor & Francis

Library of Congress Cataloging-in-Publication Data
Names: Walzer, Norman, editor. | Weaver, Liz (Nonprofit organizational
professional), editor.
Title: Using collective impact to bring community change / edited by
Norman Walzer and Liz Weaver.
Description: New York, NY: Routledge, 2018. | Series: The community
development research and practice series ; Volume 9 | Includes
bibliographical references and index.
Identifiers: LCCN 2018006551 (print) | LCCN 2018007756 (ebook) |
ISBN 9781315545073 (ebook) | ISBN 9781138682559 (hardback : alk. paper) |
ISBN 9781138682573 (pbk. : alk. paper)
Subjects: LCSH: Community development. | Community organization.
Classification: LCC HN49.C6 (ebook) | LCC HN49.C6 U5745 2018 (print) |
DDC 307.1/4—dc23
LC record available at https://lccn.loc.gov/2018006551

ISBN: 978-1-138-68255-9 (hbk)
ISBN: 978-1-138-68257-3 (pbk)
ISBN: 978-1-315-54507-3 (ebk)

Typeset in Bembo and Stone Sans
by Florence Production Ltd, Stoodleigh, Devon, UK

To Nicholas Walzer and Jacob Weaver

So that they will have better insights and tools to help
bring about positive community changes in the future

CONTENTS

Notes on Contributors   *ix*
Acknowledgments   *xiii*

1   Changing Roles and Practices in Collective Impact Usage   1
    Norman Walzer and Liz Weaver

2   Theoretical Foundations for CI Applications   17
    Craig Bradbrook

3   Network Agreements: Co-Designing Principles that
    Influence Network Culture   41
    Dustin C. Stiver

4   The Intangibles: What It Takes for a Backbone Organization
    to Succeed   56
    Rebecca Gillam and Jacqueline Counts

5   Using Systems Tools to Advance Collective Impact   78
    Kathryn Lawler, Glenn Landers, Karen Minyard, Kristi Fuller,
    and Jane Branscomb

6   Collective Impact 3.0: Extending the Collective Impact
    Vision for Community Change   97
    Liz Weaver and Mark Cabaj

7   Using Collective Impact to Move the Needle on Poverty
Reduction   116
Karen Schwartz, Liz Weaver, Natasha Pei, and Aaron Kozak

8   healthTIDE: Utilizing Aspects of Collective Impact and
Other Models of Coordinated Action to Drive Statewide
Obesity Prevention in Wisconsin   137
*Amy Korth and Amy Meinen (contributing authors Amy Hilgendorf,
Catherine Breuer, and Brian Christens)*

9   When Cultural Differences Make a Difference: The Case
of Community Change in an Arab Community in Israel   156
Smadar Somekh, Yehonatan Almog, and Fida Nijim-Ektelat

10   Progress, Challenges, and Next Steps in Collective Impact:
Collective Impact as Disruptive Illumination   175
Tom Klaus and Liz Weaver

Index   *195*

NOTES ON CONTRIBUTORS

Yehonatan Almog, MA in Public Policy from Hebrew University of Jerusalem, is the Director of System-wide Impact & Measurement Division at the Myers-JDC-Brookdale Institute. Yehonatan promotes measurement and evaluation at the inter-organizational level, through efforts of shared measurement and evaluation Collective Impact initiatives. In addition, he is involved in developing the measurement and evaluation capacities of various NGOs and Government units.

Craig Bradbrook, MPA, has more than 15 years' experience working in multi-disciplinary collaborations and establishing evaluation frameworks. He is involved in a large-scale mixed methods research project investigating what drives and obstructs collaborations. Additional interests and future research projects will focus on Social Impact Bonds.

Jane Branscomb, MPH, is a senior research associate at the Georgia Health Policy Center. She is actively involved in policy analysis and evaluation in projects related to health promotion, public health planning and health system transformation. She has a particular interest in high-leverage opportunities to advance health equity and remove barriers to health. Jane leads the center's systems thinking efforts.

Catherine Breuer, MS, is the evaluation coordinator for the Wisconsin Obesity Prevention Initiative (OPI) within the University of Wisconsin-Madison, Population Health Institute. Catherine's role is to develop and implement strategic evaluations of internal and external OPI activities using qualitative, quantitative, and mixed-method approaches to assess process, impacts, and outcomes.

Mark Cabaj, BA, MA, is president of From Here to There, a consulting company, and is an Associate of Tamarack—An Institute for Community Engagement. His current focus is on developing practical ways to understand, plan, and evaluate efforts to address complex issues (e.g. neighborhood renewal, poverty, and homelessness, community safety, education achievement, and health).

Brian Christens, PhD, is associate professor of Human and Organizational Development at Vanderbilt University. He is also a co-investigator on the Wisconsin Obesity Prevention Initiative housed at the University of Wisconsin-Madison.

Jacqueline Counts, MSW, PhD, is the Director of the University of Kansas Center for Public Partnerships & Research. Dr. Counts has been the principal investigator on numerous early childhood, systems-building, accountability and evaluation projects.

Kristi Fuller, MSW, is a senior research associate at the Georgia Health Policy Center at Georgia State University. Her areas of expertise are in aging and disability policy, long-term services and supports, and the health workforce. She also provides leadership in meeting design and facilitation for ARCHI.

Rebecca Gillam, MSW, PhD, is an Associate Director with the University of Kansas Center for Public Partnerships & Research. She has facilitated and evaluated interagency collaboration at both the state and local levels, primarily in the area of early childhood.

Amy Hilgendorf, PhD, is the associate director for engaged research of the Center for Community and Nonprofit Studies at the University of Wisconsin-Madison. Dr. Hilgendorf leads and supports research and program evaluation partnerships with community groups to advance social justice and equity.

Tom Klaus, PhD, is a nonprofit organizational consultant with diverse experience in cross-sector collaboration on social and community change issues. He is principal at Tom Klaus & Associates and an adjunct professor at Eastern University (Philadelphia) in the College of Business and Leadership.

Amy Korth, MS, RDN, is director of healthTIDE staff, housed at the University of Wisconsin–Madison, School of Medicine and Public Health. She is a dietitian with ten years' experience in public health, focused on healthy eating and physical activity. healthTIDE is a statewide network supporting policy, systems, and environmental changes.

Aaron Kozak, MSW, researches housing policy and community-based approaches to poverty reduction. He received his MA in English from the University of Victoria in 2014 and regularly organizes events in Ottawa's creative arts community.

Glenn Landers, ScD, is the director of health systems at the Georgia Health Policy Center and an assistant research professor in the Andrew Young School of Policy

Studies at Georgia State University. He plays a lead role in the center's approaches to evaluation, Collective Impact, and health system transformation.

Kathryn Lawler, MPP, serves as the first executive director for ARCHI. She brings experience in the development and implementation of cross-sector interventions to address complex social issues. She helped ARCHI develop its 28-year strategy focused on both immediate health conditions and the larger, upstream issues that result in poor health.

Amy Meinen, MPH, RDN, is director of healthTIDE staff, at the University of Wisconsin–Madison, School of Medicine and Public Health. She's a dietitian with formal training in public health and extensive obesity prevention experience at state and local levels. healthTIDE is a statewide network supporting policy, systems, and environmental changes.

Karen Minyard, PhD, is the chief executive officer at the Georgia Health Policy Center and a research professor with the Department of Public Management and Policy at Georgia State University. Her research interests include health and health care financing; financing and evaluation of health-related social policy programs; and strategic alignment of public and private health policy through Collective Impact.

Fida Nijim–Ektelat, BA in Philosophy and Political Science, Hebrew University of Jerusalem, is a Research Associate at the Engelberg Center for Children and Youth at the Myers-JDC-Brookdale Institute. In her research, Fida focuses on cultural adaptation of programs with an emphasis on the Arab community, early childhood, evaluation of programs for parents of children at risk, and policies for out-of-home placement.

Natasha Pei, BSW, MSW, brings online content to life and engages poverty reduction learners in Tamarack Institute's Vibrant Communities Canada. Natasha's education and experience is in social work, with community capacity building at the core of her practice. She volunteers with several community organizations around Ottawa.

Karen Schwartz, PhD, is Associate Dean (Research & International) in the Faculty of Public Affairs, Carleton University, and an associate professor. She is a co-investigator in a SSHRC Partnership Grant exploring the benefits to the community from campus engagement and has co-authored "Research For Social Justice: A Community Based Approach."

Smadar Somekh, MA in Organizational Studies and PhD student at the School of Public Policy and Government, Hebrew University of Jerusalem, is a Research Associate at the Center for Research on Employment of Disadvantaged Populations at the Myers-JDC-Brookdale Institute. In her research, Smadar focuses on Ethiopian immigrants and Comprehensive Community Initiatives, as well as on social policy directed at the expansion of opportunities for employment. Smadar is leading the evaluation research of Better Together, Israel's national comprehensive community initiative.

Dustin C. Stiver, PhD, is a Program Officer at The Sprout Fund. He earned his PhD in Nonprofit Organizational Leadership at Eastern University, and completed his MPA and BA at the University of Pittsburgh. Dr. Stiver's research interests include network leadership, nonprofit collaboration, philanthropy, and human-centered design.

Norman Walzer, PhD, is Senior Research Scholar in the Center for Governmental Studies at Northern Illinois University, DeKalb IL. He co-edited (with Liz Weaver and Catherine McGuire) a previous research volume on Collective Impact and community development issues. He also has actively researched local economic development issues including community supported enterprises as well as the impact of governmental structure on local public finance.

Liz Weaver, BA, MM, is Vice President and Director of Operations with Tamarack Institute. Liz provides strategic direction to the organization and leads many of its key learning activities including Collective Impact capacity building services for the Ontario Trillium Foundation. She is a nonprofit organizational professional with experience in leading cross-sector, place-based collaborations on poverty at local and national levels. She also consults with community organizations and collaborative leaders on Collective Impact and community change.

ACKNOWLEDGMENTS

Many public officials and other groups, including funding agencies, have been frustrated by the lack of long-term progress in making substantive lasting changes in programs and policies that improve conditions in communities. This frustration led to searches for improved methods of working with local groups of residents trying to evaluate and enact policy alternatives. Traditional strategic planning efforts often did not generate strategies that could be implemented successfully and bring the desired outcomes.

Collective Impact has grown in stature as a community change guiding practice since "Collective Impact" was published by Kania and Kramer in *Stanford Social Innovation Review* in 2011. Based on past experiences, that article suggested a framework that seemed to enhance the long–term outcomes from strategic planning efforts. Since that time, the usage of Collective Impact has grown across the globe with substantial success. Also true is that as with any relatively new framework, it has come under scrutiny that it is top down and not necessarily inclusive of some groups. These criticisms have generated ways in which the CI practices can be modified to bring about improved outcomes.

This edited volume comes at a very opportune time with the interest in Collective Impact being so high and suggested positive modifications forthcoming. The authors of chapters in this volume represent years of experience in working with CI efforts in many settings and on a variety of community change issues. We appreciate their willingness to share their experiences and insights into the effectiveness of CI. In addition, the editors thank Kathy Siebrasse, CGS–NIU, for her work in helping to prepare the manuscript for publication. Hopefully, this volume can add substantially to the growing literature on community change models.

Norman Walzer
Liz Weaver

1

CHANGING ROLES AND PRACTICES IN COLLECTIVE IMPACT USAGE

Norman Walzer and Liz Weaver

The Collective Impact (CI) approach to working with communities on strategic planning and community change initiatives has become a major component of many local efforts since the publication of the Kania and Kramer article in 2011. Bringing about long-term changes is often difficult due to the complexity of issues involved and the vested interests of diverse groups participating in the process. Since these efforts are usually on-going for several years, there has been a tendency for the enthusiasm to dwindle over time as the initial players are replaced by others who were not involved in the initial discussions. The loss of continuity in leadership can complicate obtaining a commitment to change process.

Many techniques to organize discussions, find a vision, and implement strategies have been tried, often with disappointment in the outcomes. Because each community and issue addressed is unique, finding a common approach or system that works in all cases is difficult and frustrating to practitioners. The complexity of the issues and the lack of lasting changes have pressured community change organizations and funding agencies trying to bring about these changes, to search for systematic conditions and procedures that can be applied successfully to other areas and issues. While many specific models or approaches had been tried in diverse efforts, their ability to bring about long-term and documented change was disappointing. They did not seem to cause the principal players and agencies to continue along a path that led to desired outcomes.

Recognizing the differences between having an isolated impact versus a Collective Impact in the community has been central to many community change discussions. While bringing about change on a specific issue may be accomplished by working with a specific group or agency, bringing about systematic change that affects the entire community requires large numbers of political leaders, agencies, and residents, not all of whom have the same goals or needs. Isolated impacts affecting a specific agency or group of residents are more easily documented, especially when they agree in principle on the desired outcome.

Bringing about change in a community, however, involves motivating many distinct organizations to pursue and value different goals, change behaviors or practices, and measure outcomes in different ways. All of these can be difficult. Thus, enhancing and measuring the Collective Impact requires different tools and performance measures than involved with isolated impact. It also means motivating groups that may have had conflicting goals and strategies in the past to refocus their actions to achieve higher objectives.

These difficulties are of special concern to practitioners such as FSG Consulting and funding agencies such as the ASPEN Institute (Kubisch et al., 2010) that have worked with communities on change projects for many years (FSG). In response to this frustration, Kania and Kramer (2011) set forth a set of conditions that, based on experiences with several change processes, identified common structural components in past activities that were more likely to bring about lasting change. With these pre-conditions, communities can create an environment in which participating organizations change their strategies and goals in such a way to reach higher goals for the entire community.

Kania and Kramer identified five elements they considered important to successful change projects including common agendas, shared measurement systems, mutually-reinforcing activities, continuous communication, and a backbone support organization to keep the effort going. These general concepts seemed to enhance the outcomes and, in practice, became considered pre-conditions to success. The elements identified were not proposed as a model or specific approach but nevertheless were thought to enhance the probabilities for successful outcomes.

The pre-conditions were adopted by many agencies and groups such as Tamarack Institute in Canada and FSG in successfully working with local agencies on community change initiatives. In recent years, they have been researched and modified to suit local conditions and, thus have evolved into a framework that other change groups can implement in different scenarios and on various local issues. The diversity of the approaches and topics is shown in later chapters in this volume, which are only a small sample of the CI applications that could have been included.

The subsequent examples and discussions have several purposes. First, the growing interest in CI practices testifies to its perceived usefulness in working with community change groups. It not only has become more popular among practitioner agencies but also has gained status in the scholarly literature (Cooper, 2017; Walzer, Weaver, & McGuire, 2017). In each case, the basic CI framework or pre-conditions have been adapted to address local issues, sometimes with more success than others. However, the authors identify and explain the limitations and efforts made to adjust for them. For instance, several subsequent chapters describe innovations in working with backbone organizations, shared measurement, and other essential elements.

While the CI framework, with adaptations, has been used successfully to bring about change on many issues in diverse settings, it also has been criticized in the professional and scholarly literatures as lacking a theoretical rationale, not based on sufficient research, and promoting a top-down strategy rather than adequately incorporating the views of participants in the process (Wolff, 2016). The debate about specific approaches continues but there can be little doubt about the effectiveness of approaching a change project from a CI type of perspective.

Second, because of past experiences with Collective Impact, there is now sufficient research and practice to assess its main strengths and limitations. Based on this evidence, there have been calls by both regular CI practitioners and others regarding what adjustments would make Collective Impact more effective in its next phases. Two later chapters (Cabaj & Weaver; Klaus & Weaver) address these issues with suggestions about ways to address some recognized limitations. There is no question, however, that it has grown in use and has made a significant contribution to how local agencies pursue strategic planning on a variety of issues (Walzer, Weaver, & McGuire 2016). Likewise, past discussions have triggered a rethinking of the CI framework that will lead to a new version incorporating suggested changes as noted by Cabaj and Weaver (2016).

The diversity of topics and conditions in which the Collective Impact framework has been applied speaks to its versatility in bringing about change and for this reason its relevance to community development practitioners. This volume contains examples of ways in which scholars and practitioners have used CI applications in working with groups in different political and economic settings as well as addresses a variety of issues related to community development.

The chapters in this volume were not selected to promote or challenge the importance or usefulness of the CI framework in working with community development issues. Rather, they illustrate that the basic CI approach, with adaptations, can be effective under a variety of scenarios involving various community development issues. Likewise, the discussions in this volume are not a handbook that can be implemented anywhere. Since community change happens over many years, it is too early in some cases to know the outcomes of the CI efforts described.

Nevertheless, readers can benefit from seeing ways community groups have used the basic CI approach, adjustments made, and subsequent outcomes as they design future community change endeavors. No two situations are the same or will benefit from the same approach but past procedures and outcomes can be informative. The following chapters fit into three categories. The first five chapters involve mainly conceptual issues regarding implementation of the CI approach including the roles of backbone organizations, using a systematic analytical approach, enhancing the capacity of participating organizations, and suggestions for the next phase of Collective Impact based on experiences in the past several years.

The next set of chapters examine ways in which the CI approach has been used regarding specific issues such as poverty, statewide obesity, and cultural issues. These examples and their outcomes show not only the versatility of the CI applications but also point to the need for adaptations in how the framework is applied. The final chapter reviews previous criticisms of the CI framework with suggestions for modifications in the next steps. The discussion recognizes limitations in how the framework has been applied in some cases and builds on lessons learned in designing the next phase.

Overview of Discussions

Perceived limitations of the initial Kania and Kramer article as summarized by Wolff (2016) in an editorial article brought new thinking and approaches to using the Collective Impact principles in community change initiatives. Wolff identified 10 ways in which the CI conditions were deficient and needed adjustments or expansions. First on the list is that "Collective Impact does not address the essential requirement for meaningfully engaging those in the community most affected by the issues." Lack of this engagement can lead to a host of other deficiencies including that the most important issues may be overlooked in the process because those affected are not included, which can make it difficult to change policies and systems essential to bringing about the lasting changes needed to accomplish the community goals.

Strategic planning or community change endeavors often engage high-level policymakers or influential leaders because they are in the best positions to bring about immediate results. However, long-term results often require policy and system adjustments that change the goals or objectives as well as ways in which organizations operate. Working only with leaders in the community can leave out many players, especially minorities, who are close to the issues but do not hold leadership positions (LeChasseur, 2016). Their commitment and involvement later will be necessary to bring about lasting effects. In short, omitting these groups can not only make building long-term commitment more difficult, it can also focus on a narrower set of goals from those that might have arisen from a broader based involvement. The lack of engagement by many groups can challenge the effectiveness of using a CI framework as a true community development practice. At the same time, this is not a cut-and-dried issue since there are varying degrees and types of engagement by residents illustrated by discussions in later chapters. The importance of inclusion, however, cannot be overstated especially in community development initiatives.

Much attention has been paid in the literature to the role(s) played by backbone organizations in early discussions of conditions needed for effective change processes on the basis that a community change process is likely to falter without long–term consistent support. Wolff makes the point that the role of the backbone organization is to build leaders and community consensus as well as provide local support and guidance for the community change effort. Its purpose is not to be a top-down agency furthering a set of goals and agenda that may not completely match community needs.

Along these lines, the CI discussions may place too much burden on the backbone organization especially in communities without sufficient budgets to carry out the assigned functions. More attention to the roles of this organization and how it can build community support can help practitioners design a system to bring about the desired changes at a viable cost. Authors of later chapters in this volume discuss various approaches used to increase the effectiveness of backbone organizations.

The initial CI work also has been criticized because it did not take into consideration or build on many years of scholarly and professional literature regarding community change efforts. Kania and Kramer draw their observations on only a few studies of successful change approaches in making their case for Collective Impact conditions. The argument can be made that a great deal of experience, literature, history, and insights could have been incorporated into the justifications to make a stronger case for key factors for successful change projects. Since the initial article was published in 2011, however, subsequent criticisms have generated many changes in how the Collective Impact approach has been pursued. The idea of considering impact on a community rather than on a specific issue is clearly embedded in the community change literature with modifications of program occurring daily. Many chapters in this volume illustrate these modifications and show their effectiveness. The flexibility of the CI approach promotes this experimentation and encourages adjustments to formats and procedures.

Engaging all three sectors—government, business, and the Third sector—is critical to achieving successes in community change approaches. Bradbook (Chapter Two) presents six theoretical foundations to help local CI leaders co-design more effective approaches that can disrupt the system. He documents how practitioners in various agencies have incorporated them into their designs in a holistic approach. Specifically, he argues that *Liberal Intergovernmentalism* and *Neofunctionalism* offer insights into ways to cause buy-in and collaboration by local agencies, each with a separate agenda and activities. For instance, providing funding for collaborative efforts can shift attention from competing for grants to designing efforts that involve more than one agency even though the focus may change from providing ultimate services.

Bradbrook also illustrates how *Elite Socialization* concepts can be effective in understanding how CI participants can move from the more defined focus of their specific organization to adopting broader goals and objectives in the community change effort. This transition is key to effective community change and depends on attitude changes by key participants.

A collaborative and multi-level governance approach is important for CI efforts to recognize broad community issues and underlying causes that must change to bring about solutions. While each level of government has specific interests and issues with which to deal, collaboration on a community development issue that impacts basic determinants will lead to more effective solutions and more lasting outcomes. Thus, it is important when defining the problem recognize the governments involved and ways in which they can address the issue in their operation.

Viewing the community issue from a multi-dimensional perspective also can provide greater legitimacy for the overall change effort. Community problems often are complex and difficult to understand. Yet for the change effort to have credibility among residents, they must see how the various aspects of the problem will be addressed and the probable impact on them. As the community effort gains momentum and some of the changes become apparent, it will gain credibility and acceptance. Bradbrook provides several examples of how this process can work.

Community change efforts involve networks of agencies and players that must be managed in a productive way even when they differ in goals and strategies. Implementation can be a major stumbling block in community change programs so special care must be taken to identify opportunities to encourage engagement by all relevant groups. Residents belong to networks in the community and these groups or arrangements will be instrumental in creating a culture to effect long-term changes. Network Agreements (NA) represent shared principles that, when used effectively, can guide and influence network activities in pursuit of long-term change.

Based on interviews with 27 Network Leaders (NL) in multi-organizational contexts in the U.S. and Canada, Stiver (Chapter Three) describes the positive roles that NAs and NLs can play in implementing CI initiatives. The agreements identified by Stiver include: leverage the power of networks; foster a supportive environment; practice honest engagement; adopt open practices; honor expertise and experience; empower people; make community-minded decisions; and fight for equity, access, and justice.

The overlaps between the perceived deficiencies of the initial CI discussions and the NA topics covered are obvious so building successful NAs in the community and finding NLs to implement them can be a major step in advancing CI implementation efforts. Especially important, though, is to recruit NLs from traditionally underrepresented groups and organizations to make sure their views and voices are included in the deliberations. The main functions of the NAs are to implement the change strategies and to monitor/record their successes. Accomplishing long-term outcomes is difficult without effective management strategies.

Effectively using networks in a community requires a major commitment not only from top leaders but throughout the organizational structures. Decentralization of authority or power and acceptance of multiple points of view can, in some cases, be hard to implement but are, nevertheless, essential in successful implementation processes. The NAs must be continually examined to make sure they are still relevant to the process goals.

NAs offer additional advantages in managing succession of change actors and other participants since a core group of NLs is unlikely to exit at the same time. Likewise, NAs and the NLs provide a record of what was intended and arrangements for implementation. While designing and managing a more decentralized structure can be difficult and time-consuming, the benefits are likely to be worth the effort based on survey results presented by Stiver.

A key ingredient in successful community change approaches is the operation of a backbone organization that can effectively maintain the momentum of the project, build leadership capacity, and assist in overall management of a decentralized and complex process. The organization requires attention to creating a culture in which participants are committed to the overall effort and follow effective procedures. Thus, the structure of the backbone organization should be examined to determine whether it is creating a work ethic or culture that allows it to play an integral role in the change process rather than pursuing top-down activities that do not adequately incorporate the views of traditionally underrepresented groups, as noted by Wolff.

Gillam and Counts (Chapter Four) provide a detailed examination of a backbone organization aimed at optimizing the well-being of at risk children, youth and families. The organization had been a backbone organization for many planning and CI projects. A focus on the intangibles needed to enable and encourage members to effectively carry out their responsibilities in catalyzing and working with NLs and other community groups can be extended to other organizations. Based on a review of the professional literature, Gillam and Counts state that six common functions of backbone organizations include: guiding vision and strategy; support aligned activities; establish shared measurement practices; build public will; advance policy; and mobilize funding.

While these tasks seem like tangible and clearly-defined responsibilities, the culture within the organization that needed to carry them out is not always understood. Behind the scenes are intangible features that can foster or limit the ability of staff to successfully meet the overall objectives. Gillam and Counts report on efforts by the Center for Public Partnerships and Research at the University of Kansas to intentionally redesign and build its internal capacity to serve as a backbone organization for various projects. Based on a correlation analysis involving surveys and discussions with 27 staff members, the authors report factors affecting staff attitudes about rules of engagement that contribute to successes in a university-based backbone organization. While these analyses focus on one organization in a university setting, they can pertain just as well to other organizations intentionally trying to enhance their ability to provide traditional backbone organization responsibilities.

Specifically, the Center included rules of engagement that staff would use in working with other agencies. The rules of engagement examined in this project include: freedom to fail; leave it better than you found it; be accountable; and work with the willing. Further analyses and interviews with personnel indicated that training could enhance their skills and understanding not only of the potential roles for a backbone organization but also guidelines for more effective operating procedures. Strategies identified include: practical tools to build staff understanding and skill development; importance of a shared struggle; creating a positive mindset; improving leadership practices; and creating a long-term sense of ability or hope to effect change.

The study of the Center is useful for several reasons. First, it demonstrates the importance of understanding the complexity of backbone organizations and the multi-faceted nature of their responsibilities. Second, educating staff and providing consistent rules of engagement to follow in working with other organizations can help significantly in achieving long-term objectives. Third, effective leadership within a backbone organization is key to effective management and successful operations. As in many operations, some, or many, of these activities are intangible and not always apparent either to those served or to providers. Nevertheless, they can be key to achieving long-term changes.

The fact that community change approaches and strategies involve complex issues involving many, sometimes competing, organizations, participants require an understanding of the system that generated the current situation including what has happened in the past, goals of current agencies involved, and likely future impacts. In other words, community change processes using CI can benefit substantially, if not require, a systems design approach rather than trying to address specific issues or concerns raised in current discussions.

Landers et al. (Chapter Five) review the systems literature as it applies to CI issues regarding the potential to help understand underlying and upstream issues that brought about the current situations with which CI is grappling. In addition to identifying and quantifying the issues being addressed, a systems approach can help create a framework for continual learning and analysis that allow the community change process to work. In making a strong case for use of systems analysis, the authors discuss efforts by the Atlanta Regional Collaborative for Health Improvement (ARCHI) initiative to bring about substantive changes in policy and their effects.

By their very nature, systems tools can effect the essential components of the CI framework. Examining the overall system in which decisions are made can attract and engage other agencies in the community change efforts because they can better see the impact on their organization as well as how they can be effectively involved in the process to bring about desired outcomes. This is especially true when key groups such as the backbone organization take a quantitative approach in showing on-going or possible future results.

Closely related is the ability of a systems approach to enhance mutually-reinforcing efforts. With a broader approach, participating agencies come to see how their actions bring about changes elsewhere in the system with a greater overall impact than seen from a more limited perspective. These effects can support efforts by the backbone organization making their tasks more viable and effective. Engaging more organizations in the overall change process adds more complexity for sure but a systems approach can increase the potential for the backbone organization and other groups to participate effectively and perhaps at lower costs.

In a similar vein, engaging participants in a systematic framework promotes continuous communications, which again helps the overall process. When various groups understand the interrelatedness of their actions and possible efforts on others, they are encouraged to collaborate, share strategies, and pursue common initiatives. Systems analysis provides tools that can be used to identify, quantify, and share outcomes in ways allowing participants to understand not only the interconnectedness of their actions but also see progress that is being made by collaborative efforts. ARCHI used system analysis tools to bring about changes that offer insights to others groups organizing community change processes. While the approach used in that instance cannot be automatically transported to other situations, it provides an excellent example regarding the effectiveness of taking a broader approach and using a systems approach.

Use of CI frameworks in community change processes has expanded exponentially since 2011, has reshaped the notion of bringing about community change in diverse settings, and has evolved with lessons learned and critiques, which are a natural progression of activities associated with any process as it evolves. Cabaj and Weaver (Chapter Six) review changes that have evolved in the use of CI and suggest ideas for ways to proceed in the future to incorporate both what has been learned from years of experimentation and stated limitations of the initial framework proposed.

Their insights are timely for at least three reasons. First, sufficient time has elapsed to identify limitations of the CI elements proposed, determine their effectiveness, and identify ways to adjust the practices to make them more useful in community change processes. Second, the usefulness of important previous research and practice that allegedly was overlook in the initial CI design can be assessed based on longer-term perspective. Third, both Cabaj and Weaver have worked intensively with CI approaches so they have relevant experiences useful in designing ways to proceed.

In line with the methods used to refine software and other programs, Cabaj and Weaver argue that the correct response in this case is more than to fine-tune the initial CI framework proposed; rather it must seriously consider the criticisms as well as the accomplishments that groups have made in the past five years or so in working with CI approaches. What has worked and what needs to be changed? They also argue that the task of upgrading and revising framework must rest with a partnership of practitioners and others associated with community change projects rather than only those who initially proposed the approach or framework.

Collective Impact can be analyzed as three phases—the community change and related practices that existed prior to the Zania and Kramer article in 2011, the period since, and the future. Thus, a Collective Impact 3.0 version could incorporate several major changes. First, the effort should consider a movement–building approach rather than a mainly managerial approach when needed to bring about lasting changes in policies and programs essential to community change. This movement must have a common vision and values shared by participants that focus on transforming the system rather than simply adjusting it when that approach is not sufficient to achieve desired outcomes.

The initial five conditions should be updated rather than replaced. The continuous communications approach can be upgraded to authentic and inclusive community engagement. This approach is consistent with the critique offered by Wolff and builds on the proposal by Landers et al., to use a systems approach and Stiver's claim of the value of Network Agreements and Network Leaders.

A second upgrade could be from a common agenda to a shared community aspiration, which is in line with a movement-building focus. While reaching a consensus of goals and vision for the community can be difficult and time-consuming, once achieved it is likely to motivate more actions in a consistent direction.

A third approach is to move from a shared measurement situation to a strategic learning initiative as part of the overall CI effort. It elicits more active engagement by participants, a better understanding of what is needed, and is likely to create more ownership within the community. An active evaluation of the project can inform participants and other community groups.

A fourth advancement is to focus on high-leverage and loose/tight working relationships. Keeping the focus on strategies that have high impact and can be achieved not only leads to successes but maintains a focus on outcomes important to residents. This approach also builds community support for the overall process.

Fifth is to change the focus from backbone support to a container for change. The backbone organization is key to the success of the change process but it plays many roles including coordinating participating agencies, building leadership capacity, arranging funding, and other activities noted by Gillam and Counts. In a Collective Impact 3.0, this organization would facilitate the learning of participants and member organizations and be an active reservoir of information about impacts and operations.

Several authors, based on past experiences, discuss the complexities in a community change process and challenges coordinating and managing the efforts of the partners. Schwarz, Weaver, Pei, and Novak (Chapter Seven) describe the organizational structure and operations of a regional initiative (Vibrant Communities Canada) to reduce poverty using community–university partnerships. The overall poverty reduction effort was complex and involved many individual organizations. It was managed by five hubs that focused on poverty reduction, violence against women, community environmental sustainability, Canadian food systems, and knowledge mobilization.

Schwartz et. al. conducted a summative evaluation of key project participants in the poverty reduction effort to determine the roles played by organizations and those played by CI principles in achieving the results. The case study involves the Poverty Reduction Hub (PRH) in Hamilton, Ontario, and examines how the main CI principles were used. Especially relevant are establishing a common agenda, shared measurement practices, and continuous communication among partners.

The PRH is chaired by Carleton University and Vibrant Communities Canada. Starting with 13 communities, it grew to more than 47 local and provincial community partners. The project processes and outcomes provide insights into managing collaborations of organizations with complementary skills as well as the potential impacts that each can have. Coordination of efforts is an especially challenging task given the diverse profiles of groups in poverty and strategies involved.

Key to the poverty reduction initiative was to encourage businesses to pay a living wage, which involved several approaches in working with private employers and local governments convincing them of the benefits from such as strategy. The authors evaluate the usefulness of these initiatives in changing systems (policy changes) and changes in individual behaviors based on previous work by Parkhurst and Preskill (2014).

Using both qualitative and quantitative analyses, the authors identified four activities that proved especially important in obtaining successful outcomes. These recommendations include:

- use a roundtable format where key stakeholders meet regularly with a common agenda and continuous communication;
- circulate reports in the community regularly to highlight the importance of the issues in bringing about change;
- have a partner research best practices for implementing ideas being considered and their impacts elsewhere so as to overcome local barriers more quickly; and
- create a recognition program to support businesses paying a living wage to encourage other businesses recognized this as a desired outcome.

These approaches use the CI practices of common agenda, shared vision, and continuous communication among partner organizations to illustrate an effective use of a backbone organization structure.

Collective Impact is especially useful in working on large scale community change types of major issues as shown by the previous example involving poverty reduction. A somewhat similar initiative involved a statewide program of controlling rising obesity rates in Wisconsin.

This issue is of special importance because of the documented link between obesity, rising costs of health treatment and other factors leading to higher mortality rates. It is important, therefore, to be able to change policies, systems, and environments (PSE) that foster increases in childhood obesity leading to higher obesity among adults.

PSE changes cannot be imposed from outside; they must involve changes within communities, so they are especially open to CI types of intervention practices. Korth and Meinen (Chapter Eight) report on a statewide initiative using CI practices to implement an obesity prevention program in Wisconsin. In an attempt to create a statewide effort to address the obesity concerns, the Wisconsin Partnership Program funded an effort to coordinate agency efforts and formed healthTIDE as a coordinative approach using CI principles. The University of Wisconsin–Madison served as a backbone organization and attended training in CI practices with guidance from other organizations experienced in CI programs such as Tamarack. This may be one of only a few statewide efforts on this specific issue so there were no models on which to pattern the organization and activities.

Four teams were created to address the relevant issues. They include: early childhood; schools; active communities; and health food retail. Each team implements the CI framework with coordination, support, and assistance from the healthTIDE backbone organization. The teams have created a common agenda and aligned mutually-reinforcing activities. They established continuous communication techniques and created shared measurement processes including short-term measurement indicators.

The authors present a mixed-methods analysis and developmental evaluation procedures to determine how the CI framework has helped bring about PSE changes to prevent childhood obesity. The importance of a backbone organization to guide and support other agencies is confirmed by the experiences with healthTIDE. Implementing some other CI practices, however, experienced more difficulties and were supplemented by alternative approaches. Continuous communication has been more difficult to bring about because of the ways in which participating organizations are located or interact. Some of these issues have been faced in other projects.

Similarly, relatively little progress in share measurement practices was reported partly because the difficulties in measuring something as complex as the obesity issue, but also perhaps because of engagement in other aspects of the healthTIDE initiative. The authors suggest that a central data collection agency may be one way to advance the measurement issue.

Korth and Meinen also report on difficulties associated with finding participants who can overlook vested interests in the status quo or their sponsoring organizations and adopt a broader perspective. In other instances, the potential of alienating the power structure in the community may prevent serious consideration of alternatives. Thus, as earlier critics (LeChasseur, 2016; Le, 2015) have suggested it is important to examine the power structure within a community, both in selecting participants and in framing potential policies or recommendations. In some cases, especially large scale projects, these issues can pose major challenges. Finally, the authors point out that CI practices represent only one framework and should be supplemented by on-going research from many other approaches and tools.

There can be little question but that the community environment in which a change process is to occur is critically important. If it is to succeed, the change process, whether CI or another approach, must adjust to these unique assets or considerations. Sometimes the attitudes or principles held by specific groups determine, or at least heavily influence, what they value or how they can participate in a change process.

Somekh, Almog, Nijim-Ektelat (Chapter Nine) report ways CI practices were used in a Better Together comprehensive community change initiative in Israel. They report on the importance of cultural barriers affecting the ways that a backbone organization must manage activities to elicit community engagement. One of the main criticisms of CI has been that it can be a top-down process. The Better Together change process occurred in an Arab community in northern Israel. A major role of backbone organizations is to build and maintain trust within the community, which is difficult with cultural conflicts in minority populations, in this case members of an Arab population.

The authors note that the preferred social structure with an Arab society centers on family with a strong patriarchal hierarchal structure, with the father as the dominant authority and the mother with responsibility for childcare and maintaining the family's integrity and stability. Since this process begins in a person's early years, it places constraints on a young girl's options to go out after dark, participate in certain types of activities or events, and related issues that may come up in community events.

In addition, while volunteerism is encouraged, it is mainly within a family or clan rather than for the overall benefit of the community. Likewise, public spaces are relatively small in some Arab communities, partly because of the importance placed on interacting within the family or clan. This aspect can limit the potential of organized meetings to address community issues.

Many Arab professionals were educated in western societies, which sometimes modified their basic value system so that while as successful leaders they are members of the same society as those in a community change activity, they may not be fully accepted. This difference can create barriers and complicate the process of organizing participants into cohesive groups around various issues.

Somekh et al. examine approaches used by a backbone organization (JDC–Ashlim) in a program operated by Better Together to improve the well–being of children and youth in disadvantaged communities by reducing their exposure to risk situations. The case examined is a relatively poor city of 4,500 residents who belong to two clans.

The backbone organization faced several difficulties. Recruiting males and girls to participate in the program was complicated because the social and community programs were not issues for which men traditionally are responsible. The families were reluctant to have girls attend functions in the evening or participate in these group functions without supervision.

The backbone organization had to modify procedures used and elicit support from parents or other groups. They also had to hold the meetings in public spaces that were acceptable to participants and/or families. Especially important was to address the differences between the two clans and find neighborhood coordinators and volunteers from each neighborhood who were acceptable to both clans and had the ability to bring them together on important issues. This study reinforces the importance of a backbone organization to recognize and accommodate cultural differences in groups involved in community change processes early in the design of the program as well as throughout the processes.

Where is CI Headed?

Previous discussions illustrate ways in which various groups have adapted the initial CI framework proposed by Kania and Kramer to address a variety of issues in diverse situations. Several have focused on the importance of a backbone organization or structure and its responsibilities while others have identified difficulties with implementing other components such as shared measurement or continuous communication. These limitations or criticisms are part of a natural development process for a technique or approach as it grows and matures with experience and usage. Nothing else should have been expected with the CI framework. It was not the intent of this volume to include other equally important work influencing the directions that CI has taken.

Klaus and Weaver (Chapter 10) review experiences with the CI procedures since the initial Kania and Kramer article in 2011, discuss the strengths and limitations that have been identified, and analyze future directions as the CI practice continues to grow. Their extensive work with CI makes them especially well-qualified to address this issue. They have worked in community change processes using the CI framework since it was first proposed, have been critical of limitations or oversights, and have experimented with alternative approaches.

The authors reviewed the professional and scholarly literature, surveyed key professionals experienced with CI activities, and then analyzed options for moving ahead to refine or expand the CI framework. Their analyses led to several conclusions. First, while the initial CI discussions were not designed as a formula or recipe, in some cases they were used in that way perhaps with only a limited understanding of the principles behind them. Rather they were intended as a theoretical framework for organizing various techniques or approaches.

Second, the initial framework was expressed as having been researched when, in fact, it was based on several identified successful approaches plus years of experience with community change approaches. However, the framework was not based on an extensive research design with formal techniques as noted by some critics, which may have led to misunderstandings by users.

Third, the CI framework was not designed specifically for community development uses but is now growing in use for these types of issues, which may have led to criticisms based on results obtained. However, not all the efforts actually fit the CI framework. The increased use in community development may be where much of the future growth will come as the CI framework is refined with more experiences.

Klaus and Weaver reviewed several major attempts to adjust or refine the CI framework in the past several years. While these approaches addressed limitations of the CI framework, they each also had a different focus and varied in emphasis. Common among the efforts, however, were perceived deficits in community participation, shared measurement, and equity issues.

Based on a review of the literature, interviews with practitioners knowledgeable about CI usage, and an examination of recommendations by other professional groups, the authors asked the key informants whether the future of CI will be "business as usual" or whether a disruptive innovation approach is preferred. There was general agreement that the business as usual description is not appropriate. This response led Klaus and Weaver to coin the term "Disruptive Illumination" since CI sheds new light on the processes associated with community change processes and their role in community development.

Future Roles for Collective Impact in Community Development Issues

What have the years since the publication by Kania and Kramer shown and what is the potential for future use of the CI framework? Discussions in this volume highlight several main topics. First, the initial discussions shed light on deficiencies with many previous community change processes and the inability to bring about long term results. The frustrations by funding agencies and practitioners created an opportunity for a changed approach.

The CI framework offers new insights in conditions that foster successful change practices although the framework did not provide a recipe or models that can be successfully applied to any and all situations. It nevertheless offered a different way of approaching these programs and was adopted by many practitioners with varying degrees of success. As is natural with most new or different approaches, the CI framework was criticized for not sufficiently including previous research and successful practices. It also did not incorporate important issues such as cultural diversity and equity.

The CI thinking has had a major impact on community change processes. From a perspective of five or more years of work with this evolving CI framework, Klaus and Weaver suggest that it will not return to business as usual approaches. Instead, CI represents a disruptive illumination where future practitioners will approach community change initiatives with new insights regarding ways to engage community participants more effectively, focus on a strategic learning process to achieve highly-leveraged outcomes, and have a strong backbone organization that supports innovation and change. This organization incorporates and builds on excellent research and practices underway in many organizations and projects.

The CI approach not only changes conversations in the community; it also fosters a movement to change both policies and agency behaviors. When used effectively, it offers many opportunities to bring about desired long-term positive community changes and is likely to continue its significant impact on community change initiatives into the future.

References

Cabaj, M. & Weaver, L (2016). Collective Impact, 3.0: An Evolving Framework for Community Change. Waterloo, Canada: Tamarack Institute Community Change Series.

Cooper, K. R. (2017). "Nonprofit participation in collective impact: A comparative case." *Community Development*, (48) 4, 499–514.

Kania, J. & Kramer, M (2011). "Collective impact." *Stanford Social Innovation Review*, Winter, 9(1), 36–41.

Kubisch, A., Auspos, P., Brown, P., & Dewar, T. (2010). "Community change initiatives from 1990–2010: Accomplishments and implications for future work." *Community Investments*. Spring 22(1), 8–12. Federal Reserve Bank of San Francisco.

Le, Vu. (2015). "Why communities of color are getting frustrated with collective impact." Available at: www.collectiveimpactforum.org

LeChasseur, K. (2016). "Reexamining power and privilege in collective impact" *Community Development*, 47(2), 225–240.

Parkhurst, M. & Preskill, H. (2014). "Learning in Action: Evaluating Collective Impact." *Stanford Social Innovation Review*, [online]. Available at: http://ssir.org/articles/entry/learning_in_action_evaluating_collective_impact

Walzer, N., Weaver, L., & McGuire, C. (2016) "Collective impact and community development issues." *Community Development*, 47(2), 156–166.

Wolff, T. (2016). "Ten places where collective impact gets it wrong." *Global Journal of Community Psychology Practice*, 7(1). Available at: www.gjcpp.org/en/resource.php?issue=21&resource=200

2

THEORETICAL FOUNDATIONS FOR CI APPLICATIONS

Craig Bradbrook

In the seven years since the seminal article by Kania and Kramer, Collective Impact (CI) has established itself as a recognized framework for addressing wicked problems, and effecting large scale change. The framework, with the five conditions for success, set the scene and introduced a typology for collaboration with a non-descript formula for progress.

These discussions brought a call to funders to think differently about how they support long-term change, referencing a previous article by Kramer, that set out four principles embedded in CI. These principles are "take responsibility for assembling the elements of a solution; create a movement for change; include solutions from outside the nonprofit sector; and use actionable knowledge to influence behavior and improve performance" (Kania & Kramer 2011; Kramer 2009).

CI is now firmly established in the Social Services sector in the United Kingdom, Canada, and Australia to name a few places. Interest in the approach has grown from both a government and funding perspective. While there are examples of the CI framework successfully achieving change at scale, for the movement to continue its momentum and for leaders/practitioners to have the necessary implementation tools, a deeper understanding of push and pull factors, and how CI may endure is needed. Deepening the theoretical basis will provide additional opportunities to frame future research projects and build additional tools for implementation.

The current chapter stresses six theoretical foundations providing CI leaders with an opportunity to better identify and plan their work. Underpinning the discussion is a focus on how the processes can improve community engagement practices including:

- ways to best structure for change;
- drivers and motivations for improved regional cooperation and integration;

- plans to work at multiple scales and levels;
- importance of establishing a coherent system of governance;
- ways to demonstrate the legitimacy of CI; and
- CI as a vehicle for managing complexity within the whole system, from pedagogical practices of frontline staff, to policy formation and politics.

As with any policy, or intervention, CI is a framework that will benefit from testing, analysis, and refinement. Theories presented in this chapter can be applied in practice and used to develop evaluation frameworks.

Collective Impact (CI): Structures for Success

Central to CI is addressing wicked problems with layers of complexity that exist in a set of complex interactions among multiple tiers of government, the Third Sector, the business sector, and communities. Understanding relationships between these stakeholders, who represent diverse and vested interests, is central to achieving the results that improve the conditions of life in target populations. Thus, a relevant question that arises when establishing, or reviewing, an existing structure for a CI initiative, is how and at what levels does the structure embed community engagement, participation and decision making?

CI initiatives have, to date, been characterized by a traditional hierarchical structure, similar to that which would be found in classical management theory. Kania and Kramer (2012) described the CI structure through "cascading levels of linked collaboration." At the top of the CI hierarchy is the membership of the cross-sector leadership group, including CEOs. Sub-committees/working groups are created to drive progress toward specific result areas, with membership in these groups including representatives from key organizations involved in the initiative.

At the lowest level of this hierarchy are community members whose input is based on constant communication regarding "what is or is not working" (Hanleybrown, Kania, & Kramer, 2012: 5). This hierarchical structure has been criticized, since it does not always meaningfully engage community members and makes CI a top-down consulting approach (Wolff, 2016). These types of structures are synonymous with classical management styles. Himmelman (2012: 278) when discussing networking, coordinating, cooperating, and collaborating as driving conditions of positive change for community, stated the issue clearly, (pre-collective impact); *"although coalitions often claim to use these strategies to foster institutional or community change, most coalitions are deeply embedded within and reinforce existing societal power relations, which constrain such change."*

Perpetuating these power relations will potentially continue the welfare dependence model that has plagued social welfare systems since their inception. An effective structure for CI must be established to ensure that end-users of systems are not only a mechanism for feedback. Instead, they must co-design strategies and interventions in partnership to truly disrupt the systems that have stalled in achieving change at scale. How can the structure of CI overcome the challenges with a multiplicity of stakeholders representing diverse interests?

Structuring for Effective Community Engagement and Co-design

The importance of embedding community engagement and participation in the structure of CI is to help address the power imbalance between decision makers who develop responses to problems, those who allocate and distribute resources, and end-users in the system. Birchfield & Crepaz (1998: 175–200) provide strong evidence that shows political institutions in industrialized liberal democracies, making decisions through political consensus, will result in lower income inequalities, while majoritarian political institutions will widen the income gap. This study offers insights as to the importance of structuring a CI that is inclusive and supports access to the public policy-making processes for community.

A holistic approach, inclusive of government, business, the Third Sector, and the community, enables consensus between the multiplicity of actors in the system if the structure is inherently community-oriented. How can a CI embed community development to become the driver for change, and influence public policy?

Collective Impact: The Hive Mt Druitt, Intentional Co-Design

Mt. Druitt is a cluster of suburbs in western Sydney, with a population of more than 60,000 residents. The region is highly stigmatized with multiple indicators of disadvantage. These include high developmental vulnerability of children, low secondary school completion rates, high rates of unemployment, mental health issues, drug and alcohol addiction, and public housing tenants (ABS, 2013). A controversial program titled Struggle Street, was filmed in Mt. Druitt. Stories of drug addiction and mental health painted a "one dimensional story of poverty", focusing on individual's deficits and challenges (Bond, 2016). The Hive, in Mt. Druitt, developed an intentional co-design approach with community that includes multiple service providers and multiple tiers of government (Legislative Council, 2015). Central to the structure, is a deliberate structured process.

The foundation for The Hive was conceived by funders, who had followed the traditional structure of any project. High level decisions makers would meet 45 kms away from the epicentre of Mt. Druitt and agree on solutions without investigating the drivers of the problems. Over time, a local leadership group would form, including all stakeholders, government, business, not-for-profits, and, most importantly, local community members.

The initial Governance Group became the Ambassador Group, who advocated for systems change. Continuous communication between the local leadership group and the Ambassador Group ensures a systems advocacy strategy built into the structure of the CI (United Way, 2016). The structure of Mt. Druitt is built from a framework of Human Centred Design. The structure provides for, and allows, community mobilization, that generates content from which decisions are made. By design, meetings provide an agenda, supported by readings, key documents, and an environment that enables innovation. There is a noticeable departure from the default *modus operandi*, resulting in a mindset and culture that delivers on community aspirations, rather than top-down imperatives (Wright, 2016). The process for engaging community happens at least twice per year, in a three-stage process:

Swarm: a facilitated discussion, representative of the diverse range of stakeholders in the community;
Incubate: a smaller group that researches specific problems requiring collective action. Solutions are tested prior to the group agreeing, through consensus, on a solution that has been co-designed specifically for the Mt. Druitt region;
Implement: local community groups or organizations take leadership to deliver the agreed-upon solutions, and they are acknowledged as most suited for these roles with the capacity and capability to implement the solutions.

The Hive Team, or backbone organization, drives the work, coordinating people, and processes. This teamwork is essential to drive systems change, supporting better coordination and integration between three tiers of government, and multiple stakeholders in the area. In a Standing Committee on Social Issues, on behalf of the New South Wales Parliament in Australia, a report cites Mt. Druitt as a best practice example.

Intergovernmentalism: Drivers for Change

The CI framework asks funders, organizations, and government agencies to think differently about how they plan, allocate, and distribute resources, and how they work collectively in a specific region, toward agreed outcomes. The remaining questions include what needs to change and what may hinder the change process?

The theory of Liberal Intergovernmentalism (Moravcsik & Schimmelfennig, 2007: 67–69) offers CI leaders insights that will support a deeper understanding of what it means for stakeholders to opt for a CI approach. There is both a *supply* and a *demand* side that can contribute to the success of integration in a service system. A scarcity of economic resources *demands* cooperation between the actors, supported by an understanding that no one organization can address these wicked problems. This *demand* supports a *supply* of, and need for, integration across the political, social, and economic systems (Cini, 2015: 65–78).

Organizational preferences are then formed by economic constraints, and an acknowledgment that coordination and integration are necessary. Within CI organizations, such as member states in the European Union, some decision-making power will be ceded to a backbone organization that provides the direction for the CI. A key actor, driving these demand and supply processes, is often the government. Competitive tendering for services in the Third Sector can become counterproductive to a CI and isolate community engagement activities.

A widely-held view among liberal democracies is that increasing competition lowers costs and improves efficiencies. Funding cycles often follow political terms, two to four years. When governments call for expressions of interest for services, organizations retreat into writing applications for funding and move away from collaborations. Once funding has been allocated and distributed, the rebuilding phase begins.

These cycles can have a detrimental impact on both delivery of services and engagement activities, since trust is lost as services change hands and new staff from different organizations are hired. It is a costly process, as the 2014 experience in Australia showed. An allocation of AUS $800 million was available for organizations to apply for with the aggregate total of all funding applications equal to AUS $3.9 billion (Department of Social Services, 2016). The Competition Review report found that competition generates more benefits to larger sectors, noting the Human Services sector as one of these sectors—"deepening and extending competition policy in human services is a priority reform" (Harper, Anderson, McCluskey, & Obryan, 2016: 35).

With competition a constant, funders and service delivery agencies have to shift from "management to movement building." As Kania and Kramer (2011) noted, funders are asked to: "see their role, from funding organizations to leading a long-term process of social change . . . funders must help create and sustain the collective processes, measurement reporting systems, and community leadership that enable cross-sector coalitions to arise and thrive."

Caution must be exercized in interpreting this proposition, however. When funders redirect funding from activities/services to collaborations, (administration/ reporting, and sustaining collaborative processes), the opportunity costs involve fewer services for those in need. Concurrently, as coalitions represent a shift from isolated to Collective Impact, most organizations will want to understand the return on investment for inputting their human and financial resources. Organizations will likely be challenged with the notion of sharing data to support shared measurement systems. These are the conditions CI is driving to achieve change across the systems.

This situation is true for government or non-government organizations, whether businesses or Third Sector organizations. Shifting toward collective goals will see a "demand for cooperation, and, the supply of integration" (Cini, 2013: 73). What incentives can CI offer organizations and governments, to move from competition to collaboration, in creating the conditions of well-being for the communities served? In a competitive market place for funding service delivery, how can CI meet the needs of self-interested organizations?

Practical Applications of Liberal Intergovernmentalism

Time is well spent identifying the motives of each stakeholder at the table in a CI effort, whether it be a Steering Committee, Working Group, or Community Engagement reference group. Three levels of motives are worth discussing. First, the motives of the organization, and why it wants to be involved in the initiative, are important. Each organization has a strategic plan, is governed by a board, and has different hierarchies of management. Does the individual representing the organization have support to maintain involvement?

Second, knowing the service or department the individual represents, along with the potential gains for the service, can help distil the motives. For example, the aim may be expansion of an existing program.

Third, what does the individual seek to gain personally or professionally from involvement in the project? These can appear to be confronting questions; however, the approach can support development of trust in the relationships and identify potential conflicts of interest among individuals, agencies represented, and the project. It can also be a useful process for identifying the skills individuals can contribute, the resources available within the stakeholders' organizations, and what may drive an organization to divorce itself from a project. Ultimately, answers to these types of questions can help in understanding factors that might drive preference formation when it comes to decision-making as a collective. While understanding these motives is important, it is also up to all parties to focus on the supply of integration.

A Case Study: The Inner West Collective Impact Initiative

The backbone for the Inner West CI is shared among multiple organizations. Representation on the steering committee is shared between Third Sector organizations and one key government department. The steering committee is led by two representatives from separate Community Service NGOs. Negatives associated with these types of backbones include "lack of accountability with multiple voices at the table, coordination challenges leading to potential inefficiencies" (Hanleybrown, Kania, & Kramer, 2012). With multiple organizations forming the membership of the steering committee, it was important to recognize that members would not be involved in the initiative for perpetuity, leading to the need for a succession plan.

The sustainability of this effort requires an in-kind investment of human resources to steer and provide leadership for the initiative. When the initiative was in its infancy, the steering committee worked through a process of identifying, and understanding the motivations of individuals, and their organizations. Doing so highlighted several people who would leave the initiative. This information allowed the Steering Committee to provide opportunities to build in succession planning for future members of the coalition.

For those leaving, it highlighted the need to work through a handover that would ensure their replacement had adequate information about the initiative.

While the Steering Committee had ten key members, only three remained with the other seven replaced by their organizations, four times in 18 months. For members who left, the Steering Committee could ensure they had both organizational support and adequate information about the initiative. Supported with key documents, including Terms of Reference, minutes, and a journey map, the succession planning worked and the initiative has grown in strength, and number of coalitions (Together SA, 2016). Expansion of the initiative included five working groups focused on key result areas including that children and young people are safe, live in supportive families, are engaged learners, are connected, and are healthy. Managing the initiatives expansion, including alignment of working groups and the influence of one key government department has been challenging (Inner West, 2017).

In a competitive market place, there may be resistance to change from organizations who compete for income generation and to maintain sustainability. Intergovernmentalism reminds leaders of CI emerging initiatives and that stakeholders will ask questions regarding their own vested interests. They will come armed with some level of expectations and expect results. While this is true in the emergent phase of improved cooperation in the competitive market place, as a CI builds momentum with a consensus among the key stakeholders, the existing structures of competition will be challenged in favor of new processes.

New processes will engage community members and enable co-design processes that make community decision-making the center of change. As agreements are reached, and the appropriate decision makers have a seat at the table, a CI can begin the process of change. For this process to be effective, multiple layers or complexity, both functional and political, will require alignment before an initiative can begin to improve the population level indicators for success. The theory of Neofunctionalism offers another perspective on the drivers of integration. Once a CI better understands the motivations of the stakeholders, and there is some agreement to change, the processes involving functional change can become almost automatic.

Neo-Functionalism

Neo-functionalism was first coined in 1958 by Ernest B. Haas (Rosamond, 2000: 50–51), who used the theory to explain how regional cooperation occurs, from the European experience to Latin America. As a CI effort builds momentum in any region, cooperation between stakeholders is necessary to work toward the common aspirations.

Three characteristics of theory are relevant to this process. First, the spill over hypothesis, which explains the dynamics of transformation processes as a coordinated effort takes hold. As the cooperation becomes embedded and change occurs, it may seem automatic, rather than an involuntary response to better coordination. A deeper analysis often shows, however, that this change results from intentional and deliberate political motivations by any number of stakeholders, which results in both intended and unintended consequences in different policy areas. There are three different typologies of spill over: functional (technical), political, and cultivated, which are discussed further in the next section.

Two, elite socialization drives this spill over hypothesis. Over time, as the momentum for a CI effort builds, individual loyalties shift from the organizations they represent to the collective. These shifts inform the third component, which in classical neo-functionalism refers to the formation of a supranational interest group hypothesis. A similar aspect in the CI framework is the formation of a backbone organization, or backbone function, to advance the effort.

In Canada, Vibrant Communities provides an excellent case study for Neo-functionalism, since it demonstrates clearly the spill over hypothesis, elite socialization and the development of multiple backbone organizations, to support different elements of the work. This multilayered, geographically diverse initiative aims to reduce poverty and improve the well-being of 50 communities across Canada. There are multiple backbone functions performed by different organizations, some specifically established for the implementation of Vibrant Communities. Community Development provides the nucleus for change, driving change at policy, funding, and regional levels. Leaders across government, the Third Sector and business, learn from and share experiences providing reciprocal support and guidance (Splansky Juster, 2013).

Spill Over Hypothesis

Understanding spill over offers leaders a more thorough and intentional approach about how a CI will achieve the common aspirations. The insights extend across the multiple spheres of influence that require alignment for an initiative to succeed. Irrespective of the common aspiration, leaders can prepare for the functional and process aspects, the political advocacy and change required (if any), and identify potential blockages within the structural relationships, that contribute to a dysfunctional system.

The relevance for CI is that it will improve the implementation, planning, governance, community engagement, and evaluation of CI initiatives. For evaluation, the spill over hypothesis offers an additional lens for investigating and advancing the understanding of various functional, political, and cultivated aspects, shared across multiple CI initiatives.

Functional Spill Over

Functional spill over is observed when an initiative takes a step towards a collective goal, and in doing so, leads to other related actions that help achieve the ultimate goal. For European Integration, the development of the single market is a prime example of functional spill over. Streamlining and standardizing industrial regulations, and health and safety for workers, was required before the free movement of labor could occur. Prohibitive trade barriers, such as tariffs, had to be removed. The functional spill over extended to regulations being standardized for workers' health and safety, across sectors and industries. The implications for sovereign states involved standardizing elements of legislation, including industrial and work health and safety. This was not the intent when creating a single market, rather, a consequence of functional spill over.

Political Spill Over

Political spill over is observed when elites and key interest groups recognize that alone no one organization or government department has the solution. There is acknowledgment of the importance of improved cooperation required to achieve the collective goal. The political will often drives the creation of backbone organizations, when it is recognized that the investment in, and maintenance of, a backbone organization will provide the necessary critical infrastructure. These situations involve shifts from traditional funding arrangements to a decentralized approach, with funding allocated and distributed based on local need, rather than a perceived need by government agencies.

Cultivated Spill Over

The European context for cultivated spill over shows that the formation of supranational organizations support, and drive forward, the process of integration. Through this process, European member states can secede authority on specific policy issues, and/or the supranational organizations can support agreements between two separate policy areas, in favor of better outcomes for both.

In CI, the supranational organizations represent the backbone organizations. Throughout the process of integration, these organizations play a pivotal role in supporting the shifting of organizational self-interests to a collective interest. This will require intense and continuous communications, and an increased level of transactions between all stakeholders. The backbone organization is supported by governmental authorities, especially when the mutually-reinforcing activities demonstrate higher levels of integration. This aspect is seen when the backbone organizations take a key role in negotiating what is in the best interests of community.

Vibrant Communities: The Spill Over

Vibrant Communities in Canada exemplifies the spill over hypothesis. Starting with acknowledgement that change was needed to continue the reduction in poverty, a pilot project with 80 stakeholders, and nearly 50 poverty reduction initiatives in one region delivered over two years, was the catalyst for further spill over effects. Local, regional, and national integration was evident, with integrated approaches to service delivery, and business partnerships between the employment sector, and vocational and tertiary institutions implemented.

The spill over was functional, political, and cultivated. Combined, there were deliberate shifts in the way funding was allocated and distributed, the political support for the project, and formation of multiple backbone organizations with specific functions. Local regions could receive grants matched by Vibrant Communities. As the work progressed to increase the number of communities involved, further changes in funding models would happen, as local partners and businesses, including municipal governments and philanthropist organizations, became involved (Splansky Juster, 2013).

In addition to new funding models, there was a paradigm shift in the way services were provided with greater flexibility for organizations delivering the services and end users to receive the supports needed (Gamble 2010: 47–70). *Political spill over* was evident in the support for developing new systems and policies, culminating in the establishment of a backbone organization, and functional support, from other newly-formed organizations, integral to the infrastructure for the project.

The organizations that formed as a result of this *cultivated spill over* include:

- the Tamarack Institute, which provided the backbone infrastructure, and support to guide strategy across other organizations providing backbone functions;
- the Caledon Institute of Social Policy, which provided awareness of the policy implications, ultimately informing the functional spill over required to advance the initiatives;
- the J.W. McConnell Family Foundation that allocated funds directly to Trail Builder communities, and developed a national strategy to support the rollout; and, a
- national government department, Human Resources and Skills Development Canada (HRSDC), that provides funding, acting as an intermediary between the key backbone supports and the government.

Elite Socialization

In its original conception, *Elite Socialization* explained the process where representatives of member states would represent their country's interest in the European Parliament, or other European organizations. While initially, the focus was intended to support the interests of their nation but, in time, their loyalty would shift to European interests (Strøby Jensen, 2013: 58–59). These representatives would return to their nations to convince the governments of the benefits from greater involvement, increased cooperation, and policy competencies transferred to the EU.

The theory holds, that as a CI initiative builds the infrastructure and sustainability of a project, including the establishment of backbone organization(s), individuals will shift their loyalties from the organizations they represent to the interests of the CI. One pre-condition of CIs, is the identification of "influential champions" (Hanleybrown, Kania, & Kraner 2012: 3). During the emergent stage of a CI these influential champions are likely to represent multiple organizations. Over time, they may transition from the organizations for which they work to the backbone organization or function. Loyalty has shifted from their organization's interest, to organizing and promoting the benefits of improved coordination and integration.

Logan Together, Queensland, Australia, is an example of how loyalties shift over time. Following a critical and violent incident in central Logan (Tapin, 2013), the *Logan Together* CI emerged in a region with high levels of poverty and racial tensions. A forum, convened in 2013, provided an opportunity to bring together service providers, government and community members. Within two years, an independent backbone organization was established and coordinated through Griffith University (Logan Together, 2015: 13–14).

The first appointed director of the backbone organization, had previously chaired the working party for Logan Together, and led youth and community development programs for the Red Cross. Note the transition from supporting the interests of an organization, the Red Cross, to chairing the working party, to being appointed the first Director for the Backbone initiative. While the transition is easy to follow, the loyalty shifting can be characterized as *Elite Socialization.* Further research, using Social Network Analysis methodology (Scott, 2013), provides an opportunity to investigate and illustrate elite socialization.

Supranational and Supranational and Backbone Organizations

When a member state of the European Union relinquishes its sovereignty, or decision-making on a policy area to the European Union, a European Organization is established to manage that issue. This process of Europeanization, changes the context of how businesses operate in a nation state, providing opportunities to trade in goods and services across the free market zone.

With increasing powers ceded to the European Union, supranational interest groups establish themselves as allies of European political organizations. With alliances strengthened, and a focus on expanding the powers of the European Union, the supranational interest groups place pressure on nation states to cede more power to the EU. What does this mean for CI? Consider the backbone organization as the European Union. As political and functional processes influence changes to existing systems there is broad acknowledgment of the need for improved integration and cooperation.

In CI, think of organizations as member states. When they transfer power to the EU to manage specific policy areas, backbone organizations are positioned to take a leadership role in breaking the mold of competitive tendering processes. To do so requires greater cooperation and a transfer of power from funding providers, both philanthropic, and government, to a backbone organization, which, through local knowledge, and processes, can allocate and distribute the funding. Here, the backbone organization plays a dual role, as both a facilitator of an initiative and an interest group lobbying for change.

Neofunctionalism Critiques and Considerations

Haas and others (Schmitter, 2005; Strøby Jensen, 2013) critiqued this theory, citing empirical and theoretical weaknesses. Empirically, as integration developed in the European Union, some could argue that it was not truly representative of the actual processes. Theoretically, the hypothesis of Elite Socialization was rejected with critics overlooking the elite socialization hypothesis, and the self-interest of the nation states being at the center of the integration process.

In the CI space, the challenge involves positioning community engagement at the center of the processes that support integration. For functional spill over, how will the processes that begin the transition to improved cooperation include community engagement activities such as the voice of the consumer? The political spill over brings a change in policy with support for backbone organizations. It also assures that the policies and processes established are both a movement building exercise that also represents a change in process. The process results in changes, including funding cycles, and traditional ways of allocating and distributing funds, reducing competition in favor of shared aspirations, and above all, keeping the community's wishes, hopes and dreams at the center of decision-making.

Spill Over and Phases of Success

Practically, for CI, functional spill over is inevitable, and will include both intended and unintended consequences. Developing a plan of action that identifies a functional pathway to achieving the end goal is time well spent. Thinking through the potential implications of achieving the end goal may foster an initiative to take the necessary steps earlier.

As an initiative gains momentum, what other resources might be needed? Tamarack Institute emphasized four components for success that happen over four key phases. The spill over effect can be seen in the *Governance and infrastructure* component for success. Phase 1—Generating ideas and dialogue. Here, the CI will convene community stakeholder meetings, and identify as well as bring together influential champions to form a coalition. By phase III, governance and infrastructure begins to embed elements of cultivated spill over with a recognition that infrastructure will be required to drive the initiative forward. Spill over must remain in perpetuity, breaking the cycle of competitive funding cycles, and should be one goal of any successful CI.

In summary, Neofunctionalism remains an adequate theory to explain the processes of economic and political integration, especially toward a common goal, while demonstrating the incremental shifts required over time to achieve the common goal. It shows the importance of groupings and alliances required to drive an initiative forward—supporting the development of backbone organizations and ensuring an appropriate infrastructure to achieve the common aspirations.

Multilevel Governance

The concept of governance is broad with many applications from private to public, local to global, land and environmental, or regulatory or participatory, and multiple typologies. Governance provides insights into the interactions of multiple actors whose aim is to influence outcomes and the allocation and distribution of resources within a region (Rhodes, 1996). Governance is especially relevant for CI. The larger the scale, the more important it is for a CI to structure itself with clear arrangements. An enmeshed Collaborative and Multilevel Governance model can provide a CI with a necessary framework to decide how to best organize for impact.

Multilevel Governance and Applications to Collective Impact

Theoretically, Multilevel Governance describes how the EU organizes itself and the decision-making processes, while being able to take a reductionist approach, and comment on specific sectors and regions (Christiansen, 2016; Tortola, 2017). CI must transcend these traditional governance methods with implicit governance structures to inform and transcend these models that are counterintuitive to the direction of large scale change. Both governments and NGOs must leave their professional arrogances behind. Emerging CI initiatives are often synonymous with addressing a key problem of homelessness, youth justice, or child protection, as examples. Time is spent working through the process of problem identification with increased attention regarding the drivers of the issues.

Why Multilevel Governance?

Focusing on governance may reveal unintended challenges and uncover multiple vested interests. When setting up for change, CI is well-advised to spend time working through the problem identification process in relation to governance issues. Identifying these governance issues from a politics, policymakers, NGO, practitioner, and community perspective will reveal the blockages and inefficiencies within existing structures. This process then informs how an initiative can better organize for action.

Underpinning most approaches will require a national strategy. At the municipal level, local level plans and actions must align with national strategies, without barriers that will prevent progress. This merging of national strategies with local level, decentralized actions, and plans that are unencumbered by politics and public policy will require agreements, and clear governance arrangements, to support joint decision-making, inclusive of government, NGO, business sectors, and local communities.

Challenges of Multilevel Governance

For CI, a Multilevel Governance will identify the power dynamics that exist within a multi-tiered or federal government system. Federalist systems such as the United States, Canada and Australia are represented by three levels of government with responsibilities identified through their respective constitutions. These arrangements are complex and CI must identify and advocate for how to address these long-rooted issues of division.

Potential challenges include tensions between not only these tiers of government, but also the multiple government departments and agencies among the three tiers that ultimately all have a role to play. Added to this complexity are initiatives that cross state or territory borders, which places a layer of complexity and governments to manage agreements. Ultimately, CI asks governments to cede some power and control for the greater good of addressing these wicked problems.

In some cases, the CI process can have a tendency to emphasize the dynamics of relationships between the backbone organizations and both local and regional actors. This can result in a multi-layered and complex interplay of competing interests without full government support. How can a CI governance structure address these challenges?

Essentials for Childhood: A Collective Multilevel Governance Strategy

A federally funded program, *Essentials for Childhood*, acknowledges the importance of federal, state, and local government cooperation, while placing community development and engagement activities central to success for the initiative. Over-arching goals and strategies for the initiative are formed at the federal level in partnership with states. The framework asserts that actions and decisions must be informed by local community and evidence-based practice. Decision-making is transferred to local health, cross government agencies, non-government organizations, and informed by community. Shared measurement systems are created to support organizations and publicize the problem.

Strategic Learning opportunities are built into the model with successes shared across the United States for all communities to review (Centers for Disease Control and Prevention, 2016). Guides are produced for media outlets on how to report effectively on issues of child maltreatment that support the who of community approach to addressing child maltreatment issues. The multilevel governance approach for the *Essentials for Childhood* is like the EU structure, local level plans are aligned with federal goals and objectives. There is access to a shared measurement system across all levels of government and strategic learning opportunities that are built into the framework. Most importantly, community engagement and development work are fundamental to the direction of an initiative at the local level.

Collective Impact and Legitimacy: Input, Output, and Throughput

How does CI claim it is a legitimate form of governance, where does its power originate? From a political perspective, a government is considered legitimate when it has the consent of the people to govern. This understanding of political legitimacy is founded in John Locke's work, or more recently, as Smismans (2015: 340) described the, "degree of trust that the governed have towards the political system." Legitimacy can be conceptualized from two key typologies "input" and "output" legitimacy.

Input refers to a political system being legitimate when citizens are happy with their involvement in decision-making processes, even if the outcomes of policy are not favorable to their position. "Output" is where the political systems are found to be legitimate, based on the outcomes they achieve.

A third, and under-theorized legitimacy, is "throughput." CI is not necessarily political, although there are indeed political aspirations that include advocating for systems and policy change, leaving questions of where, and how, can a CI find/claim to be a legitimate authority. For CI, the trick is to draw a balance that generates both "input" and "output" legitimacy.

This section discusses legitimacy from two key typologies, input and output, focusing on how a CI can demonstrate a degree of authority in an already complex system of governance with tensions for governments who attempt to demonstrate their own legitimacy.

Input Legitimacy

A normative structure for CI includes a backbone organization and other organizations that can play a backbone function. Input legitimacy refers to the processes and mechanisms for decision making, and how these link to citizen preferences. Elections provide the means with which to hold public officials accountable; but what is ultimately more important than the outcomes in a system are the processes for decision making and the level of citizen involvement. Do backbone organizations require a level of citizen input when employing staff?

The current situation for CI is that employees of backbone organizations are not voted in through an election process. With no elections, or democratic processes underpinning the appointment of officials in backbone organizations, the key decision making positions are decided through permissive consensus. That is, key representatives are selected through more traditional organizational models, characterized by interviews and selection panels. The input legitimacy of CI is characterized by permissive consensus, leaving the model subject to criticisms that it lacks democratic processes and has, potentially, a democratic deficit. There may or may not be problems associated with these processes, provided that CI can deliver the outcomes needed for change.

Child Friendly Leeds demonstrates a unique approach to input legitimacy. Leeds has three "obsessions," insure children are safe, reduce the number of children and young people not in education and employment, and improve school attendance. Weekly data are recorded on these three obsessions providing insights into how these results are trending over time. With a population over 900,000, there are over 600 organizations, businesses, and schools, all working toward 14 priorities (Leeds City Council, 2015). The voices of children and young people are central to the actions and strategies. They have established a Youth Parliament, Leeds Youth Council, when council employee staff children are invited onto interview panels, to ask questions and provide an opportunity for them to have influence on the recruitment process. This unique approach demonstrates an input legitimacy, i.e. input from the children and young people who are central to developing a child-friendly city.

Output Legitimacy

With a potential democratic deficit arising from the processes relating to the appointment of key personnel in backbone organizations, a CI's legitimacy will be achieved through its ability to achieve outcomes. At scale, a CI that does achieve outcomes for the populations it seeks to serve may well position itself as a legitimate authority for decision making as it demonstrates its ability to change the conditions of life, impact systems change, and influence public policy. Over time, this leaves questions of sustainability. Will this be enough to maintain the legitimacy of a CI in the absence of democratic decision-making processes? As previously discussed, the way in which a CI is structured will demonstrate its ability to involve community in decision making processes. Throughput legitimacy provides the methods where CI can build its argument as a legitimate form of governance and be less reliant on the input and output legitimacy for its authority.

Throughput Legitimacy

A third dimension to legitimacy exists in the less theorized "throughput" legitimacy. This concept, perhaps most important to CI, describes not just governance process, but also the quality of those processes as outlined by Schmidt (2013: 2) in relation to "efficacy, accountability, transparency, inclusiveness and openness to interest intermediation." A focus on throughput legitimacy, will uncover the extent to which the governance mechanisms support participatory decision making, and community led change. Legitimacy is not found in the ability of the initiative to demonstrate outcomes, or, by a vote of membership for the Steering Committee. Community decision making is central to establishing legitimacy for CI movements. Without throughput legitimacy and commitment to community development decision making, CI will repeat the status quo of a top-down, elitist, pluralistic approach to community change.

Throughput Legitimacy in Burnie Works, Tasmania

In the emergent stages of many CI efforts, establishing a common agenda involves an emphasis on service mapping, collating baseline population data, and consulting with community and service providers. What follows is a detailed agenda-setting process, that takes time before implementation of new projects. The legitimacy of these approaches lies in the output of the initiatives and their ability to achieve outcomes for the populations. There is no input legitimacy since members of the collective are not voted into positions and the community consultations are not designed to support decision making from community members.

When establishing the common agenda, Burnie Works (Social Ventures Australia, 2016) focused on understanding the aspirations of community and embedding the principles of collaboration that would underpin the change processes. Practically, new projects with key stakeholders and actions would be implemented almost immediately, meaning that outcomes would be achieved specific to those aspirations. One example is the ten families project where the *Burnie Works* backbone team established an integrated approach that supported families whose children were disengaging from formal education. Families opted in to the process, and were part of the decision making when setting goals. Families were then supported by the participating agencies involved (Social Ventures Australia, 2016). Following the prototype phase, the program has been scaled up to support 50 families.

Dream Big improved partnerships between the business and education sectors. It provides students with regular visits to different industries that then increase their knowledge about the diversity of employment opportunities. This exposure to an experiential learning process helps students plan for future careers at an earlier age. To date, more than 100 business are involved in the project (Burnie Works a, 2017).

Hilltop Market Garden: Food insecurity was identified as a key problem in a region within Burnie. Local residents aspired to improve health and well-being by establishing a mechanism to support the supply and production of fresh food. Unemployment is high in this area so skill development programs and accredited training are offered to residents. The success of the project has depended on the commitment of residents to establish and maintain the market gardens, learning centers, and community centers (Burnie Works b, 2017).

Throughput legitimacy is shown by the direct involvement of families in the prototyping and decision making phase that led to outcomes. Service providers understand what they need to do and how to fully support these families to achieve their goals. The professional arrogance of "service providers know best," has been left behind, in favor of families making the decisions. Other Burnie Works aspirational projects are yielding results in short amounts of time.

Summarizing Legitimacy for CI

CI will be most effective where it can demonstrate these three types of legitimacy. From the input phase, like Leeds, providing opportunities for citizens to engage in a democratic process in the appointment of staff to a backbone organization, will provide evidence of input legitimacy. Output legitimacy, will be evidenced through the CI ability to communicate its ability to show outcomes for end-users.

Accountability is one tenant of output legitimacy; shared measurement systems provide the mechanism to demonstrate the efficacy of a CI. Throughput legitimacy will be shown in the mechanism that supports inclusive community engagement and decision making processes. CI will transcend these three typologies when community development is the core of the work. For input, democratic process in the appointment of personnel in key positions for the initiatives facilitate decision making. For throughput, community aspirations and decision making drive the actions for initiative. Output includes a shared learning regarding the outcomes an initiative has achieved.

Untangling Institutional Complexity

The complexity of systems presents a challenge for CI. To frame this discussion, consider the social determinants of health and how these influence the health and developmental trajectory of children over their lifespan. There are structural determinants that include governance issues, macroeconomic policies, social policies, other public policy areas, and culture and social values. Added to the structural determinants of health are the education, occupation, and income of parents. Intermediary determinants of health include the family circumstances, housing stability, home environment, behaviors, and psychosocial factors (Solar & Irwin, 2005: 25–48). Combined, the structural and intermediary determinants of health that a child is born into has impacts on future development, income and health for the whole of life trajectory.

These structural and intermediary determinants have multiple "nested" systems (Neal & Neal, 2013: 722–737) with their own set of values, norms, and resources that exist across multiple levels, including the microsystem, mesosystem, and exosystems. These systems have multiple parts and policy that make decisions in a vacuum with little acknowledgment of their impact across other levels and parts of the system.

The current structure of these systems, layers and their parts, is inherently reductionist beginning at a political level. A government decides what policy areas to allocate to government ministers. Allocation and distribution of funding is then dispersed across these policy areas for specific purpose—employment services, housing, financial support, health.

The next layer is the department with responsibility for implementing policy, providing policy advice, and managing outsourced social and health services. Internal to each department, there is further reductionism into specific program areas. For example, the operating divisions of the U.S. Department of Health & Human Services (DHHS) has 11 administration and agency streams including Centers for Disease Control and Prevention (CDC), Food and Drug Administration, and Substance Abuse and Mental Health Services Administration. Also included is the Administration for Children and Families, and this portfolio has an additional eight program areas, including Office of Community Services, Office of Family Assistance, Administration on Children, Youth and Families (Department of Health and Human Services, 2017). Within the Office of Community Services there are a further eight grants and program streams. The types of support available across the Office of Community Services include Low Income Home Energy Assistance Program, Assets for Independence, and Job Opportunities programs.

These programs include layers that provide funding directly to states and non-government organizations. Housing assistance and support due to homelessness are provided through the Department of Housing and Urban Development. Access to health care requires users to purchase health insurance or face prohibitive costs.

CI must understand and offer a streamlined approach that reduce the complexity for individuals or families who must navigate this fragmented, and often isolated, service system. There are a diversity of government and non-government agencies implementing direct service provision with insurance based mechanisms that a family must access to provide an environment for its children to thrive. Within these government agencies, and non-government organizations delivering services are additional layers of complexity.

A single organization is a complex system. A whole systems change process will require each organization to implement its own change processes allowing it to adapt and support the entire systems change process. For an organization working in CI, change can be a bumpy incremental process, that is emergent, and requires modular and corporate transformations (Kogetsidis, 2012: 189–204).

Embedded within this complexity are levers for change. Identifying the system properties, understanding where the feedback loops break down, and the barriers to cross-sectoral integration will provide the insights that CI requires to influence systems change (Foster-Fishman, Nowell, & Yang, 2007: 197–215). The systems issues are abstract for most families and any system designed to meet individual and family needs must be designed in partnership with them. Community development approaches that enable the voices of the people who use the system to be heard will provide a much needed lens to the problems that the end users experience.

Translating Complexity into Positive Spill Over Effects

Disrupting and changing this system requires focusing on multiple levels and processes with a better understanding of system boundaries. It is necessary to take time to understand the root causes of the systemic issues and their impact. Begin with the intention to understand the problem, rather than intending to fix a problem. It is in understanding the causes that coalitions can begin the processes of change. Overarching this change process is the need for support from political leadership, to create the authorizing environment for change to flourish and, at scale, there are frameworks that support this work.

A report by The MarketShare Associates, *Disrupting System Dynamics: A Framework for Understanding Systemic Changes* (2016), provides a useful six-step framework to inform and measure systems change. First, the change begins by being disciplined and setting boundaries that can be observed during the change process.

Second, history and conditions, an environmental analysis that provides a history of the system and its current situation including identification of its potential to change.

Third, interventions that develop a vision for change and create community-driven interventions. With established feedback loops over time, all stakeholders can work through a shared learning process and continue to co-design the phases of change.

Fourth, agent level, as practitioners from different disciplines begin to deliver services differently, policy advisors provide different types of advice, and the market begins to change its behaviors, the spill over effect is observable across the system.

Fifth, collective level, when behaviors of constituents at all levels begin to change, and the desired behaviors are present. Here, it is worth highlighting the importance of building monitoring systems from the start of the change process since it allows for researchers to observe, identify, and communicate the changes that have occurred.

Sixth, development impacts, system changes require on-going monitoring of the conditions of life for the population it seeks to serve. Where negative effects may occur, these must be addressed, however, caution against a conservative view that would see the system revert to its previous state should be exercised. Again, on-going monitoring and understanding of the work underway will help to inform the next direction an initiative takes.

Systems change is a complex process with inherent norms, values and resource distribution processes governing the structures of decision making. There are then multiple interactions among multiple tiers of government departments and agencies, different levels of individuals in organizations with both balancing and reinforcing interdependencies, and interactions that can either help or hinder the change processes.

These layers of complexity contain levers for change. CI is a starting point for complex collaborative work. Initiatives must then develop a strategic action plan that acknowledges the complexity of the work, identifies the scope of the problem, and establishes strategic learning opportunities (Hanleybrown, Kania, & Kramer 2012). A systems framework helps to identify the interdependent connections that will help to drive change and locate the gaps in the feedback loops that prevent the flow of information and integration (Foster-Fishman, Nowell, & Yang 2007: 197–215). System boundaries provide the container for change and scope for influence. Outside the boundary and beyond the scope of any initiative unknown impacts can disrupt positive change. Fiscal and monetary policy, and collapse of industry and economic climates, have the potential to stop progress. Protecting our systems and communities against these deleterious economic effects that impact the developmental and health outcomes of our next generation, is easier said than done.

Conclusion

Success for CI begins with establishing a structure that incorporates community development as the central proponent for decision making at a local level, with locally designed solutions. With structures established that place community at the center of the change processes, a conceptual framework to inform the challenges when working with multiple stakeholders, and the right tools, a CI will have a greater chance of success. Both Intergovernmentalism and Neofunctionalism offer a theoretical foundation to understand the drivers of improved coordination and integration within a service system and across the business sector.

For CI, Intergovernmentalism is best applied during the emergent phase when establishing an initiative. Once the motivations for change are understood by all stakeholders and there is agreement on a common agenda, a CI can begin to advance the process of change. All stakeholders, government, non-government, the Third Sector, and the community need to acknowledge that effective change is predicated on a deliberate change of behavior. With an understanding that CI is a long-term, movement building exercise, that requires a shift from traditional ways of working, the initiative will begin the collective journey.

Neofunctionalism sets the path for action, and can be applied to small scale projects like the Burnie Works projects, or large scale initiatives like Vibrant Communities. All goals and objectives will require the identification of the key functional, political and cultivated spill over actions that must be addressed before reaching the end goal. When initiatives begin to develop or revise strategic action plans, they are advised to consider the spill over effects. Identifying key functional, political and cultivated spill over actions are necessary. Deliberate, purposive actions will provide improved transitions for change. The spill over hypothesis reminds leaders that unintended consequences and unknown actions will need to be managed throughout the processes.

As the movement building continues, elite socialization will be seen in leaders' preferences to support the collective rather than any singular organization's interests. There are opportunities for Social Network Analysis to review how these preferences have changed in a region where CI has been implemented.

Backbone organizations become a nexus between government, non-government, and the community. They are both facilitators of change and an interest group for pushing the agenda of improved integration. Multilevel governance structures connect local community participation and planning directly to policy makers, and policy networks. Community development and engagement will be the drivers for CI to be recognized as an exceptional and legitimate model. Legitimacy will be achieved by bridging the divide between formal decision making processes and aspirations of the community. Embedding community voice through the election of officials and their input into developing strategies, a CI can collectively share responsibility for the achievement of outcomes, while separating itself from traditional management paradigms.

The inclusion of community development as the key tenet that underpins CI, will be challenging in an environment where reductionism, competition and isolated impact are often rewarded. Complexity exists at a relational level between individuals, internal to any organization and agency and impacts the whole system. Scaled up, the interaction between the economic, social, cultural, and political spheres impact the individual trajectory of any organization from birth to end-of-life. CI provides a framework and community development unlocks the aspirations and ensures that community voice is central to change. Improving the conditions of well-being for whole populations will require a deliberative strategy to address the systems complexities and herein lies some of CI's greatest challenges.

References

Birchfield. V., & Crepaz, M. M. L. (1998) "The impact of constitutional structures and collective competitive veto points on income inequality in industrialized democracies," *European Journal of Political Studies*, 34, 175–200.

Burnie Works a (2017) "Dream Big," *Burnie Works Collective Impact*, viewed July 2017. Website: https://burnieworks.com.au/dreambig.html

Burnie Works b (2017) "About Burnie Works," *Burnie Works Collective Impact*, viewed March 2017. Website: www.burnieworks.com.au/about-burnie-works.html

Cini, M. (2013) "Intergovernmentalism," in M. Cini & N. Pérez-Solórzano Borragán (Ed.), *European Union Politics*, 5th Edition, Oxford University Press. pp. 65–78.

Christiansen, T. (2013) "Governance in the European Union," in M. Cini & N. Pérez-Solórzano Borragán (Eds) *European Union Politics*, 5th Edition, Oxford University Press. pp. 97–109.

Cabaj, M. & Weaver, L. Collective Impact 3.0: An evolving framework for community change, Community Change Series, Tamarack Institute, viewed September 2016. Website: www.tamarackcommunity.ca/library/collective-impact-3.0-an-evolving-framework-for-community-change

Collaboration for Impact (2017) "Build the collaborative governance structure," viewed March 2017. Website: www.collaborationforimpact.com/the-to-guide/phase-3-organize-for-impact/build-the-collaborative-governance-structure/

Department of Health and Human Services, *HHS Organizational Chart*, United States Government, viewed March 2017. Website: www.hhs.gov/about/agencies/orgchart/

Department of Social Services (2015) *Process review 2014–15 grants round*, Australian Commonwealth Government, viewed 09 October 2016. Website: www.dss.gov.au/sites/default/files/documents/11_2015/nous_process_review_of_the_2014-15_grants_round_240815_to_publish.docx

Foster-Fishman, G., Nowell, B., & Yang, B. (2007) "Putting the system back into systems change: A framework for understanding and changing organizational and community systems," *American Journal of Community Psychology*, 39(3–4), pp. 197–215.

Fortson, B., Klevens, J., Merrick, M. T., Gilbert, L. K., & Alexander, S. P. (2016) *Preventing Child Abuse and Neglect: A Technical Package for Policy, Norm, and Programmatic activities,* Centres for Disease Control and Prevention.

Gamble, J. (2010) Evaluating Vibrant Communities 2002–2010, Tamarack, pp. 47–70, viewed February 2017. Website: http://vibrantcanada.ca/files/vc_evaluation_complete_report.pdf

Hanleybrown, F., Kania, J., & Kramer, M. (2012) "Channelling Change: Making Collective Impact work," *Stanford Social Innovation Review,* viewed 24 March. Website: https://ssir.org/articles/entry/channeling_change_making_collective_impact_work

Himmelman, A. T. (2001) "On coalitions and the transformation of power relations: collaborative betterment and collaborative empowerment," *American Journal of Community Psychology,* 29(2), pp. 277–285.

Harper, I., Anderson, P., McCluskey, S., & Obryan, M. (2015) *Competition Policy Review Final Report,* Commonwealth of Australia.

Inner West (2017) Inner West Collective Impact Initiative, viewed from www.innerwest.org.au/

Kania, J., & Kramer, M. (2011) "Collective Impact," *Stanford Social Innovation Review.* Viewed March 2017. Website: www.gjcpp.org/en/resource.php?issue=21&resource=200

Kania, J., & Kramer, M. (2013) "Embracing emergence: how Collective Impact addresses complexity," *Stanford Social Innovation Review.* Viewed March 2017. Website: https://ssir.org/articles/entry/embracing_emergence_how_collective_impact_addresses_complexity

Kogetsidis, H. (2012) "Critical systems thinking: a creative approach to organizational change," *Journal of Transnational Management,* 17(3), pp. 189–204.

Leeds City Council, Leeds Children and Young People's Plan 2015: From good to great, viewed March 2017. Website: www.leeds.gov.uk/docs/Leeds%20Children%20and%20Young%20People%20Plan%202015–2019%20WEB.pdf

Legislative Council (2015) Service coordination in communities with high social needs, Standing Committee on Social Issues, New South Wales Parliamentary Library, 2015.

Logan Together (2015) Logan Together, Logan Together Working Group, Version 7.0, pp. 13–14, viewed March 2017. Website: www.logan.qld.gov.au/__data/assets/pdf_file/0010/342568/Logan_Together_Prospectus_–_June_2015_pdf.pdf

Lopez-Viso. M., Fernandez, A., & Anton, L. (2014) "Multi–level governance and social cohesion in the European Union: the assessment of local agents, a study case inside Galicia," *Revista Brasileira de Política Internacional,* 57(2), p. 204.

MarketShare Economics, Disrupting system dynamics: A framework for understanding systemic changes, Leveraging Economic Opportunities, Report 47, viewed March 2017. Website: http://marketshareassociates.com/wp–content/uploads/2017/01/Report_No__47_–_Systemic_Change_Framework_FINAL_–_508_compliant.pdf

Moravcsik, A., & Schimmelfennig, F. (2007) "Liberal Intergovernmentalism," in Wiener, A. & Diez, T. eds. *European Integration Theory,* Oxford University Press. pp. 67–69.

Neal, J. W., & Neal, Z. P. (2013) "Nested or networked? Future directions for ecological systems theory," *Journal of Social Development,* 22(4). 722–737.

Rosamond, B. (2000) *Theories of European Integration,* London: Macmillan St Martin's Press.

Rhodes, R. A. W. (1996) "The new governance: governing without government," *Journal of Political Studies,* 44(4). pp. 652–667.

Schmidt, V. A. (2013) "Democracy and legitimacy in the European Union revisited: Input, output and Throughput," *Journal of Political Studies,* 61(1), pp. 2–22.

Schmitter, P. C. (2005) "Ernest B. Haas and the legacy of neofunctionalism," *Journal of European Public Policy,* 12(2), pp. 255–272.

Scott, J. (2013) *Social Network Analysis* (K. Metzler, Ed.). London: SAGE Publications.

Smismans, S. (2013) "Democracy and Legitimacy in the European Union," in M. Cini & N. Pérez-Solórzano Borragán (Eds) *European Union Politics*, 5th Edition, Oxford University Press, pp. 339–351.

Social Ventures Australia (2016) A collective impact learning lab, SVA Quarterly. Viewed March 2017. Website: www.socialventures.com.au/sva-quarterly/collective-impact-learning-lab/

Solar, O., & Irwin A. (2005) *A conceptual framework for action on the social determinants of health.* Social Determinants of Health Discussion Paper 2 (Policy and Practice), pp. 25–48.

Splansky Juster, J. (2013) Collective Impact Case Study: Vibrant Communities, FSG, viewed February 2017. Website: www.fsg.org/publications/vibrant–communities

Stoker, G. (1998) "Governance as theory: Five propositions," *International Social Science Journal*, 50(1), pp. 17–28.

Strøby Jensen, C. (2013) "Neo-functionalism," in M. Cini & N. Pérez–Solórzano Borragán (Eds) *European Union Politics*, 5th Edition, Oxford University Press. pp. 53–64.

Together SA (2016) 'Inner Adelaide West', viewed February 2017. Website: www.togethersa.org.au/project/communities-of-action/inner-adelaide-west/

Tortola, P. D. (2017) "Clarifying multilevel governance," *European Journal of Political Research*, 56(2), pp. 234–250.

United Way (2016) Collective Impact: Insights from the Hive Mt Druitt, viewed March 2017. Website: http://unitedway.com.au/2016/12/collective-impact-insights-from-the-hive

Tapin, F. (2013) Racial tension in Brisbane as Aboriginal, Pacific Islander groups clash, Australian Broadcasting Corporation. Viewed March 2017. Website: www.abc.net.au/news/2013-01-15/an-logan-tension/4465040

Wolff, T. (2016) "Ten places where Collective Impact gets it wrong," *Global Journal of Community Psychology Practice*, 7(1), viewed March 2017. Website: www.gjcpp.org/en/resource.php?issue=21&resource=200

Wright, O. (2016) Insights from a Collective Impact initiative in Australia, Collaboration for Impact. Viewed March 2017 www.collaborationforimpact.com/insights–from–a–collective–impact–initiative–in–australia/

Further Reading

W. Ulrich, *A brief introduction to critical systems heuristics (CSH)*. ECOSENSUS project, Open University, Milton Keynes, UK. Provides a detailed framework for systems analysis. (2005). P.M. Senge, *The dance of change: the challenges of sustaining momentum in learning organizations* (New York: Currency/Doubleday 1999), supporting managers and executives to build organizational capability for complex systems change. J.M. Bryson, *Strategic planning for public and nonprofit organizations: A guide to sustaining organizational achievement* (Hoboken: John Wiley & Sons, 2011), a resource providing a detailed approach to strategic planning, useful for any CI initiatives.

3

NETWORK AGREEMENTS

Co-Designing Principles that Influence Network Culture

Dustin C. Stiver

Introduction

The term *networks* refers to "multi-organizational arrangements for solving problems that cannot be achieved, or easily achieved, by single organizations" (Agranoff & McGuire 2001: 296). Provan, Fish, and Sydow (2007) described whole networks as those that are consciously formed, organized, and goal-directed. The professional literature on this topic shows that most networks share the following elements: social interaction, relationships, connectedness, collaboration, collective action, trust, and cooperation (Popp et al. 2014). High-performing multi-organizational networks are built on a foundation of principles agreed upon by both leaders and members. The following analyses examine the core elements and processes guiding the development of *Network Agreements* (Stiver 2017).

Multi-organizational networks are a mechanism to organize a community's resources to accelerate positive change. Nearly all sectors—from education to public health to community development—are pressured to operate more efficiently and achieve greater outcomes more quickly (Camarinha-Matos & Afsarmanesh 2014). Networks help communities collaboratively contend with society's most vexing challenges and create lasting community change (Bryson, Crosby, & Stone 2015). This condition is especially true when addressing wicked problems that are more multifaceted and entangled than any one person or organization can tackle individually (Rittel 1973). In those cases, "networks provide a plausible alternative for productively organizing the diverse expertise needed to solve complex . . . problems" (Bryk, Gomez, and Grunow 2011: 6).

The pursuit of novel and effective solutions to complex problems routinely involves collaboration between individuals and organizations with a diverse array of experiences and expertise (Leonard & Swap 1999). Soliciting contributions from actors who reside in different organizations and different sectors is an important part of building a successful network (Bryson, Crosby & Stone 2015; Mumford et al. 2000). Indeed, inter-organizational and cross-disciplinary collaboration is at the heart of initiatives designed to achieve Collective Impact (Kania & Kramer 2011).

Network-building has become a common strategy for leaders who see the world through a holistic, systems perspective (Senge & Sterman 1992). Practitioners in many fields are adopting network-based approaches to solve or mitigate complex social problems (Cullen-Lester & Yammarino 2016; Popp et al. 2014). To wit, "networks have been established in the public and nonprofit sectors to create collective solutions to complex problems through cross-boundary action" (Popp et al. 2014: p. 1). Structurally speaking, networks are a hybrid organizational form that enable allied institutions to pursue collectively held goals (Popp et al. 2014; Provan et al. 2007).

Some networks engage people to work on behalf of the network; these people are considered *Network Leaders* (NLs). NLs are individuals who steward network activity, either because they hold a formal position of authority or because they are influential in other ways. NLs are the individuals responsible for motivating people to be part of something bigger and leveraging the power of collaboration to create change in the face of "domain level problems" (Trist 1983). NLs are action-oriented and pragmatic (Huxham & Vangen 2000). They move beyond rhetoric by facilitating processes through which more creative, inventive, and impactful solutions can be devised and implemented. Ansell and Gash (2012) described collaborative leaders as "stewards, mediators, and catalysts" (p. 6). NLs are collaborative and they must work across boundaries to cultivate contributions from people who will help the network achieve its mission (Linden 2003).

Research on NLs suggests that they live by a motto of *lead as one among many* (Stiver 2017). Successful NLs recognize their place as one among many and come alongside stakeholders to leverage the power of the collective. *Rise of the Network Leader*, a 2014 CEB report, stated that "network leadership is more about influence than control; it is also a more indirect than direct form of leadership, requiring leaders to create a work environment based on autonomy, empowerment, trust, sharing, and collaboration" (p. 11). Network leadership is not hierarchical; it is horizontal. NLs actively acknowledge their positionality alongside and in support of *Network Members* (NMs). NLs acknowledge the fact that they serve at the pleasure of NMs and must rely on them to enact change.

Constructivist Grounded Theory research has been used to examine how NLs catalyze collective action (Stiver 2017). One strategy used by NLs is to co-design principles that influence network culture. These principles are called *Network Agreements* (NAs), which are shared principles that influence network activity and explicitly name network values. The word *agreements* emphasizes the point that NAs must be *agreed to* by all members of a network. NMs must have a shared understanding of the NAs and a willingness to work in accordance with those values.

NAs represent a lens through which NLs and NMs can view and evaluate their work. NLs are encouraged to work with NMs to co-design custom NAs based on local conditions. Lee (2008) stated that co-designing "is based on the idea that all people have different opinions and should collaborate in any design process" (p. 34). When co-designing NAs, NLs must design processes that incorporate the views of as many NMs as possible. When practiced, NAs can lead to the development of a welcoming, inspiring, and more equitable network culture.

Collaboration is commonly regarded as a productive strategy for dealing with complex problems but it can also lead to confusion and consternation. NLs sit at the crux of the energy generated when collaborative intentions meet real world challenges. In an increasingly connected society, NLs must orchestrate the creative chaos occurring when people engage in collaborative innovation processes (Goh, Goodman, & Weingart 2013). NLs must weave together a multitude of voices into a powerful collective and empower people to work together to contribute solutions to shared challenges. Ultimately, NLs are charged with creating the conditions for productive and meaningful collaboration. Developing a reliable set of NAs can help NLs ensure that NMs understand the values governing their shared pursuits.

Methodology

The research informing this chapter involved subjects who were professionally engaged as NLs and sought to uncover strategies that NLs employ when performing their unique role. Data were collected and analyzed using the Constructivist Grounded Theory method (Charmaz 2006). Klenke (2008) neatly defined Grounded Theory as "a research method in which theory emerges from the data and is grounded in it" (p. 186). Grounded Theory "comprises a systematic, inductive, and comparative approach for conducting inquiry for the purpose of constructing theory" (Bryant & Charmaz 2007: 1). The primary research question was: How do NLs catalyze collective action? The emergent, iterative, and responsive nature of Constructivist Grounded Theory allowed the research topic to be studied in a prudent and effective way (Patton 2002).

The research used criterion sampling. Participants were selected from a variety of networked-based settings, including but not limited to Collective Impact networks, to collect data from NLs working in a range of operating environments, settings, locations, and content areas. All participants were active NLs working in the United States or Canada. Participants included individuals employed as independent facilitators, NMs specifically tasked with leading network activity, and staff of backbone organizations. The average time on the job for interviewees was more than four years. Data were collected through intensive interviews with 27 participants (Kvale 1996). For more details about the data sources and the data collection process, see Stiver (2017).

In accordance with Grounded Theory, initial sampling and theoretical sampling were utilized (Charmaz 2006). These sampling methods enable researchers to identify data-rich research participants based on pre-determined criteria (Ritchie et al. 2013). In Constructivist Grounded Theory research, data analysis is systematic

TABLE 3.1 Demographic Information about Study Participants

Gender Identification		Age of Participants		Race of Participants		Time Served as NL (yrs)		Length of Interview (mins)	
Female	16	30–39	11	White	20	Avg Time	4.10	Average	55
Male	11	40–49	12	Black	3	Median	3.25	Median	59
		50–59	1	Other	4	Min	0.83	Min	17
		60+	3			Max	11.00	Max	74

and begins as soon as data becomes available. Data were analyzed using qualitative coding—evolving from initial to focused to theoretical. Constant Comparative Analysis, a hallmark of Grounded Theory, was used throughout the data collection process (Charmaz 2006). As data was collected and analyzed, memos were written about themes emerging from the data. As the process continued, additional data was collected and analyzed until saturation was reached.

A few limitations arose. Data was collected from individuals working as NLs in specific context; data was gathered voluntarily from research subjects in the United States and Canada during late 2016 and early 2017. The geographic restriction was implemented to ensure that research subjects worked in comparable environments. NLs working in other locales and under dissimilar conditions might have responded differently.

Adherence to several best practices in qualitative research assured the trustworthiness of the study. Information-rich participants and other data sources were used in data collection. A systematic research method was utilized (Lincoln & Guba 1985; Patton 2002). The findings and conclusions are grounded in the data and the analysis process was both judicious and fitting (Charmaz 2006). Triangulation of the data helped to document and report multiple perspectives (Patton 2002). Lastly, the construction of rich, thick descriptions ensured that the research process was complete.

About the Findings

Research has identified a set of eight *Network Agreements* (NAs) that are relevant to Collective Impact efforts and other collaborative networks (Stiver 2017). NAs are shared principles that influence network activity and, in turn, network culture. These agreements represent a framework through which NLs and NMs can view and evaluate their work. The NAs outlined in this chapter are conceptualized as a starting point. NLs are encouraged to work with NMs to modify these principles by co-designing custom agreements based on the local operating environment. NAs must be developed in a participatory fashion, ratified by NMs, and benevolently enforced by NLs. When practiced, NAs can help create a healthy network culture.

The findings presented next are informed by anonymous participant quotations, paraphrases and summaries of interviewees' comments from recent research (Stiver 2017). Most participant quotations are presented verbatim; however, some have been edited for readability and to ensure confidentiality.

Co-designing Network Agreements

One of the primary ways that NLs create parameters for action is by *shaping the network*. This phrase describes the variety of network leadership responsibilities related to network design. The notion of *shaping* a network is reminiscent of Mintzberg's[sj1] (1987) essay about *crafting* strategy. Shaping a network is a craft that requires skill and expertise. A network's structure must be molded to meet the needs of its members.

Shaping the network is about creating an organizing framework and giving structure to a network. Interviewees emphasized the value of creating networks that are responsive, adaptable, and even liberating. Shaping the network involves developing nimble processes, procedures and mechanisms that enable NMs to collectively achieve the network's goals. The overriding principle is to use "minimal interventions to make sure that the network is headed in the direction that it needs to go."

NLs cannot shape the network by themselves; instead, they must create a culture that encourages NMs to creatively and meaningfully contribute to the overall form of the network. Interviewees described the importance of properly developing a framework for action, as illustrated by this quote: "having a frame is the only way to navigate chaos." Designing a reliable network structure, and iteratively improving on it, helps NLs navigate chaos in positive ways and provides NMs with a clear understanding of how they can contribute to shared goals.

NLs face many design challenges when shaping a network. Each network has a set of unique design constraints such as limited staff capacity, relying on a transient population of NMs, working across vast geographies, and jockeying for people's time. NLs must be prepared to design within such constraints. To effectively shape a network and develop winning strategies, the current research shows that NLs must understand the constraints impinging on the network and be responsive to them.

When designing a network, it is important to consider localization, which can be described as *leading in context*. To be effective, NLs must have a firm grasp on the local landscape they are navigating. Interviewees emphasized that NLs must recognize the importance of context and the fact that what works in one community may "not look the same in every zip code." Networks must be grounded in the local context. Whenever NLs are developing strategies, they must customize their approach, or *shape their network*, to meet local needs.

The process of shaping a network involves many elements such as crafting a theory of change, developing shared messaging, building an identity, fundraising for network activities, and setting common, measurable goals. However, this chapter focuses solely on one specific element of shaping a network: Co-designing

Network Agreements. NLs must develop processes to help NMs identify and adopt shared commitments.

Interviewees underscored the importance and difficulty of developing shared commitments, as represented by this quote: "One of the hardest parts is the alignment piece. In my mind, that is always the hardest part of a Collective Impact. Getting people aligned around specific goals." NMs must be invested in achieving shared outcomes. NLs must help NMs find commonalities that draw them together and identify shared values and practices. To create a healthy network culture, interviewees emphasized the need to select focus areas, determine priorities, and co-develop NAs. NLs must possess excellent facilitation skills, a hefty dose of patience, and an unwavering commitment to community change in order to align the network to a common agenda.

Interviewees also mentioned the importance of developing and enforcing quality standards. Again, NLs cannot determine these standards alone but they can do so in tandem with an advisory group comprised of NMs. The majority of interviewees said that it is important to establish expectations about network participation, accurately communicate those expectations to NMs, and be candid about non–negotiables. Ultimately, NMs must make commitments about how they will advance the work of the network. Having a shared set of NAs is beneficial because it allows NLs and NMs to clearly set expectations regarding how people will operate within the network.

The Network Agreements

Current research has identified eight NAs that are applicable to multiorganizational networks: (1) leverage the power of networks; (2) foster a supportive environment; (3) practice honest engagement; (4) adopt open practices; (5) honor expertise and experience; (6) empower people; (7) make community-minded decisions; and (8) fight for equity, access and justice (Stiver 2017). These NAs are a starting point, not an exhaustive list; nor are they necessarily right for each network, which is why NLs must implement a Network Agreement Development Process with their NMs to determine which agreements match the local context.

NLs must work with NMs to co-design custom NAs that reflect the network's goals, approach, and local conditions. NLs must design processes that incorporate the opinions of as many NMs as possible. Human-Centered Design (HCD) approaches to facilitation are a promising way to incorporate NMs into the process of developing shared NAs. When adopted and practiced, NAs can lead to the development of a welcoming, inspiring, and equitable network culture. The following sections describe eight fundamental NAs expressed by modern-day NLs.

Leverage the Power of Networks

Networks are powerful because they unleash the collective energy and expertise of people who share similar passions. NMs must adopt a "network mindset" that prizes collaborative action (Scearce 2011). Tracey and Stott (2017) coined the term "social extrapreneurship" to describe "the process of interorganizational action that facilitates alternative combinations of ideas, people, places and resources to address social challenges and make social change" (p. 55). Interviewees emphasized that networks are a viable strategy when a challenge is so complex and interwoven that there is no way to respond to it as one organization or institution. It is in those instances when people must leverage the power of networks to achieve uncommon outcomes.

Networks are a promising vehicle for responding to complex problems because they connect disconnected nodes, but here's how one interviewee described the current reality:

> It was clear that there was really amazing work happening in many different places. Lots of solutions were emerging from the ground that were locally driven and empowering and rethinking how people could be a force for good in communities. Yet those nodes were disconnected.

NLs are the "informed connectors" that help stitch together the threads of collaboration by working across organizations. Networks can go where organizations cannot: the spaces between institutions. NLs and NMs toil in the in-between spaces that require them to cross boundaries and break down silos.

Networks are strong when they leverage the power of distributed leadership, collective expertise, and interpersonal connections. Indeed, believing in the power of the collective is core to network life. This quote makes the point well: "Understanding one's impact within networks and how to leverage networks is the key skill going forward for personal, professional and civic life." This echoes Raine and Wellman's (2012) research on networked individualism. NMs must see themselves as part of a networked world.

Interviewees touted the benefits of networks by saying that they help reduce duplication, streamline the use of limited resources, and align the major players working within a field of interest. In short, networks exist to solve shared challenges through intentional collaboration. Interviewees were clear that "we have a lot to gain from collective intelligence and collective experience." NLs must create the conditions that enable NMs to leverage existing resources, increase cohesiveness, and scale great work. The collective opinion of interviewees can be summed up by saying that "systemic issues require coalitions, collectives, collaboratives, and networks." Capitalizing on a belief that collectively we can do more than we can do alone, NLs leverage the power of networks to catalyze collective action.

Foster a Supportive Network Environment

Interviewees clearly indicated the importance of developing cultural practices, creating rituals, and establishing norms within a network. NLs and NMs must recognize that every decision they make contributes to the development of a network culture. Interviewees stressed that NLs must endeavor to create an environment that is warm, friendly, and inviting. It is important to build a culture that welcomes people and treats them with respect.

NMs must care deeply about one another and their common cause. One interviewee summarized the sentiment by saying, "I think it's important for people to feel like they're part of a loving community that has the interests of others in mind." Wei-Skillern and Silver (2013) echoed this point when they wrote about four counterintuitive principles for network collaboration: focus on mission before organization; build partnerships based on trust, not control; promote others rather than yourself; and build constellations rather than stars.

NLs and NMs must strive to create a supportive environment that encourages people to learn from one another. Interviewees emphasized the importance of embracing an inquiry-based approach and adopting a learning stance—a disposition emphasizing the need to learn from other people and acknowledging that no one person has all the answers. Interviewees mentioned the need for NMs to develop the confidence to share their work and not be ashamed to ask for help when needed. The data revealed that people are more willing to be vulnerable when they are in a network culture that feels safe. In short, the goal is to foster a supportive network environment that is welcoming and inviting, and results in the development of a loyal and caring community.

Practice Honest Engagement

Network-building is predicated on the development of strong, meaningful relationships. Interviewees emphasized the importance of engaging with people at a human level, as colleagues and friends. A preponderance of interviewees discussed the need to truly, honestly, and genuinely engage participants. The word *honest* accurately captures the earnest and authentic spirit of the data. Honest engagement is not vapid or veiled; it is sincere and involves a mutual exchange of value. NLs must be truthful, open, candid, and forthright. Avolio and Gardner (2005) provided an overview of the authentic leadership behaviors related to honest engagement.

NLs must design ways to genuinely involve NMs in network activities and enable NMs to contribute to shared goals. NLs must devise ways to help NMs learn about, connect to, benefit from, and take on network projects. NLs must focus people's energy and expertise and funnel them toward places where their talents can be used most effectively. Interviewees also stressed the importance of identifying ways to increase engagement by NMs. Once people find their place in the network, then NLs must offer people unique leadership roles.

NLs must be mindful of the network engagement lifecycle, from salutation to valediction, to ensure that NMs genuinely contribute to the network's goals in ways that are both personally and collectively beneficial. NLs must intentionally design ways for people's participation to ebb and flow so that they do not burn out. Still, some NMs may reach a point where it makes the most sense for them to exit the network. People need to know how to start engaging with the network, ramp up their involvement, be given ways to sustain their participation, take leadership roles within the network, and either continue to be involved or gracefully exit.

Scaffolding learning is a popular notion in education. Pea (2004) described a scaffolding model that includes focusing a learner's attention on a more advanced task, modeling the more advanced activity, then fading away and allowing the person to work autonomously at a deeper level. A similar idea could be applied to network engagement, scaffolding engagement. NLs should make it easier for members to become involved and empower them to stay involved. It is important to provide multiple ways for people to engage with the network and grow their engagement over time. The scaffolding metaphor is an evocative way to describe how NLs can help NMs increase their involvement and engage in more autonomous network activity (Stone 1993, 1998).

Adopt Open Practices

It is important for NLs to encourage NMs to adopt open practices. Santo, Ching, Peppler, and Hoadley's (2016) description of "working in the open" and engaging in "collective professional learning" is relevant to network leadership (p. 280). The authors describe five practices that are emblematic of working open: (1) public storytelling and context setting; (2) enabling community contribution; (3) rapid prototyping; (4) public reflection and documentation; and (5) creating remixable or replicable work products (Santo et al. 2016).

All interviewees discussed the importance of helping good ideas spread throughout the network; sharing with each other, deeply; and keeping people apprised of what's happening within the network. One way to accomplish those goals is by adopting open practices. This quote summarizes the point well: "There's a piece about open source culture, open source practices, and an open source ethos that is actually the blueprint for doing networked work better and more thoughtfully." An opportunity exists to "evolve open source processes and social practices and apply them to broader network thinking."

Interviewees stressed the importance of documenting and archiving one's work. Process and documentation are imperative to open source thinking and NLs must be "be highly intentional about what they document, how they share it, and what kind of experience they want their users to have." After all, without process and documentation, it's all ephemeral.

NLs must model behaviors that are desired within the community when it comes to "working open." Interviewees encouraged NMs to adopt open practices, share their thinking through open platforms, open up their archives, and to take advantage of the wisdom of the crowd. NLs must make clear the shared problems of practice that NMs need to address in order to achieve the network's collective goals. It is important to encourage people to openly reflect on challenges and share their reflections with others. Networks that adopt open practices engender a culture of sharing, iteration, and continuous improvement that can lead to accelerated outcomes.

Honor Expertise and Experience

A majority of interviewees expressed a desire to enable individuals to exercise their personal agency. Ahearn (2001) defined agency as "the socioculturally mediated capacity to act" (p. 112). There is an important distinction between giving people agency, which presumes they do not have any or they do not have enough, and freeing people to utilize their existing agency, which, in effect, enables them to express themselves more fully. NLs must create structures that empower NMs to make meaningful contributions to shared goals. NMs should possess the capacity to act be compelled to do so. Edwards' (2006) notion of relational agency recognizes the need to work with others, especially in professional environments and at the boundary of organizations. Ultimately, interviewees emphasized that NMs must feel a sense of agency and belonging in order to be a valued member of a network.

It is safe to assume that those who adopt a network–based approach see value in the collective. Therefore, honoring the expertise and experiences that others bring with them is fundamental to network life. NLs rely on the expertise of others. Instead of being a gatekeeper of knowledge, interviewees reported that NLs must respect the knowledge of members and honor individuals' capabilities. Moreover, interviewees clearly said that NLs should yield to other people's expertise, defer to people with more subject matter knowledge, and recognize that NMs are the most important source of information related to the network.

An important part of *leading as one among many* is acknowledging the value of NMs and their lived experience. NLs must adopt an orientation that recognizes the expertise of their members and NMs should seek to learn from the experiences of their peers. By honoring the expertise of NMs, NLs give them a chance to express their agency and contribute to the network in meaningful ways. NLs should strive to provide high quality, empowering, capacity-building leadership that equips NMs to apply their knowledge, skills, abilities to the mission of the network.

Empower People

Networks are nothing without the people who contribute to them. NLs must remember that. They work in support of NMs and their collective aims. NMs must be motivated to contribute to the network and NLs cannot force people to participate; they must want to be involved. So much of what networks can do is empower people to build connections with one another by sharing their stories and learning from each another.

Empowerment, in a networked setting, is about encouraging individuals to feel emboldened to express themselves in ways that are both personally meaningful and additive to the goals of the network. Rowland's (1995) tripartite conception of empowerment is aligned with the research presented in this chapter. Similarly, Bandura's (2006) discussion of collective agency is also relevant. Interviewees said that when people feel empowered, they can face their challenges and access the information that they need to succeed.

In practical terms, empowering people also helps NLs get things done. When a network member is well-suited to handle a challenge, and they possess the resources necessary to tackle it successfully, they need to be empowered to act. It is important to note that not all projects require collaboration. Instead of actively orchestrating every activity, many NLs choose to put the power in the hands of the NMs to lead projects and activities on behalf of the network. It is important to empower people to be themselves and make unique contributions to the network. Ultimately, NMs must feel inspired to do work that benefits the network's mission.

Interviewees also referenced the power of using a network's identity to endorse the actions of NMs—in effect, giving them freedom to act, to try new things, and to take risks. Networks can endorse the activity of their members and provide a stamp of approval or the imprimatur to act. Networks can empower people by giving them the freedom to express themselves, leverage their expertise, and utilize their agency in support of network goals.

Make Community-Minded Decisions

NLs are not heavy-handed rulers from on high; they are active facilitators who engage the group in making decisions, often by consensus. Designing processes that enable NMs to make sound decisions is a key role of NLs who are responsible for creating space for collective decision making. Routhieaux's (2015) emphasis on shared decision-making and building a culture of shared leadership align with the findings reported here. Some interviewees prefer all decisions to be network-led while others said that certain decisions have to rest with the network leader, either for expediency or because of fiduciary arrangements. Either way, it is imperative that NLs go where the network wants them to go and always have the network's best interest in mind when making decisions on behalf of the group.

NLs must steward decision-making processes that include as many voices as possible and encourage NMs to make community-minded decisions. Diverse networks are stronger and more vibrant than homogeneous networks, but welcoming diverse perspectives means that NLs must be excellent listeners with the skills to incorporate multiple viewpoints. As one interviewee said, NLs must "reconcile a set of competing ideas and advocate for benefits that different stake-holders want out of the experience."

NLs must acknowledge their biases and chart a path forward that is inclusive of different points of view and different ideas. With many stakeholders and diverse opinions, NLs must weather tensions to make community-minded decisions. There will always be many roads to travel; NLs must help their network determine which route is best.

Fight for Equity, Access, and Justice

NLs are often charged with increasing equity and creating greater access to opportunities. Interviewees frequently mentioned combatting various types of inequality. Structural barriers are those that are ingrained in the system, perpetuated by hegemonic influences, and are related to persistent inequalities. Networks are a vehicle that can be used by community leaders to confront such challenges. Interviewees spoke passionately about their desire to shine a light on inequity and work toward a more equitable world. Wolff et al's (2017) six principles for collaborating for equity and social justice are a useful guide for NLs.

One reason that people work together is to increase the volume and intensity of their voices. Most interviewees noted the importance of amplifying the voices of NMs. NLs are responsible for encouraging NMs to share their unique opinions and perspectives, recognizing when voices are missing, and making sure the loudest voices are not the only ones making waves. NLs must strive to ensure that oft-marginalized voices are heard and that quieter voices have a chance to speak, and learn how to navigate difficult discussions around equity.

To *lead as one among many*, NLs must actively distribute leadership to NMs by sharing ownership and giving NMs opportunities to lead. Network leadership is a highly social role grounded in building and maintaining relationships that are built on trust. NLs serve at the pleasure of NMs and they are beholden to the will of the group. NLs should ensure that increasing equity, access, and justice is a thread that runs through all network-based activity.

Conclusion

The eight NAs described in this chapter are a starting point for NLs seeking to develop principles to guide network activity. Better yet, developing custom NAs is a useful way to codify a network's values. NLs can use the list of NAs described here to begin crafting a customized set of NAs that apply to their work. Readers are encouraged to modify the list of NAs, remove those that are not applicable, or add new agreements. However, it is important to develop a manageable number of principles, because individuals must be able to remember them and incorporate them into their network lives.

Promoting the active use of NAs is an important way to create a welcoming and respectful network culture. Once a network has a set of NAs, NLs can devise strategies to infuse them into their workflow and ensure that the community adopts and abides by the agreements. NLs and NMs must strive to incorporate NAs into their everyday routine. The NAs must be clearly communicated to the network and made accessible to all NMs. NLs must make them visible by displaying them on the network's website, printing well-designed posters that illustrate the NAs, reminding people of the NAs at the beginning of meetings, highlighting examples of NAs in action, and devising other ways to help them percolate throughout the network. The agreements should guide all aspects of network activity.

Finally, it is valuable to routinely re-evaluate NAs to make sure that they are still relevant, compelling, and actionable. NAs should be evaluated every three to five years to determine their past, present, and future value. If some of the NAs no longer add value or could be more eloquently explained, they should be *re-shaped*, so to speak. Remember, networks are not static; they are dynamic. It is important for a network's structure to remain malleable over time so that it can be reformed and recast as needed. NLs and NMs are encouraged to work together to design custom NAs that clearly express their network's guiding principles, infuse those agreements into the network, and regularly re-evaluate them over the life of the network. Regularly practicing NAs can lead to a better understanding of a network's values and, ideally, the development of a more welcoming and equitable network culture.

References

Agranoff, R., & McGuire, M. (2001) Big questions in public network management research. *Journal of Public Administration Research and Theory*, 11(3), 295–326.

Ahearn, L. M. (2001) Language and agency. *Annual Review of Anthropology*, 30, 109–137.

Ansell, C., & Gash, A. (2012) Stewards, mediators, and catalysts: Toward a model of collaborative leadership. *The Innovation Journal*, 17(1), 2–21.

Avolio, B. J., & Gardner, W. L. (2005) Authentic leadership development: Getting to the root of positive forms of leadership. *The Leadership Quarterly*, 16(3), 315–338.

Bandura, A. (2006) Toward a psychology of human agency. *Perspectives on Psychological Science*, 1(2), 164–180.

Bryant, A., & Charmaz, K. (2007) Introduction: Grounded theory research methods and practice. In: Bryant, A. & Charmaz, K. (eds.) *The Sage handbook of grounded theory*. Thousand Oaks, CA, Sage Publications, pp. 1–28.

Bryk, A. S., Gomez, L. M., & Grunow, A. (2011) Getting ideas into action: Building networked improvement communities in education. In: Hallinan, M. T. (ed.) *Frontiers in sociology of education*. Dordrecht, Netherlands, Springer Science+Business Media, pp. 127–162.

Bryson, J. M., Crosby, B. C., & Stone, M. M. (2015) Designing and implementing cross-sector collaborations: Needed and challenging. *Public Administration Review*, 75(5), 647–663.

Camarinha-Matos, L. M. (2014) Collaborative networks: A mechanism for enterprise agility and resilience. In: Mertins, K, Bénaben, F, Poler, R, Bourrières, J. P. (eds.) *Enterprise interoperability VI*. Cham, Switzerland, Springer International Publishing, pp. 3–11.

CEB, Inc. (2013) *Rise of the Network Leader*. [Online] Available from http://ceb.uberflip.com/i/199263-the-rise-of-the-network-leader/1

Charmaz, K. (2006) Constructing grounded theory: A practical guide through qualitative analysis. Thousand Oaks, CA, Sage Publications.

Cullen-Lester, K. L., & Yammarino, F. J. (2016) Collective and network approaches to leadership: Special issue introduction. *The Leadership Quarterly*, 27(2), 173–180.

Edwards, A. (2006) Relational agency: Learning to be a resourceful practitioner. *International Journal of Educational Research*, 43(3), 168–182.

Goh, K. T., Goodman, P. S., & Weingart, L. R. (2013) Team innovation processes: An examination of activity cycles in creative project teams. *Small Group Research*, 44(2), 159–194.

Huxham, C., & Vangen, S. (2000) Leadership in the shaping and implementation of collaboration agendas: How things happen in a (not quite) joined-up world. *Academy of Management Journal*, 43(6), 1159–1175.

Kania, J., & Kramer, M. (2011) Collective impact. *Stanford Social Innovation Review*, 9(1), 36–41.

Klenke, K. (2008) *Qualitative research in the study of leadership*. Bingley, UK, Emerald House Publishing Ltd.

Kvale, S. (1996) *InterViews: An introduction to qualitative research writing*. Thousand Oaks, CA, Sage Publications.

Lee, Y. (2008) Design participation tactics: The challenges and new roles for designers in the co-design process. *Co-Design*, 4(1), 31–50.

Leonard, D., & Swap, W. C. (1999) *When sparks fly: Igniting creativity in groups*. Boston, MA, Harvard Business School Press.

Lincoln, Y. S., & Guba, E. G. (1985) *Naturalistic inquiry* (Vol. 75). Thousand Oaks, CA, Sage Publications.

Linden, R. M. (2003) Working across boundaries: Making collaboration work in government and nonprofit organizations. San Francisco, CA, Jossey-Bass.

Mintzberg, H. (1987) Crafting strategy. *Harvard Business Review*, 65(5), 66–75.

Mumford, M. D., Zaccaro, S. J., Harding, F. D., Jacobs, T. O., & Fleishman, E. A. (2000) Leadership skills for a changing world: Solving complex social problems. *The Leadership Quarterly*, 11(1), 11–35.

Patton, M. Q. (2002) *Qualitative evaluation and evaluation methods* (3rd ed.). Thousand Oaks, CA, Sage Publications.

Pea, R. D. (2004) The social and technological dimensions of scaffolding and related theoretical concepts for learning, education, and human activity. *The Journal of the Learning Sciences*, 13(3), 423–451.

Popp, J., Milward, H. B., MacKean, G., Casebeer, A., & Lindstrom, R. (2014) *Inter-organizational networks: A review of the literature to inform practice*. [Online] IBM Center for the Business of Government. Available from www.businessofgovernment.org/report/inter-organizational-networks-review-literature-inform-practice

Provan, K. G., Fish, A., & Sydow, J. (2007) Interorganizational networks at the network level: A review of the empirical literature on whole networks. *Journal of Management*, 33(3), 479–516.

Raine, L., & Wellman, B. (2012) *Networked*. Cambridge, MA, MIT Press.

Ritchie, J., Lewis, J., Elam, R. G., Tennant, R., & Rahim, N. (2013) Designing and selecting samples. In: Ritchie, J, Lewis, J., McNaughton Nichols, C. & Ormston, R. (eds.) *Qualitative research practice: A guide for social science students and researchers*. Thousand Oaks, CA, Sage Publications, pp. 111–145.

Rittel, H. W., & Webber, M. M. (1973) Planning problems are wicked. *Polity*, 4, 155–169.

Routhieaux, R. L. (2015) Shared leadership and its implications for nonprofit leadership. *The Journal of Nonprofit Education and Leadership*, 5(3), 139–152.

Rowlands, J. (1995) Empowerment examined. *Development in Practice*, 5(2), 101–107.

Santo, R., Ching, D., Peppler, K., & Hoadley, C. (2016) Working in the open: Lessons from open source on building innovation networks in education. *On the Horizon*, 24(3), 280–295.

Senge, P. M., & Sterman, J. D. (1992) Systems thinking and organizational learning: Acting locally and thinking globally in the organization of the future. *European Journal of Operational Research*, 59(1), 137–150.

Scearce, D. (2011) *Catalyzing networks for social change: A funder's guide*. Washington, DC: Grantmakers for Effective Organizations.

Stiver, D. C. (2017) Catalyzing collective action: A grounded theory of network leadership. (Unpublished doctoral dissertation). Eastern University, St. Davids, PA.

Stone, C. A. (1993) What is missing in the metaphor of scaffolding? In: Forman, E., Minick, E. & Stone, C. (eds.) *Contexts for learning: Sociocultural dynamics in children's development.* New York, NY, Oxford University Press., pp. 169–183.

Stone, C. A. (1998) Should we salvage the scaffolding metaphor? *Journal of Learning Disabilities*, 31(4), 409–413.

Tracey, P., & Stott, N. (2017) Social innovation: a window on alternative ways of organizing and innovating. *Innovation: Organization and Management*, 19(1), 51–60.

Trist, E. (1983) Referent organizations and the development of interorganizational domains. *Human Relations*, 36(3), 269–284.

Wei-Skillern, J., & Silver, N. (2013) Four network principles for collaboration success. *The Foundation Review*, 5(1), 10.

Wolff, T., Minkler, M., Wolfe, S. M., Berkowitz, B., Bowen, L., Christens, B. D., Butterfoss, F. D. (2017, January 9) Collaborating for equity and justice: Moving beyond collective impact. *Nonprofit Quarterly*. [Online] Available from https://nonprofitquarterly. org/2017/01/09/collaborating-equity-justice-moving-beyond-collective-impact/

4

THE INTANGIBLES

What It Takes for a Backbone Organization to Succeed

Rebecca Gillam and Jacqueline Counts

Intermediary agencies have acted as project managers to move collaborative projects forward long before the term "backbone organization" was coined. While it may be straightforward to organize meetings and perform basic backbone functions, the mindset and the skills necessary to be an effective and competent backbone organization do not come from following a checklist or claiming to be one. As will be described in the current analysis, many intangibles are really the black box of how an organization takes on the role of backbone and effectively moves Collective Impact forward. This chapter describes experiences with a backbone organization that made a concerted effort to address those intangibles using a variety of practices intended to increase staff engagement and facilitate cross-project collaboration. The results of those efforts are reviewed below.

As a designated research center at the University of Kansas, the Center for Public Partnerships and Research (the Center) has served as a backbone organization during the past decade for several federal initiatives to promote systems work in child maltreatment prevention, early childhood, and out-of-school time. Examples of the Center's function as a backbone include:

- the facilitation and implementation management of the Kansas Early Childhood Comprehensive Systems (KECCS) plan;
- the design and application of an accountability framework for using funds from the Tobacco Master Settlement to support policy that aligns early childhood programming and distributes funding based on impact;
- project management and evaluation of Delivering Change, a collaborative to reduce infant mortality;
- visioning, coordination, technical assistance, and sustainability planning for out-of-school programs; and

- programmatic and evaluation support for several early childhood, health and wellness, and behavioral health programs with tribal communities.

Feedback from partners shows that the Center is valued for efficient and effective Collective Impact management, providing the vision and strategy, cohesiveness, communication, and structure to keep the work moving forward and to make an impact.

In 2013, with the arrival of a new director, the Center initiated a critical look at its own adherence to CI principles and collaboration strategies. While the Center was achieving outcomes on individual projects and contributing to the field in various disciplines, there was little cross-center sharing of knowledge and lessons learned. Staff were informed of the goals and objectives of their own respective projects, but had limited understanding of how their work contributed to co-workers' projects that were part of the same system. These team siloes restricted innovation, synergies across projects, and the application of lessons learned. Consequently, the Center was missing opportunities to learn from each other, share data that could inform strategies, and leverage successes. In effect, staff were working in siloes while asking partners to work collaboratively.

To effectively act as a backbone, leadership realized the importance of applying the same approach internally as was used with partners. The Center needed to be mission-driven, utilize shared metrics, communicate effectively and efficiently, and determine how to integrate and align 45–50 separate projects to mutually-reinforce a common agenda—a mission to optimize the well-being of children, youth, and families. In addition, the Center needed to find methods to model collaboration. Prompted by this need, leaders explored how the Center, as a backbone organization with many grants and funding sources, could move from a collection of disparate projects to an adaptive, entrepreneurial entity that effectively employed an internal and external CI approach that cultivated sustainable social change.

This chapter shares findings of a study that explored the impact of the Center's approach on organizational culture and staff engagement. The chapter starts with the current literature on backbone organizations. It then describes the Center's journey to move from a siloed organization in a competent backbone organization comprising a cohesive confederation of individuals committed to the mission. Of special interest is the Center's use of four "Rules of Engagement" that guide staff in *how* to work together to facilitate CI. Quantitative and qualitative findings are presented showing how Center staff perceive these Rules and the degree to which they apply to their work. The chapter concludes with a discussion of how the Center used these findings to develop practical tools for staff and management, and continue to promote workplace culture.

Literature Review

Backbone support is one of the five key conditions for Collective Impact (CI) success, in addition to common agenda, shared measurement, mutually reinforcing activities, and continuous communication (Turner, Merchant, Kania, & Martin 2012). The backbone organization must function as an effective catalyst to achieve community-level progress by carrying out six common activities identified unsuccessful CI initiatives. Backbone organizations guide vision and strategy, support aligned activities, establish shared measurement practices, build public will, advance policy, and mobilize funding (Turner, Merchant, Kania, & Martin 2012). In theory, these are tangible and specific roles that an organization can take to support a collaborative effort. However, simply checking off a list of these activities is not enough to successfully move the needle on social problems. Translating this theory into practice requires a deeper dive into how intangible elements such as competence, commitment, objectivity, data and information, networking, and visibility establish an organization as respected facilitator of CI (Turner, Errecart, & Bhatt 2013A). The following literature review weaves these intangible elements with the functions of a backbone.

Vision & Strategy. Competent backbone organizations with content knowledge and experience in strategic planning and problem-solving provide leadership, which allows the backbone to guide a collaborative's course of action. Backbone staff with strong interpersonal skills can exert more influence, which allows constituents to develop trust and effectively work together. Successful backbones also have an adaptive leader who excels at managing relationships and keeping key people informed and engaged. Partners need to feel included and valued in the process (Turner, Errecart, & Bhatt 2013A).

Backbones are most influential when viewed as a trusted and impartial entity with no personal stake or competitiveness in the collaboration's outcomes and course of action. This objectivity for backbone organizations is crucial for their effectiveness and partnership with the community. Such arrangements gain more trust from constituents, allowing for more buy-in and sustainable outcomes (Turner, Errecart, & Bhatt 2013A). Practicing inclusion demonstrates to constituents and community leaders that all viewpoints are welcome and encouraged, creating safe spaces for difficult conversations. This inclusiveness cultivates influence by appealing to shared values of all (Turner, Errecart, & Bhatt 2013A). When partners see that an organization's motivations are honest and aligned with the common good, trust increases (Bhargava 2012).

Support aligned activities. To keep partners moving in the same direction and performing aligned activities, backbone organizations must rely on their communication savvy and networking skills (Kania & Kramer 2011). Those organizations with strong connections to cross-sector partners and community members are well-positioned to broker and mediate relationships between individuals and groups.

A backbone's reputation and overall likeability are also critical. Organizations that are high in competence with high likeability are sought after as work partners (Bhargava 2012), but likeability is more than just being nice and "liked." It is about creating trust with partners; demonstrating the relevance of the work; being unselfish in commitments; communicating with straightforward and non-jargon language; and knowing when to act (Bhargava 2012). Effective network management in other fields uses these principles to be deliberate and intentional about interactions with partners (Kort, Verweij, & Klijn 2015).

Research has established the importance of cross-sector partnerships (Foster-Fishman et al, 2001). Public–private cooperation generates higher information exchanges and pooling of knowledge, yielding more innovation with better quality products from the backbone organization and policy changes for social problems (Kort, Verweij, & Klijn 2015).

Shared measurement. Data and information provide the backbone credibility and influence. Backbones are most successful and cohesive when they produce quality research and data that help constituents understand the problem, promote accountability, and foster learning, allowing for continuous quality improvement (Ammerman et al. 2016). Perspectives from community members and media channels in connection with strong data are critical to reach a tipping point in both public will and securing funding (Friedman 2005). Community leaders from coast-to-coast are embracing data and generating ongoing improvements to systems and initiatives by relying on backbone organizations to use tools like the Three I's: Identify, Interpret, and Improve (Edmondson & Hecht 2014).

Establishing uniform measurement practices enables initiatives to reach consensus early on indicators of progress. Backbones can help partners identify appropriate data to collect at appropriate intervals (Edmondson & Hecht 2014). Backbone organizations can play a vital role in presenting and interpreting data in real time in meaningful ways. Such real-time and digestible data enable organizations to improve efforts on the ground by training practitioners to make data-driven decisions and engage in continuous quality improvement (Edmondson & Hecht 2014).

An example of these concepts is a partnership in Dallas, TX, called the Commit! Partnership, which identified schools that had achieved notable improvements in third grade literacy: "The backbone staff worked with practitioners to identify the most promising schools and interpret data to identify the practices that led to improvements" (Edmondson & Hecht 2014). Using data, the backbone organization empowered district leaders to spread refined practices across the area to facilitate continual improvement (Edmondson & Hecht 2014).

Building public will. Commitment is visible when backbone organizations are influential leaders with a strong track record and ongoing involvement in similar initiatives. The ability to pivot and adapt to contextual factors also demonstrate that backbone organizations are stable and committed to long-term outcomes. In addition to proven success and a reputation of being trustworthy and likeable, backbones must also be visible and relevant to partners and community members to be effective. Relevance comprises three elements—active listening, a meaningful point of view, and context (Bhargava 2012). The backbone organization staff must demonstrate that they understand the issues, are willing partners, and are ready to listen. To be considered relevant, these staff must be seen as adding value to the initiative and conversations. They must do more than document partners' goals. Rather, they must be highly aware of contextual factors, synthesize information, translate partner ideas to action opportunities, and identify and interpret nuanced cues (Bhargava 2012). Backbone organizations also must be curious, ask questions, make suggestions, and recognize connections.

Advancing public policy. By having evidence generated through shared measurement systems, backbone organizations can support the advancement of public policy (Turner, Merchant, Kania, & Martin 2012). For example: backbone organizations ". . . in Ohio and Kentucky have focused on measuring progress and using data to improve kindergarten readiness." Data from a collaborative is hard for policymakers to ignore (Turner, Merchant, Kania, & Martin 2012). Over time, CI initiatives have driven policy changes at the organizational and systems levels, which lead to more effective systems and better community outcomes (Turner, Merchant, Kania, & Martin 2012).

Mobilizing funding. Collaboration-building is a time- and resource-intensive activity that requires significant investments at all levels of an organization (Bachmann et al. 2009; Bolland & Wilson 1994; Bunger 2010; Moran et al. 2007). In partner organizations where funding is often tenuous and caseloads are full, research has shown that "[d]edicated resources are needed to support the management and administrative functions of multi-agency working. Lead professionals should not be expected to implement and manage change without protected time and funding for this role" (Townsley et al 2004: 33). Backbone organizations provide the infrastructure to build and maintain the momentum of an initiative by providing staff who focus on the collective rather than the organizational perspective in terms of data, activities, and funding.

Staffing considerations. The role of a backbone organization is challenging. To successfully implement a CI initiative, highly competent and flexible staff in the backbone roles are key (Kania, Hanleybrown, & Splansky Juster 2014). Collaboratives struggle with whom to entrust their common agenda. All things being equal, partners want to work with the entity that has the highest likeability factor, that demonstrates leadership qualities, and, that understands the principles of collaboration (Bhargava 2012; Kouzes & Posner 2012; Kania, Hanleybrown, & Splansky Juster 2014). Staff who possess these traits tend to build stronger informal relationships; convey confidence and drive toward a common purpose; and be humble in their accomplishments (Bhargava 2012; Kania, Hanleybrown, & Splansky Juster 2014).

The Intentional Transformation of a Backbone Organization

Assembling a group of individuals who understand the principles of CI, possess the requisite skills and intangible elements to support, and have high likeability is no easy feat. But if social change is to happen, the backbone must be strong enough to withstand internal and external challenges. The current study explored the results of an intentional and strategic transformation of a confederation of teams with disparate approaches to a mission-driven collaborative that used a Collective Impact approach.

In the Center example, the organization functioned as a backbone, yet staff were very focused on individual projects that remained siloed, missing opportunities to learn from each other. Leadership began the transformation in 2013 by conducting a six-month landscape assessment of the types of projects, core values, and resources needed for sustainability. A common agenda (or mission) emerged from this process that was broad enough to accommodate the Center's diversity, but sharp enough to ensure that all staff were working in the same direction for social change: *to optimize well-being of at-risk children, youth, and families.*

Once the common agenda was established, leadership and staff identified mutually-reinforcing activities that would extend reach, generate knowledge, and increase capacity to serve partners plus enhance the quality of the Center's products. On the surface, CI components seemed easy to understand. However, experience showed that the work is complex and requires a high level of tolerance for ambiguity and comfort with productive tension (Turner, Errecart, & Bhatt 2013B).

Within an organization, tolerance for ambiguity varies based on individuals, their role in the organization, and affinity for uncertainty. Initially, the Center forced CI through meetings where staff discussed project intersections and ways that project activities reinforced each other. This technique proved too rigid, failed to allow natural connections to occur, and forced unnatural alliances. Leadership then stepped back to assess the approach and encouraged a more dynamic approach that recognized the complexity of work. Staff were encouraged to develop prototypes and try new ideas and communication strategies to build relationships and alliances (Darnell & Means 2016). This organic approach was intended to be more natural and lead to mutually reinforcing activities.

From this period of "seeing" (Scharmer 2009), conversations in staff meetings changed. The Center collectively embraced the struggle, and common themes continued to surface. These themes focused on risk-taking, responsibility, and partnership, and were the basis for four Rules of Engagement: 1) Freedom to Fail (or fail forward); 2) Be Accountable to each other and the Center; 3) Work With the Willing; and 4) Leave It Better Than You Found It. The Rules were introduced at a staff retreat to provide context, discuss real-life examples, and to come to a collective understanding of what they meant and how they could be applied in the work setting. The Rules of Engagement started to guide how the Center worked together and helped to address staff discomfort with complexity (D'Souza & Renner 2014).

Freedom to Fail. Being a successful backbone organization requires an element of entrepreneurial spirit and the resilience to recover in the face of setbacks (McGrath 1999). As an organization with smart, successful, young staff, the Center was experiencing a fixed-mindset approach to the work, where staff were adverse to projects or activities where success was not guaranteed (Dweck 2006). Research on Millennials has found that this emphasis on growth–mindset is an important and difficult shift (Dweck 2006; Howe & Strauss 2007).

Freedom to fail addressed this pervasive issue by giving staff permission to experience failure in a protected and developmental way. *Freedom to Fail* as a Rule was an attempt to allow staff to experiment, take risks, and push boundaries with the potential for positive impact. A cross-center team of emerging leaders developed a Best Practices guide for supervisors and staff to operationalize each Rule (Table 4.1). The guide forced staff to create more tangible examples of what the Rules look like in practice, and it provided a common language for meaningful conversations to emerge.

Be accountable. The Center had established a reputation as a trusted backbone organization that was accountable to CI partners. However, when the expectations shifted to internal, cross–team work, staff defaulted to traditional organizational hierarchies and struggled to hold each other accountable. Clear expectations and communication were lacking. Holding others accountable requires mutual trust and respect. This Rule established the expectation that the way of working with each other internally is the model for the way the Center works with partners (Table 4.2).

Work with the willing. Collaborative work is easy to agree to; follow through is much harder. While individuals sign on as partners to a CI initiative, their level of willingness to make unselfish decisions and compromises varies significantly. Many Center staff were not prepared with the skills or understanding of what was needed to navigate these roadblocks. This Rule gave permission for staff to invest their energy in the willing and committed partners. Instead of letting a certain few slow down the process, backbone staff were asked to be adaptable and flexible enough to focus on the willing. The Rule draws on the diffusion of innovations

TABLE 4.1 CPPR Best Practices for Supervisors and Staff, Freedom to Fail

Supervisor behaviors	*Staff behaviors*
Provide context for the project: • Set a goal and define boundaries for innovation. • Clarify the background, including players, politics, and potential landmines. • Communicate what is at stake and be prepared to take responsibility.	Develop a plan and get started: overcome perfection paralysis by generating action steps, trying it out, and asking for feedback early and often.
Build in time for the iterative process.	Use feedback from your supervisor to refine or expand plans, or change course.
Encourage innovation and try new skills.	Take a risk and get outside your comfort zone! Try new skills!
Allow staff to develop their own way of doing things with your coaching, guidance, and oversight.	Take ownership of your projects and your approach. Be prepared to justify your choices.

TABLE 4.2 CPPR Best Practices for Supervisors and Staff, Be Accountable

Supervisor behaviors	Staff behaviors
Be available for regular check-ins and use the Risk-to-Impact Matrix to help your supervisee know when to check in.	Check in with your supervisor regularly and use the Risk-to-Impact Matrix to help guide when to check-in. Take ownership of meetings with your supervisor: come prepared to get what you need from him or her.
Set clear expectations for quality work and define the quality assurance process.	Use the Center tools to guide work quality. Build in time for review and revision.
Share your expectations and vision with your new staff. Encourage them to get to know others within the Center.	Introduce yourself to other members of the Center and get to know your co-workers and supervisor. Be curious and ask questions.
Communicate project goals, expectations, and deadlines early and often. Use the Effort-to-Impact Matrix and the RACI framework to guide specific expectations about deliverables.	Clarify how the work plan will be executed (RACI). Ask for help and provide status updates early and often. Know and meet deadlines.
Model the way by promoting a positive work culture and climate.	Adopt a positive attitude. Establish a strengths-based mindset toward your work and relationships.
Maintain accurate calendars and be responsive, including when on professional travel.	Maintain accurate calendars and be responsive, including when on professional travel.

theory recognizing that individuals adopt change at varying rates (Rogers 2003). This Rule encourages staff to focus on the innovators and early adopters to gather momentum for collective success (Rogers 2003). In practice, Work with the Willing meant reflecting, connecting, and moving forward, despite late adopters and laggards who are resistant to change (Table 4.3).

Leave it better than you found it. The Center provides no direct services that offer instant feedback on the success of the work. Systems-level work focuses on long-term outcomes that can make it difficult to recognize progress. To address this gap, staff needed some form of validation other than occasional praise from supervisors, or summative reports that are often years in the making. This Rule encourages staff to leave work every day knowing that they made some contribution to making a situation better. On the project level, it may mean reading someone else's report and editing. On the people level, it may mean having a difficult conversation and having productive conflict that leads to clearer expectations and deeper relationships. For work culture, this rule is enacted when staff are invested in maintaining a positive work climate and model the Rules of Engagement (Table 4.4).

While these tenets provide guardrails for operation, they do not ensure that team members have the confidence and boundary fluidity to test them. To create this culture, leadership used a variety of communication techniques, including dashboards, walking meetings, First Monday stand-up meetings, ongoing temperature checks using clicker technology, organic huddles, lunch club, and the

TABLE 4.3 CPPR Best Practices for Supervisors and Staff, Work with the Willing

Supervisor behaviors	Staff behavior
Connect the work to the Center's mission and rules of engagement.	Align your daily work with the Center's mission and rules of engagement.
Collaboratively problem-solve apparent roadblocks. Coach staff on navigating personal and professional challenges.	Know yourself, acknowledge limitations, and seek opportunities to reframe or redirect efforts.
Facilitate cross-team activities and discussions.	Participate in and seek out cross-team activities and discussions.
Model the way: model engagement (i.e., be active and present), how to represent the Center, and the behaviors you expect in staff.	Reflect well on the Center by demonstrating professionalism in dress, communication style, posture and non-verbal body language, and social media. Show up on time for internal and external meetings and for the weekly stand-up.
Acknowledge frustrations or resistance and encourage open discussion.	Be willing to explore frustrations and to change your approach.
Provide timely, constructive feedback with context in the spirit of development and growth.	Openly receive and use feedback. Reflect upon the message and intent of the feedback and actively work to apply feedback in future tasks.

TABLE 4.4 CPPR Best Practices for Supervisors and Staff, Leave It Better Than You Found It

Supervisor behaviors	Staff behaviors
Identify formal and informal professional development opportunities that challenge staff to grow.	Take initiative for your own growth. Find ways to apply the knowledge and skills you have gained from professional development opportunities.
Accept and encourage different approaches to getting work done.	Create and propose next steps aligned with the goals of the work, and accept feedback graciously.
Own, learn, and discuss your mistakes: fail forward with others.	Own, learn, and discuss your mistakes: fail forward with others.

director's weekly blog, to name a few. During this process, the Rules of Engagement were well-received. However, it was unclear how they were operationalized in the workplace. In particular, Center leaders wanted to better understand how the Rules influenced collaboration and contributed to the Center's role as a backbone organization.

Methodology

An internal study was conducted to understand how Rules of Engagement influence perceptions of work culture in a backbone organization. Specifically, authors asked the research question: Do Rules of Engagement impact staff perceptions of work culture? The authors tested several hypotheses: a) staff can apply Rules of Engagement in their work; b) Rules of Engagement lead to improved staff perceptions of workplace culture; and, c) staff describe the organization in positive terms that address backbone competence.

The present study used data collected from staff in a backbone organization. The Center is multi-disciplinary, with staff from psychology, sociology, anthropology, social work, education, law, and related fields. Staff are mostly highly educated white women. Responses were submitted via an online survey using *SurveyMonkey*, as well as in small group sessions. Twenty-seven survey responses were submitted, a 60% response rate. And all surveys were complete with no missing data. The survey used a combination of questions with staff asked to: 1) rate their level of agreement with a series of statements on a 4-point Likert scale, 1 being "strongly disagree" to 4 being "strongly agree"; and 2) provide open-ended responses about their perceptions of the organization.

Survey data was analyzed for descriptive statistics and Pearson correlations using IBM SPSS 23.0. Open-ended responses were analyzed for frequency of words used to describe the organization. Linguistic Inquiry and Word Count (LIWC) was used to assess meaning in text (LIWC 2015). This computerized text analysis method calculates word counts in language categories and demonstrates the psychological state of the writer. Small group discussions functioned like focus groups with staff asked to share their interpretations of the Rules, how easy/difficult they thought it would be to apply, and potential struggles they might encounter.

Quantitative Results

Results were used to answer the research question: Do Rules of Engagement impact staff perceptions of work culture? Table 4.5 displays descriptive statistics for staff responses to the statement: "I can truly follow each of the following Rules of Engagement in my work."

Mean scores for each of the four Rules range from 2.89 (Freedom to Fail) to 3.56 (Leave It Better Than You Found It and Be Accountable), with an average across the four Rules of 3.3. Minimum and maximum scores show that Freedom to Fail elicited the largest range of responses, and this Rule has the lowest mean

TABLE 4.5 Descriptive Statistics

Rule of engagement	Mean	Min.	Max.	"Agree" or "Strongly Agree"
Freedom to Fail (Fail)	2.89	1	4	74%
Leave It Better Than You Found It (LIBTYFI)	3.56	2	4	93%
Be Accountable (BA)	3.56	3	4	100%
Work With The Willing (WWW)	3.19	2	4	82%
Overall	3.30	1	4	87%

at 2.89. However, the vast majority of staff (74%) agreed or strongly agreed that they could truly follow this rule in their work.

Be Accountable showed the smallest range of the Rules; 100% of staff agreed or strongly agreed they truly could be accountable in their work. This is probably not surprising, as this rule is likely the easiest to interpret as directly within an individual's personal locus of control Freedom to Fail, Leave It Better than You Found It, and Work With The Willing imply engaging with and perhaps pushing boundaries.

Be Accountable may fall, for some, within non-negotiable boundaries such as deadlines and external pressures, including client expectations. In these situations, staff understand the desirability of operating within these confines and feel confident in their ability to Be Accountable. Overall, descriptive statistics suggest that staff find the Rules of Engagement highly applicable to their work, and a high level of uniformity across staff and Rules. These findings support Hypothesis 1: Staff can apply Rules of Engagement in their work.

In addition to whether they felt they could follow the Rules of Engagement in their work, staff were asked to respond to the following statements:

- "I usually leave work with a feeling of accomplishment" (Accomplish);
- "I feel supported in my work" (Supported);
- "I feel as if I am free to speak my mind" (Speak);
- "I feel valued by CPPR" (Valued);
- "CPPR management communicates a clear sense of direction for our organization" (Direction); and
- "I feel like my work is reflective of CPPR's mission" (Mission)

Table 4.6 shows Pearson correlation coefficients between staff responses to these statements and the degree to which they felt they could apply the Rules of Engagement to their work. Given the small sample of 27 respondents, the number of significant positive correlations between variables is noteworthy suggesting these results are fairly robust and also speaks to the high degree of support among staff members for all of the statements.

TABLE 4.6 Pearson Correlations

	Fail	LIBTYFI	BA	WWW	Accomplish	Supported	Speak	Valued	Direction	Mission
Fail n=27	1.00									
LIBTYFI n=27	.37	1.00								
BA n=27	.27	.55**	1.00							
WWW n=27	.39*	.59**	.44*	1.00						
Accomplish n=27	.21	.38	.16	.22	1.00					
Supported n= 27	.63**	.08	.22	.11	.53**	1.00				
Speak n=27	.71**	.11	.24	.10	.32	.56**	1.00			
Valued n=27	.63**	.14	.08	.29	.62**	.78**	.569**	1.00		
Direction n=25	.51**	.57**	.55**	.48*	.28	.35	.508**	.385	1.00	
Mission n=27	.31	.33	.55**	.13	.14	.32	.487*	.338	.63**	1.00

* Correlation is significant at the 0.05 level (2-tailed)
** Correlation is significant at the 0.01 level (2-tailed)

As in the descriptive statistics, Freedom to Fail (Fail) stands out as distinct from other Rules of Engagement. The only other Rule of Engagement with which it is correlated is Work With The Willing (WWW), and that is the only Rule correlated with all the other rules. However, Fail was significantly correlated with four of the six statements: I feel supported in my work (Supported); I feel as if I am free to speak my mind (Speak); I feel valued by CPPR (Valued); and, CPPR leadership communicates a clear sense of direction for our organization (Direction). In other words, how people respond to Fail seems mainly connected with the way people feel at work—if they feel supported, valued, and free to speak their mind, they also feel free to take risks and sometimes fail.

In contrast, the other three Rules were all correlated positively and significantly, but not with most other feelings about one's work or the organization. This finding may suggest that as a set, the Rules act as a kind of a credo, that people identify with or they don't, regardless of how they feel about their work life.

And, in fact the descriptive statistics suggest most people do identify with them, with little variability across staff members or Rules.

The final especially interesting result is that Direction significantly positively correlates with all of the rules indicating that the Rules are strongly associated with leadership. Staff may think of leaders as the direction of the organization, or at least the mechanisms by which the organization moves forward. Interestingly, Speak your Mind is the only attitudinal item about how people feel at work that is significantly correlated with Direction. This may indicate a link between the freedom for staff to say what they are thinking and clarity on leadership's part about the direction the organization is going. Staff may also free to speak their mind when they feel like leadership is clearly communicating.

Overall, results from correlational analysis showed that, for the most part, the Rules of Engagement were significantly and positively related to each other and to staff perceptions of workplace culture (see Table 6). This finding supports Hypothesis 2: Rules of Engagement lead to improved staff perceptions of workplace culture.

Qualitative Results

In addition to the scaled questions, the survey asked staff to list three adjectives that they would use to describe the organization. A total of 112 words were submitted as open-ended responses. Responses were analyzed using LIWC to assess whether descriptions of the organization were positive. Positive emotions in this study included words like "dedicated, fun, nurturing." In this study, 19.3% of words used by respondents were positive emotions. By comparison, examples of negative emotions included "overwhelmed, unorganized, stressful."

Only 3.4% of responses given in the organizational description were negative. Cognitive processes are also relevant to the analysis and include words related to insight, causation, discrepancy, tentative, and certainty. Of the descriptors, 14.3% of responses were cognitive processes, indicating that staff are an introspective group. More than 10% of staff offered words that demonstrate the importance of relationships at the office (social words).

Finally, the score of 99.0 for Emotional Tone is a composite of both positive and negative emotion. Higher scores mean a more positive overall tone (Cohn, Mehl, & Pennebaker 2004). The results show that nearly all word responses indicated a positive emotional tone, and connection to the organization (Table 4.7).

Overall frequencies of specific word use were analyzed to further understand staff perceptions of the organization. Eight words made 29% of the total responses, indicating alignment of purpose and vision with organizational culture. Table 4.8 displays the words and their frequencies.

Results support Hypothesis 3, that staff describe the organization in positive terms about backbone competence and presence of the intangible qualities contained in the literature review.

TABLE 4.7 LIWC Results

Traditional LIWC dimension	Study results
I-words (I, Me, My)	0.0
Social words	10.1
Positive emotions	19.3
Negative emotions	3.4
Cognitive processes	14.3
Emotional tone	99.0

TABLE 4.8 Words and Frequencies

Word	Frequency
Supportive	7
Fast–paced	5
Engaging	4
Friendly	4
Growing	3
Innovative	3
Productive	3
Transition	3

Finally, small group discussion notes were analyzed using standard qualitative analyses (Patton, 2002). Perspectives on each of the Rules of Engagement support Hypothesis 2, that the Rules of Engagement lead to improved staff perceptions of workplace culture.

Staff indicated that Freedom to Fail was the most difficult Rule in practice, shedding further light on the quantitative results indicating the Freedom to Fail had a fundamentally different relationship than the other rules and an important connection to feelings of being valued, supported, and free to speak one's mind. This finding is also consistent with the research on mindset and millennials (Dweck 2006; Howe & Strauss 2007). Despite this discomfort, for many staff, Freedom to Fail was their favorite Rule, because it implies an implicit expectation to try new ideas and take risks, and gave them permission to do so.

Overall, staff had a difficult time distinguishing between what has become known as big 'F' failures and little 'f' failures. A big 'F' fail happens when deadlines are missed, projects are poorly managed, and when teams do not communicate effectively. A little 'f' fail is a temporary state and is necessary for individuals and organizations to grow. These fails are when you try something that doesn't work—a new activity in a meeting, a new way of presenting data—and learn from that experience. These types of safe-to-fail risks encourage new ideas and create a safe space to learn from projects that did not go as planned.

Be Accountable is the rule that is easiest to understand at first glance. Staff understood it as supporting each other and the Center. In some ways, this rule seemed obvious to staff. However, some staff expressed a potential tension between this expectation and being responsible for their own tasks and project objectives. To address this concern, staff recommended being clear about timelines, expectations, and roles and responsibilities.

Work With the Willing was challenging for staff to understand and they interpreted this rule on two levels: 1) being the willing, and, 2) working with willing partners. There was discussion about how to work with partners who are not willing; these are the individuals who say there is not enough money, not enough information, etc. While unwilling partners are a reality of collaboration, this rule focuses on the bright spots as the catalysts for change (Heath & Heath 2010). Working With the Willing means identifying those individuals who are committed to moving forward and finding solutions.

Leave It Better Than You Found It resonated with most staff. Staff discussed how this rule means adding value to all situations—projects, people, and the work culture. It is not about perfection. For the types of complex social problems that the Center addresses, it would be easy to become discouraged because progress is not immediately evident. On many of the prevention and early childhood projects, results are many years down the road. Leave It Better Than You Found It allows staff to recognize and celebrate the incremental milestones in long-term social change.

Discussion

The results provide useful insights into how work culture impacts key functioning of a backbone organization. The Rules of Engagement appear to resonate with staff after a short period of implementation. Freedom to Fail is the lowest mean score (2.89), and yet is most highly correlated with the statements about connection and engagement. This suggests five strategies worth considering by backbone organizations: 1) practical tools to build staff understanding and skill development; 2) the importance of shared struggle; 3) mindset; 4) leadership practices; and 5) hope.

Practical tools. The Rules of Engagement provide simple guidelines for working effectively as a backbone organization. However, the nuances and intangible qualities do not manifest by simply knowing the rules. Rather, through practice and intentional integration, the rules become an engrained approach that influences what staff do and how they do it. One way the Center put the rules into practice was by developing supervisory best practices providing tangible examples of expectations and behaviors for both supervisors and supervisees. The best practices document (Tables 4.1–4.4) has been used in new staff orientation, regular supervision meetings, and annual performance reviews to guide conversation and establish expectations that are clear and in line with the Center's work culture and philosophy as a backbone organization.

The importance of shared struggle. When staff feel supported and valued they are more likely to practice the freedom to fail or to take calculated risks that stretch their abilities. In their book *Team of Teams*, McChrystal et al. (2015) discuss this shared struggle as fundamental to building teams capable of addressing complex situations. For many organizations, this is a significant departure from business as usual. "Command" organizations that function as hierarchies give directives to staff to complete discrete tasks. This approach works well in factories, or even in some direct service organizations where staff are tasked with assessing clients and providing services to meet those needs. Such organizations tend to have predictable days where staff know what to expect and what specific tasks they will complete. Work is proscribed and requires a deft command of technical skills that address complicated problems.

However, in backbone organizations, the demand to move the needle on complex problems, such as poverty, health disparities, or homelessness, requires a different set of skills and a different structure. As McChrystal et al. (2015) state, "team building . . . is all about horizontal connectivity" (McChrystal et al. 2015: 97). Sharing the struggle is a big part of the work, as are alignment of personal and organizational purposes.

In line with the idea of having the freedom to fail, "resilience thinking" is another important concept for successful teams working in complex systems (McChrystal et al. 2015). Organizations that embrace resilience thinking are not perfectionists. While they value quality work and want to succeed, they do so by "creat[ing] systems that roll with the punches, or even benefit from them" (McChrystal et al. 2015: 78). In other words, they are willing to try, adjust strategies, and expect the unexpected. Staff are more likely to do this when they feel supported, and when, despite the difficulties encountered, they have a sense of accomplishment at the end of the day.

However, because backbones are not able to witness day-to-day client-level breakthroughs or significant changes in indicators, it is important that organizations establish other ways to measure and acknowledge success or progress. The need to mark advances and progress underscores the need for the Leave It Better Than You Found It Rule of Engagement.

Mindset. Fundamental to all of the Rules, and to the role of a backbone organization, is Carol Dweck's work on Mindset. Mindset is closely connected with the idea of failure. In Dweck's framework, there are two basic mindsets: a fixed mindset, in which your abilities are limited, or a growth mindset, in which you believe that you can always improve. In her 2006 book, *Mindset: The New Psychology of Success*, Dweck outlines how these mindsets play out in the business world. She states: [T]hose with growth mindset kept on learning. Not worried about measuring – or protecting – their fixed abilities, they looked directly at their mistakes, used the feedback, and altered their strategies accordingly (Dweck 2016: 111).

Mindset can be a significant challenge in CI work. To effectively address complex social problems, a growth mindset is essential. When partners come to the table with a fixed mindset, even the most adept backbone staff's change management techniques will not turn the collective into champions for the work. Backbone organizations play a critical role in building a growth mindset culture within a CI initiative. Before infecting a collaborative with a growth mindset, the backbone needs to get its own house in order and develop a culture that fosters an empowered, future-oriented staff.

Applying Dweck's mindset framework to the workplace means embracing challenges, persisting in the face of setbacks, being willing to put in the effort, learning from criticism, and embracing a team-based structure (Table 4.9). Because mindset is such a critical factor to empower others to act, we suggest that organizations assess their internal mindset by using the Mindset Scale (Dweck 2006). This exercise is informative for the overall orientation of the organization. If the members of the backbone do not believe they can empower others to change, it is highly unlikely that they will be effective Collective Impact leaders who convey confidence in the process or the project.

Leadership. All of the Rules of Engagement were significantly correlated with the statement "[Center] management communicates a clear sense of direction for our organization." This finding underscores the importance of leadership, especially in organizations that perform backbone functions. Kouzes and Posner (2012) state that:

Leaders *envision the future by imagining exciting and ennobling possibilities.* You need to make something happen, to change the way things are, to create something that no one else has ever created before . . . [V]isions seen only by leaders are insufficient to create an organized movement or a significant change in a company (Kouzes & Posner 2012: 18).

Leaders of backbone organizations are critical to success (Piha 2014). Further, capacity to fulfill the backbone role, connecting, staff skills, and teamwork were the top characteristics that influenced the effectiveness and readiness of a backbone organization (Piha 2014). These characteristics of leaders and staff align with the key components of CI and the functions of a backbone organization (Table 4.10).

TABLE 4.9 Mindset in the workplace, adapted from Dweck 2006

Fixed Mindset	*Growth Mindset*
Work culture is static	Work culture can be developed
Desire to maintain the status quo	Desire to grow and change
Avoids challenges	Embraces challenges
Gives up easily	Persists when obstacles get in the way
Sees effort as fruitless	Sees effort as the path to mastery
Ignores opportunities to change	Takes feedback and grows
Feels threatened by success of others	Finds lessons and inspiration in the success of others
May not adapt to complexity, achieving less than full potential	Reach ever higher levels of achievement

TABLE 4.10 Backbone Function Alignment with The Leadership Challenge Framework

Backbone Functions (Kania & Kramer 2011)	The Leadership Challenge Exemplary Practices (Kouzes & Posner 2012)
Guide Vision & Strategy	Inspire a Shared Vision
Support Aligned Activities	Model the Way
Establish Shared Measurement Practices	Enable Others to Act
Build Public Will	Inspire a Shared Vision
Advance Policy	Challenge the Process
Mobilize Funding	(Artifact of success of above)

Moreover, they align with The Leadership Challenge framework, and the attributes of leaders: honest, forward-looking, competent, and inspiring (Kouzes and Posner 2012).

Encourage the Heart, the fifth Exemplary Practice from The Leadership Challenge, does not explicitly align with the functions of a backbone organization. However, it is key to the work, both within the backbone and with partners in the Collective Impact initiative. Kouzes and Posner describe what Encourage the Heart looks like (Kouzes & Posner 2012: 271):

"Leaders give heart by visibly recognizing people's contributions to the common vision."

"Leaders express pride in the accomplishments of their teams."

"Leaders find creative ways to celebrate accomplishments."

In a backbone organization, all staff are leaders. Regardless of reporting structures within the organization, staff are the leaders of the CI work, performing backbone functions on behalf of the organization. Rules of engagement may be one way of operationalizing The Leadership Challenge in the work environment, especially in a backbone organization where leadership attributes and behaviors of all staff are key to success.

Hope. Positive descriptions of a backbone organization are more than a feel-good self-assessment. Positivity is a relationship-building strength (Rath 2007) that can influence both an organization and a Collective Impact effort. An important, although implicit, role of a backbone organization is to spread hope. Hope is defined as the belief that the future can be different, and that you have the power to do something to make it so (Lopez 2013). When individuals lack hope, they are more likely to have poor educational outcomes and lower job and life satisfaction (Lopez 2013). In situations where staff of an organization or members of a CI initiative do not actually believe that it is possible to solve the kind of complex social problems being addressed, the chances of successful outcomes are significantly limited. Backbone organizations spread hope by making others feel excited about the future and modeling and supporting others (Snyder 2003; Lopez 2013). This is more likely to occur when staff have a positive view of their organization, their work, and the collaborative effort.

Limitations

Several limitations of the study should be noted. The small sample size limits generalizability of findings. However, the results indicated statistical significance and strong positive correlations in spite of the small sample size. In addition, although the survey did have a high (60%) response rate, we should note that respondents were not randomly assigned, but rather self-selected, making it possible that the data have selection bias. In particular, there is reason to question whether staff who chose to take the survey were systematically different from those who chose not to participate in a way that might bias results. Qualitative data collected on a larger sample of the staff largely confirm quantitative results, suggesting any such bias is not pronounced. Further plans include a larger, randomly chosen sample with a focus on demographics, including age, length of time at organization, career status, and overall job satisfaction.

The survey questions were specific to the organization and its strategic plan. Pairing of the questions with other valid and reliable measures, such as the hope and mindset scales would strengthen the results.

LIWC analysis is generally conducted on full narrative style pieces. This study used LIWC to analyze descriptive words. The results, particularly the percentages of word count, still provide insight into staff perceptions. Typically, emotion words are less common in full–text writing samples, where positive emotions average 3.91% of the text. While asking for more narrative rather than a few descriptors may have resulted in a lower percentage of emotion words, this difference (19.3% to 3.91%) demonstrates that staff have a positive view of and feel connected to the organization.

Finally, the data presented here cannot conclusively demonstrate the causal direction of the relationships between variables. While a range of formal and informal observations have led us to conclude that the Rules of Engagement have positively contributed to workplace culture and improved staff perceptions, we acknowledge the possibility that positive attitudes toward work may be shaping staff members' embrace of the Rules, or that support for the rules and perceptions may be shaped by a third exogenous factor.

Conclusion

Backbone organizations are a key component of the CI framework. The functions of a backbone are useful in guiding the work, but organizations should not assume that implementation of the activities alone will be sufficient to move the needle on complex social problems. Bringing about social change is hard work, and progress is sometimes difficult to see.

It often feels like two steps forward, one step back with many twists and turns along the way. With other competing demands, partners may become distracted or disengaged when the common agenda seems to stall or progress does not come as quickly as desired. In addition to being the facilitator and the glue that hold the change partners together, backbone staff must also bring the intangibles, including a growth mindset and a healthy dose of assurance that things are moving forward. These intangible qualities, along with the data from the shared measurement system, are critical elements for keeping members engaged. The experience at the Center shows that it is critical to start within your organization to be taken seriously as a credible backbone organization with the wherewithal, grit, and urgency to deliver.

This chapter reviewed the literature on backbone organizations, and found many checklists for how to be a backbone, but fewer tools that dive into the intangibles. We discussed what the Center did to move from silos to an integrated mission-driven organization, all with the goal of being an effective backbone organization. Especially important were the Rules of Engagement, which provided guardrails for *how* we work together to support CI. We analyzed survey and focus group data around the Rules of Engagement and how staff felt about their work life and the Center, and found ample support and applicability of the Rules. Staff understand and apply them strategically and intentionally.

There is no magic behind being an effective backbone organization. Yet, having Rules that guide the work improved the ability to guide vision and strategy, support aligned activities, establish shared measurement practices, build public will, advance policy, and mobilize funding (Turner, Merchant, Kania, & Martin 2012). Embracing the struggle and identifying tools and practices like mindset, leadership, and hope are key to success.

References

Ammerman, R. T., Putnam, F. W., Kopke, J. E., Gannon, T. A., Short, J. A, Van Ginkel, J. B., Clark, M. J., Carrozza, M. A., & Spector, A. R. (2007). Development and Implementation of a Quality Assurance Infrastructure in a Multisite Home Visitation Program in Ohio and Kentucky. Journal of prevention & intervention in the community. 34. 89-107. 10.1300/J005v34n01_05.

Bachmann, M.O., O'Brien, M., Husbands, C., Shreeve, A., Jones, N., Watson, J., Reading, R., Thoburn, J., Mugford, M., & The National Evaluation of Children's Trusts Team. (2009). Integrating Children's Services in England: National Evaluation of Children's Trusts. *Child: Care, Health and Development*, *35*(2), 257–265. doi:10.1111/j.1365-2214. 2008.00928.x

Bhargava, R. (2012). *Likeonomics*. Hoboken, NJ: Wiley.

Bolland, J. & Wilson, J.V. (1994). Three Faces of Integrative Coordination: A model of Interorganizational Relations in Community. *Health Services Research*, *29*(3), 341.

Bunger, A. (2010). Defining Service Coordination: A Social Work Perspective. *Journal of Social Service Research*, *36*, 385–401. doi: 10.1080/01488376.2010.510931

Cohn, M., Mehl, M. and Pennebaker, J. (2004). Linguistic Markers of Psychological Change Surrounding September 11, 2001. *Psychological Science*, 15(10), pp.687–693.

Darnell, J. and Means, T. (2016). United States Association for Small Business and Entrepreneurship Proceedings. In: *Entrepreneurship Everywhere*. San Diego, pp. DY1–DY6.

D'Souza, S. and Renner, D. (2014). *Not Knowing: the art of turning uncertainty into possibility*. London: LID Publishing.

Dweck, C. (2006). *Mindset: The new psychology of success.* New York. NY: Random House.

Foster-Fishman, P., Salem, D., Allen, N., and Fahrbach, K. (2001). Facilitating Interorganizational Collaboration: The Contributions of Interorganizational Alliances. *American Journal of Community Psychology,* 29(6), pp.875–905.

Friedman, M. (2005). Trying hard is not good enough: How to produce measurable improvements for customers and communities. Victoria, BC: Trafford.

Heath, C. and Heath, D. (2010). *Switch: how to change things when change is hard.* New York, NY: Random House.

Howe, N. and Strauss, W. (2007). *Millennials go to college.* Great Falls, VA.: LifeCourse Associates.

Kania, J., Hanleybrown, F., and Splansky Juster, J., (2014). Essential mindset shifts for collective impact. *Collective Insights on Collective Impact,* pp.2–5.

Kania, J. & Kramer, M. (2011). Collective Impact. *Stanford Social Innovation Review.*

Kansas Early Childhood Comprehensive Systems Plan. (2011). *Implementation project: 2011 evaluation report.*

Kort, I.M., Verweij, S., and Klijn, E.H., (2015). In search for effective public–private partnerships: An assessment of the impact of organizational form and managerial strategies in urban regeneration partnerships using fsQCA. *Environment and Planning C: Government and Policy,* 34(5), pp.777–794.

Kouzes, J. and Posner, B. (2012). The leadership challenge: How to make extraordinary things happen in organizations. 5th ed. San Francisco, CA: Jossey-Bass.

Liwc.wpengine.com. (2015). *LIWC | Linguistic Inquiry and Word Count.* [Software] Available at: http://liwc.wpengine.com/

Lopez, S. (2013). *Making hope happen.* New York, NY: Atria Books.

McChrystal, S., Collins, T., Silverman, D., and Fussell, C. (2015). *Team of teams.* New York: Penguin Publishing Group.

McGrath, R. (1999). Falling Forward: Real Options Reasoning and Entrepreneurial Failure. *The Academy of Management Review,* 24(1), p.13–30.

Moran, P., Jacobs, C., Bunn, A., and Bifulco, A. (2007) Multi-agency Working: Implications for an Early-intervention Social Work Team. *Child and Family Social Work,* 12, 143–151. doi:10.1111/j.1365-2206.2006.00452.x

Patton, M.Q. (2002). *Qualitative Research & Evaluation Methods.* Thousand Oaks, CA: Sage Publications.

Piha, S. (2017). The important role of intermediaries in Collective Impact work. Washington D.C: The Forum of Youth Investment.

Preskitt, J., Fifolt, M., Ginter, P., Rucks, A., and Wingate, M. (2016). Identifying Continuous Quality Improvement Priorities in Maternal, Infant, and Early Childhood Home Visiting. *Journal of Public Health Management and Practice,* 22(2), pp. E12–E20.

Rath, T. (2007). *Strengths finder 2.0.* New York: Gallup Press.

Rogers, E. (2003). *Diffusion of innovations, 5th Edition.* 5th ed. New York: Free Press.

Scharmer, C. (2009). *Theory U.* Oakland: Berrett-Koehler Publishers. Forwarded by P. Senge.

Snyder, C. (2003). *Psychology of hope.* New York: Free Press.

Suárez, D.F. and Esparza, N., (2015). Institutional Change and Management of Public-Nonprofit Partnerships. *The American Review of Public Administration,* 47(6), pp. 648–660.

Townsley, R., Watson, D., & Abbott, D. (2004). Working Partnerships? A Critique of the Process of Multi-agency Working in Services to Disabled Children with complex Health Care Needs. *Journal of Integrated Care,* 12(2), 24–34C.

Turner, S., Errecart, K. and Bhatt, A. (2013a). Exerting Influence without Formal Authority. *Stanford Social Innovation Review.*

Turner, S., Errecart, K. and Bhatt, A. (2013b). Measuring Backbone Contributions to Collective Impact. *Stanford Social Innovation Review.*

Turner, S., Merchant, K., Kania, J., & Martin, E. (2012). Exerting Influence without Formal Authority. *Stanford Social Innovation Review.*

5

USING SYSTEMS TOOLS TO ADVANCE COLLECTIVE IMPACT

Kathryn Lawler, Glenn Landers, Karen Minyard, Kristi Fuller, and Jane Branscomb

The application of the Collective Impact framework to modern challenges of community development can be enhanced through the use of systems tools (Minyard, Lawler, Fuller, Wilson, & Henry, 2016). Regardless of the topics collaboratives are tackling—poverty reduction, obesity among adolescents, early childhood development, or health disparities—a deep understanding of the issues, current data, internal and external forces, and any relevant historical context is essential to achieve success. Collaboratives can barely begin to apply the pre-conditions of Collective Impact—influential champions, urgency of the issue, and adequate resources—or the five core conditions of CI—a common agenda, shared measurement, mutually reinforcing activities, continuous communications, and a backbone infrastructure (Kania & Kramer, 2011)—without a strong foundation in the larger system, whose design created the present challenge and related issues.

Systems tools can be employed to deepen stakeholders' shared knowledge, which is essential to developing an effective strategy, establishing consensus, and setting priorities. Systems tools can be well-suited for CI work, which is designed to address adaptive rather than technical problems (Kania & Kramer, 2011). Specifically, systems tools can help CI efforts:

- understand the underlying, and often upstream, issues that are the root causes of the complex, social problems faced today;
- quantify the challenges that CI work is best designed to address; and,
- provide the framework for the continual learning and analysis necessary for the emergent wisdom, insight, and strategies that are critical to Collective Impact success.

Collective Impact starts with the assumption that there are many factors contributing to a problem and that many organizations must be part of the solution.

But as an emerging practice, CI is not always well-understood by all stakeholders or potential investors in a community. Using systems tools can help organizations, community leaders, local governments, and philanthropists understand how the CI team is defining the problem and why this strategy will be the most effective.

This chapter explores how the Atlanta Regional Collaborative for Health Improvement (ARCHI), a CI initiative in Atlanta, GA, utilized systems models to quantify local health disparities, align stakeholders, and identify potentially effective strategies to improve health, as well as educational and economic opportunity, for all living in the metro Atlanta area. Specifically, the chapter will examine the use of systems tools in the fields of public health and community development, detail the history of the ARCHI collaborative and its use of the ReThink Health model and the REMI (Regional Economics Model), and explore the larger implications of this work for community development disciplines.

Systems Tools and Community Development

Every person and every collaborative can use some level of systems thinking to build strong collaboration, more clearly understand the local context, develop a shared vision of the desired future, and prioritize actions. These are important ingredients for overcoming resistance and making transformational change. Systems thinking is especially important for collaboratives that seek to transform local health, well-being, and health care because the system is complex and ever-changing.

Heifetz and Linsky describe the importance of adaptive thinking in complex situations (Heifetz & Linsky, 2002). Routine problems are easily defined, there is an obvious, proven solution, or there is an expert on whom to call to solve the problem. In contrast, adaptive challenges are hard to define, have no clear solution, require collaboration to solve, are viewed differently by various people, and do not have experts with the answer. Solving complex, adaptive problems is fundamentally different from solving routine problems and requires a new way of thinking and working together that can be supported by systems tools.

The Formula for Change, pioneered by David Gleicher and later adapted by Richard Beckhard and Kathy Dannemiller (Beckhard & Harris, 1987; Dannemiller & Jacobs, 1992), is used when approaching complex problems. The DVF formula is defined as $RC < D \times V \times F$, where the resistance to change (RC) must be less than the product of dissatisfaction (D), Vision (V), and first steps (F). If any of the elements on the right side of the equation (dissatisfaction, vision, first steps) do not exist then the product becomes zero and resistance to change cannot be overcome.

Dissatisfaction with the current state often surfaces when participants in the change process have access to data. Having data that stimulates dissatisfaction with the status quo creates an environment that is ripe for building a shared vision for the future. When participants in a change process can envision a future of which they would be proud and are willing to work toward it, the change process can happen more easily and more quickly. Accurate data and a shared vision help to overcome resistance to change.

Another important ingredient to the change process is taking action. Even a few first steps can be enough to launch a change process. Once participants are looking together at a shared and desired future, it is natural to identify first steps for moving forward.

Systems thinking skills and tools can support the change process. Conversational skills; simple tools like behavior over time graphs and stock and flow maps, and more complex computerized models, can all aid the change process.

Barry Richmond (1993) proposed that decision makers could evaluate the outcome of different systems thinking activities by the value derived from that activity relative to the amount of time, resources, and effort required to engage in that activity (Richmond, 1993). For example, a team could simply ask a set of questions that are systemic (e.g., what's the trend? Are there potential unintended consequences to this policy?). This process would take little time, but could improve the quality of the conversation. They might gain additional value by developing a simple map or model, which could help them "see" where an intervention might impact system behavior. Or, they could even spend much more time and build a full-scale simulation model and rigorously test policy interventions. The point of the graphic is to indicate that systems thinking can infuse a range of activities, all with some likely benefit, but that does not all require a year-long modeling analysis project to obtain sufficient value and insight (Minyard, Ferencik, Phillips, & Soderquist, 2014).

Several key principles define systems thinking, including that all systems are composed of interconnected parts; the structure of a system determines its behavior; system behavior is an emergent phenomenon; feedback loops control a system's

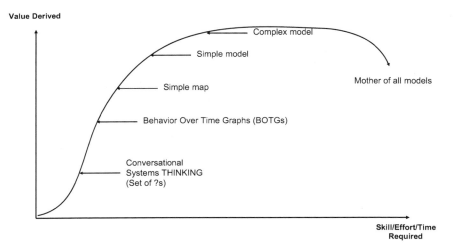

FIGURE 5.1 Value and Effort of Systems Tools

Source: Adapted from Richmond, B. (1993) Systems Thinking: Critical Thinking Skills for the 1990s and Beyond. *System Dynamics Review*, 9(2), 113–133.

major dynamic behavior; and complex social systems exhibit counter intuitive behavior. When there is an adaptive problem, embedded in a complex system that requires powerful collaboration to solve, systems tools can help. An issue for many groups has been how to successfully use systems tools.

In 2013, the Center for Disease Control and Prevention's (CDC) Division of Violence Prevention and the Georgia Health Policy Center at Georgia State University convened an expert panel of 30 researchers, modelers and practitioners. They explored what is collectively known to work/not work in the area of complex system sciences, what can accelerate learning and how to help practitioners use models and maps more effectively (*Modeling Expert Panel Meeting: A Collaborative Think Session*, 2013). While numerous systems dynamic models and maps exist, the field is still learning how to help practitioners use models more effectively. Some current unanswered questions this panel started to discuss include:

- How do you use the tools of maps and models to most effectively facilitate stakeholder and community change?
- What types of models or maps work in which type of situation?
- What do we know about our experience with models and adult learning theory, adaptive leadership, meeting design and facilitation, and organizational learning theory that can accelerate learning and action with these models?
- What types of supplementary materials are needed to 'wrap-around' existing maps and models to increase adoption and use while motivating action?

The expert panel identified a process framework for creating successful model use that included five phases of model development and use—discovery, definition, preparation, interaction and evaluation. Further, the group discussed what activities, information, skills, players, materials, and challenges/risks exist, or are needed, to successfully use system dynamics models to effect positive change and impact. The panel identified the following practice principles to make the most effective use of systems thinking tools (such as models and maps) to catalyze change:

- The purpose for using a model is clearly identified and supported by the client.
- Tools are as simple as possible, but no simpler.
- Tools can be tailored to the readiness and the level of engagement of participants, as well as the goals and the outcome of the process.
- The modeler or facilitator has the adaptive and technical skills to use the tools.
- The tools are used as a part of a larger change process.

ARCHI was able to use the ReThink Health (RTH) system dynamics model to chart the course toward a 28-year future. The RTH model is a realistic, but simplified, portrait of a regional health system. Representing a U.S. city, county, state, or region, the model simulates changes in population health, health care delivery, health equity, workforce productivity, and health care costs by quarter-year increments from 2010 to 2040 (Homer, Milstein, Hirsch, & Fisher, 2016). The model contains more than 20 options for simulating strategies either individually or in combinations.

ARCHI was well-positioned to effectively use the RTH model. The collaborative's original leaders understood the complexity of the challenge faced. They were interested in making broad, sweeping, impactful change in the region and understood that they faced an adaptive, rather than a routine, problem.

The components of the DVF formula provided support. As leaders and partners reviewed data about the region, they were dissatisfied with the current state. The RTH model provided a vehicle for a large group of stakeholders to envision a future of which they could be proud. Using the RTH model, they could explore various scenarios and chose the one with majority support. Without the model, they would have been unable to see the whole ecosystem in a way that helped them chart a future path.

ARCHI was at the point on Richmond's graph where the value derived and the effort expended were maximized. The complex RTH model was not built specifically for ARCHI, but was calibrated using regional data. Without knowing it, ARCHI followed the process and principles identified by the expert panel because there was a clear purpose for the model and the model could be tailored to the needs of the group through calibration. The RTH modelers and the ARCHI leadership had the adaptive skills to facilitate the process and the model was used within the context of a larger change process.

Systems Tools to Develop a Common Agenda

Eleven Atlanta-based organizations came together in 2011 to explore how local health systems might collaborate on several new requirements in the Affordable Care Act. Representing a wide range of sectors, this group met to discuss how it could provide incentive for a joint community health needs assessment (CHNA) that could support the needs of multiple health system and public health departments. The idea was based on the premise that collaboration would be efficient and cost effective, since each health systems had to accumulate the same data and complete the same analysis. So rather than hiring separate consultant teams to produce what would amount to, largely the same report, a single analysis could save each of the systems and all of the public data partners time and money. The idea was relatively simple because the systems were only being asked to work together on data analysis—not strategic planning, not shared priorities, not joint implementation—just data.

While justified in its simplicity, efficiency, and cost-effectiveness, this idea was also driven by changes occurring in the broader health ecosystem. The U.S. Congress passed the Affordable Care Act (ACA) in 2010. The next two years brought much discussion about new regulations, penalties, and incentives stemming from implementation of the ACA. The rules governing CHNAs were only one of many major changes to which health systems were rapidly responding. As an extension of the law, the federal government expressed interest in the idea of regional health needs assessments and issued guidance to clarify how such a joint assessment could meet ACA requirements. The U.S. Centers for Disease Control and Prevention (CDC) had a staff person in the U.S. Department of Treasury and the 11-organization group in Atlanta benefitted from working directly with this staff person as it provided a potential joint assessment to each of the seven health systems with a service area that included the core metro area.

Over one year, this group went from an informal gathering of colleagues to actively soliciting involvement and investment from other partners. Three organizations emerged to serve in a leadership capacity—the Georgia Health Policy Center (GHPC), the Atlanta Regional Commission (ARC), and the United Way of Greater Atlanta (United Way). This leadership team exemplified the cross-sector approach of the original group and brought a wide range of skills and relationships to the task of soliciting the involvement of the health systems. In addition, with influential and well-known individuals leading each organization, the emerging group was supported by a powerful team of local champions.

However, after months of meetings and conversations and proposal development, only two of the seven health systems agreed to work together—Grady Health Systems and Kaiser Permanente of Georgia. The leadership team from GHPC, ARC, and the United Way met and prepared to inform the rest of the group that they no longer needed to gather monthly as had been their practice. It simply was not the right time for the larger scale, regional, joint assessment initially envisioned.

However, the core group refused to accept that the work was over. By meeting together, they had begun to articulate a grander shared vision than just a joint health assessment. They shared a vision for an improved local health ecosystem based on the fundamental idea that drivers of health and well-being lie mostly outside the walls of health care institutions, while most of the dollars lie within these institutions. The group also believed that it was this mismatch between what makes people healthy and how health dollars are spent in the United States, in Georgia, and in Atlanta that kept some areas of the metro region at the bottom of national health statistics. The leadership group went back to the drawing board.

These three leaders committed to meet every month—no matter what time of day or day of the week it had to be scheduled. After a while, the group became affectionately known as the three-headed executive, or the executive trio, and their monthly meeting still continues, eight years later. As the trio worked through options in the first quarter of 2012, several critical issues emerged—in order to tackle the multigenerational health disparities that held back too many in Atlanta's communities, they agreed to:

- take a broad view of the health system;
- spend time building a common understanding of the relationships between health and education, health and transportation, health and workforce development, health and housing, etc.;

- build the infrastructure for a decentralized investment strategy since it seemed clear that while individual organizations might support a single agenda, they were not going to turn over their resources to a single fund; and
- assemble a substantial partnership that included organizations and individuals who could unite diverse sectors around an organized change strategy.

A new name also emerged and the group now became known as the Atlanta Regional Collaborative for Health Improvement (ARCHI). The original founding organizations became the steering committee, led jointly by the executive trio.

Returning to the collaborative, the executive trio presented a four-part convening series, open to anyone who was frustrated by Atlanta's poor health outcomes and tremendous disparities and interested in learning about innovations and best practices from across the country. This series culminated in the exploration of a shared agenda for change. Organizational champions, inspired by what they saw as a very different approach to community change, agreed to meet quarterly at the Commerce Club, where corporate and political leaders long had been meeting to make major decisions for Atlanta.

Each meeting was designed to explore the group's understanding of the system dynamics that were causing the health inequities and would have to be overcome in any strategy for health improvement. The first meeting was held in July 2012, just after the Supreme Court ruled that the majority of the ACA would stand. The agenda covered much ground: a panel of local leaders representing local government, the business community, public health, and the insurance industry discussed the need for a collective approach to health improvement. Leaders from the CDC discussed examples of Collective Impact from across the country and leaders from the ReThink Health Initiative of the Rippel Foundation demonstrated its health systems model and described its use by communities nationally.

Building on this same momentum, the second meeting in September 2012 featured local Atlanta leaders both past and present. Ambassador Andrew Young shared the collaborative history of the Atlanta region and Doug Hooker, executive director of ARC, highlighted the role that community health plays in the region's economic success. Explaining the role that community and faith-based organizations can play in achieving health outcomes, guests from the Memphis HealthCare system shared their extensive partnership experience with local Methodist congregations. Together they have a track record of not only reducing health care expenses, but also changed lifestyles.

In October 2012, the collaborative took a deeper dive into other critical areas of the health ecosystem. Speakers profiled the recent completion of a resident-led photo audit, during which a community about to undergo a significant redevelopment used photography to capture their hopes and fears about the impending change in their community and how it might impact their health. The group was introduced to the stewardship work of Elinor Ostrom (Ostrom, Burger, Field, Norgaard, & Policansky, 1999), and the five core conditions of Collective Impact.

Finally, a senior executive from Langdale Industries, a 118-year-old, diversified forest products company, shared how the company has improved the health of its workforce and saved over $29 million in healthcare costs since 2000. Specifically, the company both reduced the number and costs of claims and reduced the annual health insurance premium growth rate significantly below U.S. trends by taking a holistic approach to the health of employees and their families.

Attendance continued to grow with each quarterly meeting. Initially, 30 people attended the July 2012 meeting but by the November 2012 meeting more than 80 stakeholders joined the dialogue. The meeting was organized into three parts: an overview of the CHNA that ARCHI completed despite not having buy-in from all seven health systems, an extensive review of the RTH model first introduced at the July meeting, and action planning in small teams.

The CHNA showed what many already knew—that health status and disease prevalence varied widely across the two metro Atlanta counties (DeKalb and Fulton) and were highly correlated with rates of poverty, unemployment, educational attainment and race. There was clear consensus among attendees that something had to be done.

Prior to the meeting, ARCHI steering committee members had worked with faculty from Georgia State University to calibrate the RTH model to reflect the specific details of the health system in DeKalb and Fulton counties. Data covered health status and a full range of health conditions, demographics, socioeconomic information, and the current health care finance system. The model demonstrated that without any changes to the way services are delivered or health care is financed, Atlanta health care costs would continue to rise while key indicators of health, the effectiveness of the health system, and the economy would continue to decline.

It was time to move from agreement about the problem to an action agenda for the future. Meeting attendees were divided into groups of eight to 10 people. Each was given a lengthy set of interventions they could chose to deploy in the Atlanta area over a 28-year period (2012 to 2040). These interventions included changes in the delivery of care, expansion of certain kinds of care including primary care and behavioral health services, increases in healthy behaviors, a range of upstream interventions that addressed education and income, and a variety of new methods of financing service delivery. Based upon evidence-based interventions, as well as their knowledge of the health ecosystem, the Atlanta community, and the data from the CHNA, each group proposed the combination of changes to services, the service delivery system, and health care financing they believed would make the biggest impact on the health of Atlanta residents.

The combinations of interventions and financing from each small group were then entered into the model and run live, so all stakeholders could see the results of each group's proposed solutions. The model allowed the assembled stakeholders to compare and contrast the impact different scenarios could have on the larger health ecosystem and the economy. Several themes emerged, including that sustainable financing would be essential to ensure that the impacts would last.

Interventions, if solely restricted to the clinical setting, were not as effective as interventions that included both medical and nonmedical practices. Increased access to both care and insurance would have to be expanded and provider capacity had to increase.

The broader group then used electronic voting to determine which change scenario it would adopt and collectively pursue. With 87% support from the diverse stakeholders gathered, the approach that became known as the Atlanta Transformation Scenario (Figure 5.2) was adopted as the preferred scenario.

The Atlanta Transformation Scenario

There are seven key elements of the Atlanta Transformation Scenario: two assumptions regarding future health system trends (contingent global payment levels and rates of non-insurance), two financing propositions (an innovation portfolio and a capture and reinvest scheme), and three priority areas for intervention (healthy behaviors, pathways to advantage, and care coordination). These factors and their roles in the health ecosystem are described below.

Health Insurance Coverage

RTH allows users to establish the trends they anticipate in health insurance coverage (or uninsured rates) among the disadvantaged and those covered by private insurance. ARCHI members left insurance coverage for the disadvantaged at status quo for the Atlanta Transformation Scenario, since Georgia opted not to expand Medicaid eligibility under the ACA. They posited declines in the portion of the advantaged population that remains uninsured based on uptake of private insurance due to various features of the ACA.

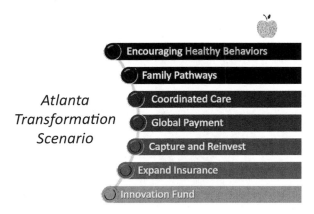

FIGURE 5.2 The Elements of the Atlanta Transformation Scenario

Source: Created by the Authors; Georgia Health Policy Center, January 2013

County Health Rankings & Roadmaps data showed the portion of adults under age 65 years who were uninsured in 2010 as 27% in both DeKalb and Fulton counties. For adults in Georgia, overall, the uninsured rate was 27 percent. In Fulton County, 11% of children were uninsured, as were 12% in DeKalb County versus 10% in the state overall.

Contingent Global Payment

The goal of various payment reform models, as illustrated in Figure 5.3, is to promote higher quality care, while lowering the cost of care. Further along the spectrum of payment reform is the contingent global (or bundled) payment approach, in which the provider is paid a fixed amount to cover all of the care an individual requires for a given condition. The provider receives a share of any savings that result from their providing high quality, lower-cost care. In ARCHI's preferred change scenario, contingent global payment is set to 50% of the care provided through Medicare, Medicaid, and commercial payers.

Innovation Portfolio

ARCHI's preferred intervention priorities all require funding. RTH allows users to specify the dollars and duration of an innovation fund to be used in carrying out the specified interventions. If some of the available funds are not required in a given year, RTH rolls the remainder over to the next year. Any such rollovers can be used even after the designated termination of the innovation fund. If, based on the model's assumptions, not enough money is available to implement the chosen interventions at specified levels, the level of intervention intensity is

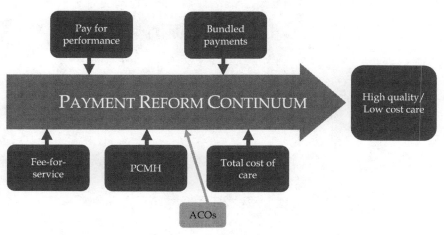

FIGURE 5.3 Continuum of Payment Reform

Source: Created by the Authors; Archi Playbook, November 2013

reduced proportionately. ARCHI members simulated the Atlanta Transformation Scenario with an innovation fund of USD $100 million per year during the first five years, a total of USD $500 million.

Capture and Reinvest

Capturing and reinvesting savings is another financing option in the RTH model and one selected by ARCHI members for the Atlanta Transformation Scenario. The strategy involves negotiating arrangements with payers whereby they calculate health care cost savings against appropriate benchmarks and then return some fraction of those savings to the community. This money, combined with the innovation fund, can then be used to finance scenario initiatives. In ARCHI's preferred scenario, the negotiated split of savings with each payer—Medicare, Medicaid, and commercial—is 50%. Figure 5.4 plots the annual funds this strategy could generate under the Atlanta Transformation scenario over the next 25-plus years.

Healthy Behaviors

As simulated by the RTH model, promoting healthy behavior and preventing risky behavior can lead to reductions in the onset of mild and severe chronic, physical illness, the likelihood of urgent events (e.g., heart attacks from cigarette smoke), and the onset of mental illness associated with drug use. It also reduces

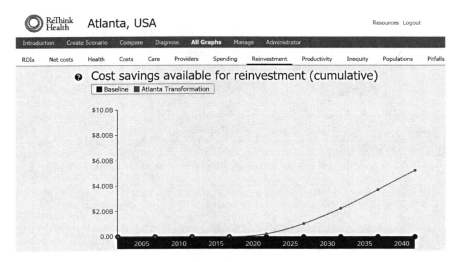

FIGURE 5.4 Atlanta Transformation Scenario Reinvestment of Savings

Source: Reproduced with Permission from Rethink Health, an Initiative of the Rippel Foundation (November 2012).

the need for medications for lifestyle-related disorders, including asymptomatic hypertension and high cholesterol. Based on the literature, the model estimates that risky behavior prevalence declines by a factor of 2.5 over time as cessation increases and that new onset of disease decreases by 50 percent. It estimates implementation costs at $100 per person per year for the population engaging in risky behavior and assumes that interventions are targeted at specific populations and/or neighborhoods.

ARCHI is focused on the five healthy behavior areas that are included in the RTH model: reducing smoking and tobacco use, improving diet and nutrition, increasing exercise and physical activity, reducing alcohol and drug use, and reducing incidence of unprotected sex and sexually transmitted infections, and a sixth focus area, increasing regular preventive care for physical and mental health.

Pathways to Advantage

Advantage is defined as having annual income that is at least twice the federal poverty level. Evidence indicates that economic advantage plays multiple roles in the health and health care ecosystem. The model reflects that the advantaged are more likely to be insured, seek care, and engage in self-care activities, compared to the disadvantaged. The advantaged are also are less likely to engage in unhealthy behavior, live in hazardous or high-crime environments, or go to the hospital for non-urgent care. Because of these and other factors, the advantaged are less likely to develop chronic physical or mental illness.

Care Coordination

As defined in RTH model, health care coordination includes coordinating patient care and providing patient and physician coaching to reduce duplicative or unnecessary care and costs. Using integrated information systems, coaching arrangements, protocols for shared decision-making, and increased use of generic drugs when appropriate. These elements of care coordination can result in fewer referrals to specialists, less ambulatory testing and procedures, and fewer hospital admissions, without adversely affecting outcomes.

RTH estimates that it takes about a year for an office-based physician to implement components of care coordination, with an initial investment of $30,000 per physician. Subsequent maintenance of the integrated information system and on-going physician coaching are estimated to cost $3,000 per year, per office-based physician.

Evidence is emerging on care coordination strategies, but gaps still exist. Because these practices are in their infancy and only one met the highest standard for evidence of effectiveness, the care coordination working group agreed to include promising and emerging programs in its recommendations for consideration.

Using Systems Tools to Attract New Partners

After the Atlanta Transformation Scenario was adopted at the end of 2012, ARC, a member of the executive trio, integrated the results into another systems tool—the REMI Econometric Model (Treyz, Rickman, & Shao, 1991). The Atlanta region had been using a locally calibrated version of the REMI dynamic model to understand and predict trends in the local economy since the mid-2000s. The model, like other systems tools, is designed to understand components of the economy and their interactions with each another. Specifically, it examines relationships between population and labor supply, labor and capital demand, market shares, wages, prices and costs, state and local government spending, and other investments. Issues affected by the health improvements quantified in the RTH model, including longer life expectancy, increased utilization of health care services, and enhanced worker productivity, are all likely to impact the region's economy. Without the use of systems tools, the impact of these effects, both the potential costs and benefits, could only be offered as an educated guess. But because ARCHI had employed the RTH system dynamics model, staff at the ARC were able to incorporate the results and rerun the region's economic forecast. The results were compelling.

If through the implementation of the Atlanta Transformation Scenario, ARCHI and its partners could achieve the desired improvements in the health care system, in health outcomes and in worker productivity, the models demonstrated that the economy would also benefit from an increase in employment, population and gross domestic product for the metro region. These results are powerful and through the integration of these two systems models, were quantified.

In both cases, these systems tools changed the dialogue and the agenda around community change. While the associations between health and the economy, health and workforce development, health and education are clear to many in the field, these connections are relatively new to many policymakers. The systems models—both RTH and REMI—clearly demonstrate these interactions and broaden the platform on which the change agenda is built. For ARCHI, this additional use of the REMI tool helped to recruit and engage the business sector, economic development industry, and local government.

Applying Systems Tools to Collective Impact Beyond a Shared Agenda

Because health and health care are so complex, there is an opportunity to employ systems tools as practitioners work to improve community conditions. As described earlier, systems tools can range from simple to very sophisticated. ARCHI's use of the RTH model was presented as an example of the application of a fairly sophisticated systems tool that assisted in galvanizing a multi-sectoral collaborative around a common vision of community improvement over a 28-year timeframe. The process led to the creation of a common agenda (the Atlanta Transformation

Scenario and the *ARCHI Playbook*) that illustrates an actionable path forward. This section explores the potential application of systems tools to the four other conditions of Collective Impact: mutually reinforcing activities, continuous communication, backbone infrastructure, and shared measurement (Kania & Kramer, 2011).

Systems Tools and Mutually Reinforcing Activities

The advantage of using systems tools and frameworks—even in the simple forms of strategy maps, strategic visioning, and strategic frameworks—to delineate how mutually-reinforcing activities relate to a common agenda has been described by others (Barberg, 2017; Irbyis, 2014; Kania & Kramer, 2013). As detailed in the previous section, while the RTH model was employed to galvanize many individuals around a common agenda, ARCHI envisioned a distributed approach to advancing ARCHI's work (as suggested by CI). This meant that members were encouraged, supported and recognized for aligning decisions and activities with these priorities within and across their spheres of influence.

In support of this approach, ARCHI and its partners drafted the *ARCHI Playbook* (begun in 2013 and completed in 2014). The Playbook is a compendium of evidence-based strategies organized in the seven areas of the Atlanta Transformation Scenario. Since its adoption, it has guided and aligned ARCHI members to achieve progress toward ARCHI's shared agenda. All of the Playbook's suggested interventions are evidence-based in an effort to minimize the risks that partners often have to take to adopt mutually-reinforcing activities.

Stakeholders investing in an intervention want to know there is evidence of its effectiveness (having credible reasons for expecting the positive results they seek). Evidence of effectiveness has two components. First is the level of evidence—the amount and quality of information available that speaks to an intervention's likelihood of producing desired results. Second is the degree of effectiveness—the magnitude of results that can reasonably be expected from the intervention. One would typically prefer to invest in interventions with strong evidence of large, positive effect. However, not only are such choices not always available, but the specific context may call for different priorities. Sound investments are based on careful consideration of the level of evidence, degree of effectiveness, and contextual factors.

The level of evidence ranges from low to high; from solid logic to multiple, rigorous research studies. Some considerations include: Is the cause–effect relationship plausible? Is it backed by established theory? Has the intervention or something similar been tested in practice? Have studies been published in peer-reviewed journals? Have they been replicated independently? Were research designs rigorous?

The degree of effectiveness also varies along a continuum. Considerations include: Is the intervention likely to produce a small change, a large change, or possibly an unacceptable type of change? Will it affect an outcome of primary interest, such as deaths averted, or an intermediate one, such as smoking prevalence? Will the effect be distributed evenly across the population or might it reduce or exacerbate an existing disparity?

Figure 5.5 illustrates the combined domains of evidence and effectiveness. In the green area, there is some level of evidence for some degree of positive effect. Thus, consideration is justified for any intervention that falls in this zone. Strategies in the gray area must be rejected, as there is evidence of ineffectiveness or harm. Thus, there is reason to expect that implementing these interventions would be, at best, futile, if not unethical. Point A represents a strategy that has been demonstrated through multiple, rigorous studies to produce a positive, though small, effect. Point B is one that may be untested, but for which sound logic and theory suggests has potential for a large, positive impact. Point C is a strategy that has strong evidence for a large-scale effect. All of these interventions are reasonable to consider. The context might argue for A or B, even though C is most compelling at face value.

As suggested by the blurred regions along the axes, there are some interventions for which the level of evidence and/or the effect size is non-zero, but so negligible that it should be treated as zero. Simple hunches and research results that are not statistically different from zero are examples. The Playbook offers a menu of strategies informed by the best available evidence in each priority intervention and financing area. Because the quality and quantity of evidence varies across these areas, no single standard for evidence of effectiveness could be applied in determining inclusion. Thus, these lists are not exhaustive, as some strategies worthy of consideration may be missing because the evidence base is just emerging. In other cases, because the body of evidence is so large, only strategies in the

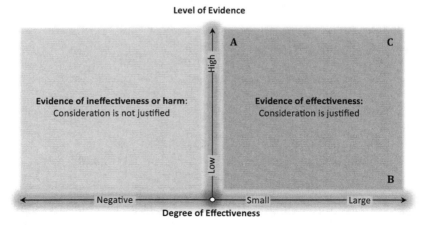

FIGURE 5.5 Framework to Evaluate Evidence, Effectiveness of Potential Interventions

Source: Created by the Authors; Archi Playbook, November 2013

upper tiers of effectiveness were included. Still, the use of a simple evidence framework aids in determining how various interventions fit within the overall agenda.

Systems Tools and Continuous Communication

It is more obvious how systems tools can support a common agenda and help delineate mutually-reinforcing activities that might support a common agenda than it is how systems tools might support continuous communication. According to Kania and Kramer, "Developing trust among nonprofits, corporations, and government agencies is a monumental challenge. Participants need several years of regular meetings to build up enough experience with each other to recognize and appreciate the common motivation behind their different efforts" (Kania & Kramer, 2011).

It was previously shown how a simple diagram plotting evidence and effectiveness can aid in delineating various choices among a range of activities. The example below illustrates how mapping patterns of group behaviors, communications, or actions might provide a platform for honest reflection of group dynamics so that a collaborative can learn from its actions and strive for high performance.

In this simple example, a collaborative grapples with new information or ideas presented at regularly scheduled meetings. The new information has the effect of causing excitement among membership and potentially increases morale. At the same time, though, the repeated introduction of new information—new ideas or potential activities—can alter the group's continuity of direction. If this continuity is interrupted, action and progress may be impeded, which can, in turn, lower group morale.

Conversely, maintaining continuity of direction might support action and progress and increase group morale. A collaborative can get bogged down in these repeating patterns and may not be aware of how they interact and affect the group's progress. Intentionally mapping these group behaviors, communications, or actions—and making them a regular part of the group's reflection and learning— can support clarity.

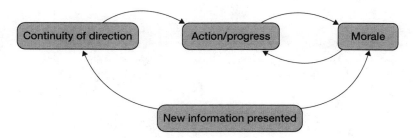

FIGURE 5.6 Sample Pattern Map of Collective Impact Progress

Source: Created by the Authors; Georgia Health Policy Center, June 2016

As a tool in evaluating Collective Impact progress, the authors have used similar mapping exercises to draw a group's attention to how they might be repeating behaviors that facilitate or hamper progress. The use of a simple pattern map as a tool enables open and honest communication by, perhaps, depersonalizing the action or behavior within a broader system of elements playing out at once among members.

Systems Tools and Backbone Support

Backbone organizations are evolving along with the entire field of CI (Cabaj & Weaver, 2016). While it may be relatively easy to initially identify an organization to serve as backbone support, over time it is a common pitfall to revert to older more traditional roles away from the backbone model. As the work moves from vision and strategy to implementation, communities can sometimes struggle to differentiate the role of an organization designed to provide backbone support to a collaborative with the more traditional roles of lead agency, administrative home, or fiscal agent. Systems tools can be very helpful to both focus the work of the backbone and the work of the larger collaborative on the interdisciplinary, cross-sector strategy that originally drew it to the CI framework.

Systems tools can be ongoing reminders of the larger system the Collective Impact effort is seeking to change. Using the systems maps or other tools that supported the original strategy as a reference point, the backbone organization can guide the collaborative through its ongoing decision making, priority and goal setting and the development of annual work plans. It will ensure that as the implementation and evaluation work must inevitably dive into the weeds, the goals and measurements can remain tethered by the systems tools to the larger objectives. The role of backbone support is to guide and keep the momentum moving forward, not to lead unilaterally. Systems tools can provide a valuable check to ensure that the backbone support is moving all the parts of the work ahead and not reverting to other more traditional work. As the backbone organization supports the leadership team in attracting new leaders and transitions individuals from one role in the collaborative to another, systems tools can be an important orientation tool.

Lastly, as the collaborative builds and evolves, the backbone organization often takes on the work of external communications and building public will. As a graphic visualization of the collaborative's strategy, of the problem that the collaborative is trying to fix, or of the collective approach to change, systems tools can in one page, several images, or simple, concise statements explain very complex problems, issues, strategies, and the proposed solutions, thus, further galvanizing shared purpose.

Systems Tool and Shared Measurement

Shared measurement has been held out by some as the holy grail of Collective Impact (Rose, 2014), and significant time and effort has been spent addressing the topic since the CI term was coined in 2011 (Hamilton & Fielden, 2015; Pearson, 2014; Weaver, 2014; Wood, 2016). According to Schuchter and Jutte,

> Measurement can help community development and health practitioners align and optimize their investments and leverage additional resources to achieve shared goals. It should be no surprise, then, that systems tools, which, at their most basic are designed and intended to delineate all the parts of a complex system, can provide a roadmap for a robust shared measurement system.
>
> Schuchter & Jutte, 2014

Returning to the chapter's first example, employing the RTH Model and developing the Atlanta Transformation Scenario enabled ARCHI to delineate very specific targets across a range of broad activities. Namely, the effort seeks to reduce the rate of uninsured from 27% in both Fulton and DeKalb counties; increase contingent global payment across public and private payers to at least 50% of the market; raise or reallocate $100 million in health spending per year for five years in support of an innovation fund; achieve systems savings across payers and reallocate 50% of those savings as shared incentives for population health interventions; increase tobacco cessation by 50%; increase graduation rates (benchmark as yet to be determined); and reduce duplicative physician office testing through the use of care coordination.

As ARCHI turns its focus more intently to evaluation, it has several systems outputs at its disposal from which to craft an evaluation framework, including the original model baselines and outputs, a theory of change diagram, various systems maps that outline relationships among partners and activities, and multiple program logic models. By focusing on the entire system that it seeks to impact, ARCHI ensures that mutually-reinforcing activities are kept at the forefront, rather than focusing exclusively on individual partner or program outcomes to the detriment of the greater effort.

Using systems tools to keep the collaborative focused on shared, rather than individual, measurement is not a panacea. Because partner organizations must still be held accountable to their own boards and funders, there is always the tendency to focus on the specific, programmatic target rather than system impacts. Systems tools enable a collaborative to regularly reorient the group to its higher purpose.

References

Barberg, B. (2017). Implementing Population Health Strategies. In Bialek, M., Beitsch, L. M., & Moran, J. W., Solving Population Health Problems Through Collaboration. New York: Routledge.

Beckhard, R., & Harris, R. (1987). Managing Organizational Transitions. Reading, MA: Addison-Wesley.

Cabaj, M., & Weaver, L. (2016). Collective Impact 3.0 – An Evolving Framework for Community Change. *Community Change Series 2016*, 1–14.

Dannemiller, K. D., & Jacobs, R. W. (1992). Changing the Way Organizations Change: A Revolution of Common Sense. *The Journal of Applied Behavioral Science, 28*(4), 480–498.

Hamilton, J., & Fielden, S. (2015). The Power of Collective Impact. *British Columbia Medical Association*, 115–165.

Heifetz, R. A., & Linsky, M. (2002). A Survival Guide for Leaders. *Harvard Business Review*, 80(6), 65–74.

Homer, J., Milstein, B., Hirsch, G. B., & Fisher, E. S. (2016). Combined Regional Investments Could Substantially Enhance Health System Performance and be Financially Affordable. Health Affairs, 35(8), 1435–1443.

Irbyis, M. (2014). Aligning Collective Impact Initiatives. *Stanford Social Innovation Review Fall 2014, 12*(4), 15–16.

Kania, J., & Kramer, M. (2011). Collective Impact. Stanford Social Innovation Review Winter 2011, 9(1), 36–41.

Kania, J., & Kramer, M. (2013). Embracing Emergence: How Collective Impact Addresses Complexity. Retrieved from https://ssir.org/articles/entry/embracing_emergence_how_collective_impact_addresses_complexity

Minyard, K. J., Ferencik, R., Phillips, M. A., & Soderquist, C. (2014). Using Systems Thinking in State Health Policymaking: An Educational Initiative. *Health systems, 3*(2), 117–123.

Minyard, K. J., Lawler, K., Fuller, E., Wilson, M., & Henry, E. (2016). Reducing Health Disparities in Atlanta. *Stanford Social Innovation Review, 14*(2), 22–23.

Modeling Expert Panel Meeting: A Collaborative Think Session. (2013). Georgia State University. Atlanta, GA.

Ostrom, E., Burger, J., Field, C. B., Norgaard, R. B., & Policansky, D. (1999). Revisiting the Commons: Local Lessons, Global Challenges. Science, 284(5412), 278–282.

Pearson, H. (2014). Collective Impact: Venturing on an Unfamiliar Road. *The Philanthropist, 26*(1), 49–53.

Richmond, B. (1993). Systems Thinking: Critical Thinking Skills for the 1990s and Beyond. *System Dynamics Review, 9*(2), 113–133.

Rose, L. (2014). Community Knowledge: The Building Blocks of Collective Impact. *The Philanthropist, 26*(1), 75–82.

Schuchter, J., & Jutte, D. P. (2014). A Framework To Extend Community Development Measurement To Health And Well-Being. *Health Affairs, 33*(11), 1930–1938.

Treyz, G. I., Rickman, D. S., & Shao, G. (1991). The REMI Economic–Demographic Forecasting and Simulation Model. *International Regional Science Review, 14*(3), 221–253.

Weaver, L. (2014). Q & A with John Kania and Fay Hanleybrown. *The Philanthropist, 26*(1), 125–132.

Wood, D. M. (2016). Community Indicators and Collective Impact: Facilitating Change. *Community Development, 47*(2), 194–208.

6

COLLECTIVE IMPACT 3.0

Extending the Collective Impact Vision for Community Change[1]

Liz Weaver and Mark Cabaj

Collective impact was coined and introduced by Kania and Kramer of FSG Consulting. Their *Stanford Social Innovation Review* article (2011) of the same name introduced and distilled some of the key ingredients of successful community efforts to move "from fragmented action and results" to "collective action and deep and durable impact." These ingredients (also known as the "five conditions") are a common agenda, shared measurement, mutually reinforcing activities, continuous communication, and backbone support (Kania & Kramer, 2013).

This initial article was followed in subsequent years by articles in the *Stanford Social Innovation Review* that built upon the original. These included *Channeling Change: Making Collective Impact Work* (Hanleybrown, Kramer, & Kramer, 2012); *Understanding the Value of Backbone Organizations in Collective Impact* (Turner, Merchant, Kania, & Martin, 2012); and *Embracing Emergence: How Collective Impact Addresses Emergence* (Kania & Kramer, 2013); *Essential Mindset Shifts for Collective Impact* (Kania, Hanleybrown, & Juster, 2014); and *The Dawn of System Leadership* (Senge, Hamilton, and Kramer, 2015).

The impact of CI on the field of community change has been electric. Innovators whose work the article described praised its distillation of the key elements of an approach to community change. Paul Born, a CI pioneer, said: "Kania and Kramer understood the work we were doing so well, and described it so effectively, that they essentially laid out a new operating system for community change" (Born, personal correspondence, 2015). Connor, an early practitioner and coach for community-wide collaboration, noted:

> I am grateful to FSG for what they have done. We have been trying in our own way to describe these ideas for so many years, trying in our own way to explain it clearly. We can spend more time doing the hard work on the ground.
>
> Connor, 2015

The original article excited early adopters even more. Countless community organizations, government agencies, philanthropies and socially-minded businesses embraced CI hoping it would help them make deep and durable changes in the social, economic, and even environmental challenges facing their communities. Wolff, an experienced coalition builder, who is also a vocal critic of CI, described in an April 8, 2016 blog post, the response as a "revolution" in the way that governments and funders thought about and approached community change (Wolff, 2016).

Wolff has not been alone in his criticism of Collective Impact and has been joined by others who have raised concerns about the role of shared decision making and community participation in CI initiatives. In addition, criticisms concerning inclusivity and equity have also been leveled at the CI framework. Others including Klaus and Weaver (this volume) question the quality of research undergirding the framework.

FSG and other CI advocates have done much to expand and elaborate the original five conditions described in that first article. In subsequent articles they described the pre-conditions for CI, the phases of the approach, a variety of key practices (e.g., strategy, governance, funding, evaluation), and eight key principles of practice. The Collective Impact Forum, an online community administered by FSG, was designed to be a comprehensive resource on community change and a platform for practitioners to share and build knowledge, skills, and tools for the work. Collective Impact has become a permanent—even dominant—part of the landscape of community change.

An Evolving Vision

It is time for an evolution in the revolution. While the CEO of one philanthropic organization argued that support and buy-in for CI is now at "fever pitch," there are two compelling reasons to upgrade—not simply elaborate upon—the original CI framework (Carson, 2012). First, there has been sufficient experimentation with CI by communities working on diverse issues in a variety of settings to shed light on its limitations. These include: insufficient attention to the role of community in the change effort; an excessive focus on short-term data; an understatement of the role of policy and systems change; and an over-investment in backbone support (Robinson, 2014 blog post). Holmgren (2015) warned that if these limitations are not taken seriously, the field may experience a "pendulum swing" away from collective change efforts.

The FSG team welcomed the critiques on the CI Forum, admitted the framework's shortcomings, and worked diligently with others to address them or expand on areas that deserve elaboration. The Collective Impact Forum continues to develop and publish resources designed to assist the field in advancing its work. In 2015, it released the *Collective Impact Principles of Practice* as a response to critiques about engaging citizen voice, advancing Collective Impact through an equity lens and ensuring that the collective effort effectively reflects the community context.

The *Collective Impact Principles of Practice* provide a foundation for collaborative planning tables to build their shared approaches.

Karen Pittman (2015), head of the Forum on Youth Investment, noted: "Kania, Kramer and the FSG team get high marks in my book for being consistently open to adapting their theory to better reflect practice."

Still, criticisms of CI have continued to surface. Like all frameworks, CI reveals a great deal about how people tackle tough issues at scale, yet is simply unable to capture the full complexity of the work. It has been important for those who have devoted their lives to community change to identify gaps and weaknesses, because the stakes are so high.

Second, in the rush to embrace CI, many in the field have ignored the less well-packaged and promoted frameworks of community change developed by other organizations and practitioners. Some of these include the Bridgespan group's work on Needle Moving Collaboratives, the Aspen Institute's work on Comprehensive Community Initiatives and the grassroots Turning Outward model of the Harwood Institute (Harwood, 2014). Each approach is based on solid experience and research, offers alternative perspectives on community change, and deserves to be taken seriously. Many of the observations and strategies in these community change approaches can be woven into effective CI implementation.

Are CI's limitations significant enough to warrant throwing it away? No. The framework has too much "roughly right" and has been too successful in expanding the work to build stronger communities. The better response is to move beyond simply fine-tuning the original framework and upgrade it to reflect important criticisms and limitations. Hardware and software developers relentlessly upgrade operating systems to reach the next level of capability and performance. This should be the same improving the Collective Impact framework.

The task does not need to fall on FSG alone. The framework's redevelopment is simply too much work for one organization—and it disempowers the rest of the field. If CI is to reach the next level, community change practitioners and those who support them must step up to design and build framework's next iteration.

Collective Impact 3.0

This article is the first of a series in which the authors and, others from Tamarack Institute, will propose a number of upgrades to the CI framework. The Tamarack Institute regularly publishes articles on Collective Impact intended to advance the field of knowledge and practice. In the 2016 series of articles, Holmgren (2015) explored the how to effectively land on strategies around which to build CI efforts. In Summer 2017, Cabaj released a paper called *Shared Measurement*. The why is clear, the how continues to develop (Shared Measurement: The How is Clear, the Why Continues to Develop Webinar, Tamarack Institute, accessed Jan. 7, 2018), which deepens the dialogue about the benefits and challenges of integrating a shared measurement approach into Collective Impact efforts.

Collective Impact 3.0 is a term that emerged during the Tamarack Institute's Collective Impact Summit in Vancouver in 2015. At that event, the authors described the evolution of CI in three phases. The 1.0 phase referred to the days prior to 2011 when diverse groups organically prototyped CI practices without knowledge of, or reference to, the patterns identified by FSG. The 2.0 phase spanned the five years following Kania and Kramer's seminal article. During that period, many communities adopted the five conditions CI framework and FSG tracked, codified, and assessed the second phase of CI initiatives. The third phase, Collective Impact 3.0, focuses on deepening, broadening, and adapting CI based on yet another generation of initiatives.

The authors and Tamarack Institute have been deeply involved in community change initiatives for more than 20 years, which includes the sponsorship of Vibrant Communities, an evolving network of prototypical CI initiatives focused on poverty reduction. Tamarack made CI one of its top five themes. Its staff and associates have been involved in scores of CI efforts across North America and beyond.

Tamarack Institute is committed to the basic structure of CI, which provides a solid framework for community change efforts seeking to move the needle on complex issues like poverty, homelessness or educational achievement. However, many of the ideas and practices need to be reconsidered given the limitations of the original framework, the insights of other frameworks, Tamarack's experience, and FSG's own work. Collective Impact 3.0 is not the only iteration of CI or the best one. All practitioners are prisoners of their own experience and limitations. The authors are no exception and, hopefully, the next generation of CI practitioners will continue to adapt and advance the framework. Community development and change need diverse voices and perspectives moving forward.

Adapting the Collective Impact Paradigm

The evolution to Collective Impact 3.0 begins by revisiting the foundational elements of the CI framework and providing a fresh look at the five conditions and the Leadership Paradigm underlying it. Table 6.1 from Collective Impact 2.0 to Collective Impact 3.0 suggests several shifts from the original CI framework. Some of these shifts are significant and some are modest. All broaden the original elements laid out in Kania and Kramer's 2011 article.

In the management paradigm, leaders of institutions, who are responsible for a domain such as health, education, or criminal justice, come together to achieve better outcomes than they might achieve independently. While consulting with the broader community on the nature of the problem and how it might be addressed, they perceive themselves to be primarily responsible for developing and implementing new responses to an issue. As a result, CI participants employing a managerial approach often focus on improving existing systems through such measures as data-sharing, coordination of services, and joint action on policy or regulation barriers.

TABLE 6.1 From Collective Impact 2.0 to Collective Impact 3.0

From	To
The Leadership Paradigm	
Management	Movement Building
The Five Conditions	
Common Agenda	Community Aspiration
Shared Measurement	Strategic Learning
Mutually Reinforcing Activities	High Leverage Activities
Continuous Communication	Inclusive Community Engagement
Backbone	Containers for Change

Source: Compiled by authors.

A management paradigm can generate results. For example, in the case of Strive in Cincinnati, featured in the 2011 CI article, educational institutions and community agencies agreed to organize their activities around a comprehensive "cradle to career" framework with 60 key measures. They succeeded in getting dozens of organizations to align their efforts and produced a score of innovations. Cumulatively, these have resulted in improvements in reading and math scores, high school graduation rates, and post-secondary enrollment and completion (Strive Cincinnati).

The movement-building paradigm works a bit differently. Etmanski and Cammack, two Canadian social innovators, have developed a simple philosophy to guide their efforts: "Act like an organization, but think like a movement" (Etmanski, 2016). Would-be change-makers must tend to the day-to-day tasks of research, raising money, planning, and management. The chances that their efforts will achieve scale improve dramatically if the work is undergirded with relationships based on a common vision and value—relationships that span diverse organizations, sectors, and political affiliations.

In the movement-building paradigm, the emphasis is on reforming and transforming systems where improvements alone will not make a difference. Movement-building leaders bring together a diverse group of stakeholders, including those not in traditional institutions or seats of power, to build a vision of the future based on common values and narratives. Etmanski and Cammack further state that movements "open up peoples' hearts and minds to new possibilities," "create the receptive climate for new ideas to take hold," and "embolden policymakers" and system leaders (Etmanski, 2016). Movements change the ground on which everyday political life and management decisions occur.

For example, participants in End Poverty Edmonton focus on creating a movement to end—not reduce—local poverty within a generation (End Poverty). To achieve this end, one of their game-changing priorities is to eliminate racism, including a six-point plan to support reconciliation between Aboriginal and non-Aboriginal people. Racism, participants assert, is at the root of the difficulty many residents experience when securing adequate housing, education, human services, and income. This commitment has cleared the way for the community to pursue some atypical initiatives. One approach involves training local police and safety officials to improve their cultural literacy and reduce the stigmatization of racialized groups. More importantly, this initiative also challenges all the city's residents to become actively involved in dozens of little ways. The End Poverty Edmonton movement is in its early stages, but the effort is impressive and the prospects for large-scale impact seem much greater under the movement-building paradigm.

To be clear, a CI management paradigm can change systems. Between 2010 and 2014, hundreds of organizations in New York state came together to reform a broken criminal justice system. Youth who committed even minor offenses encountered an array of programs and regulations so disconnected and ill-designed they tended to increase, not decrease, the likelihood of re-offending or committing even more serious crimes. Through a variety of innovations, such as serving young offenders in local day programs rather than residential programs, the number of youth in custody fell by 45 percent without an increase in youth crime. Buoyed by these successes, state leaders decided to work on a bill to raise the criminal age of responsibility from 16 to 18, a key move to reduce the number of youth exposed to the harsher edges of the adult system (FSG).

Mainstream institutions have led several other successful CI efforts. Nonetheless, the prospects for impact are dramatically better if change makers would use a movement-making paradigm. When CI initiatives operate from a management paradigm, the emphasis tends to be on improving systems rather than changing them. Holding to a management paradigm, stakeholders and participants in the initiative may be suspicious of bold measures. They can resist or block transformative ideas because their orientation is to preserve systems they manage. As Bonabeau, CEO of Icosystems, observes: "Managers would rather live with a problem they can't solve than with a solution they can't fully understand or control"(Brenda Zimmerman at the Collective Impact Summit, Tamarack Institute, posted October 25, 2014).

Consider how the leaders of two major Canadian cities approached the challenge of ending poverty. In one western city, several reputable nonprofit leaders made the case that reducing wage inequity and introducing a guaranteed annual income should be key features in the poverty reduction plan. Key philanthropic leaders vetoed the idea. They argued such measures were unlikely to gain widespread support in a community that celebrates "pulling yourself up by your bootstraps." Moreover, the proposed tactics risked alienating several of the philanthropic leaders; generous conservative contributors.

In the other Canadian city, however, the chair of the poverty roundtable declared poverty a public health crisis on the scale of Severe Acute Respiratory Syndrome (SARS). A guaranteed annual income and living wage policy, the chair argued, were as key to poverty reduction in the 21st Century as the abolition of slavery and child labor were in the 19th Century. Rather than alienate local leaders, the call to action inspired them. The municipality, the Chamber of Commerce and local school board signed on as living wage employers (CBC Hamilton. More Hamilton Employers Pledge to Pay Workers $15 per Hour, CBC Hamilton, last update June 30, 2015).

Leaders in community change are right to heed the interests of the organization they are paid to operate. However, broad, deep, and durable changes in communities are more likely when CI initiatives embrace a movement-building rather than a management paradigm. By approaching CI as a movement, it is more likely to "shift boundaries for what is socially acceptable and politically expected" (Eight Questions for Thinking and Acting Like a Movement, Al Etmanski).

An Upgrade to the Five Conditions of Collective Impact

Kania and Kramer identified five conditions that community change initiatives must fulfill to move from isolated impact, where organizations operate independently and scale is achieved through the growth of individual organizations, to Collective Impact. These include: agreement on a common agenda; development of a shared measurement approach; leveraging resources through mutually reinforcing activities; building continuous communications; and a backbone structure to mobilize the collective effort. The five conditions which form the CI framework provide a broadly-defined approach and are close yet are too narrowly framed to capture how successful CI initiatives actually operate when efforts are imbedded in a movement-building approach to community change. The following section describes how each of the five conditions can be upgraded to work within a movement-building paradigm.

Authentic Community Engagement upgraded from Continuous Communication

A frequent and significant critique of the original Five Conditions of the CI framework has been its apparent failure to put community at the center of the change process. While FSG had not intended to diminish the role of community in the work, a strong emphasis on "CEO-level cross-sector leaders" in early CI articles was interpreted in ways that resulted in the elevation of these leaders over other community members. Kania and Kramer's fourth article (2015) in the CI series, *The Equity Imperative in Collective Impact*, focused on the importance of equity and argued that inclusion in the change process of the people most affected by an issue is "imperative." More recently, of their Eight Collective Impact Principles of Practice, three concern equity, the inclusion of community members, and relationship, trust and respect.

Nonetheless, the original 2011 article on CI identified "continuous communication" as a condition for mobilizing stakeholders, building trust, and structuring meaningful meetings and work. Yet these hardly convey all the work that is involved. "Authentic community engagement" tends to reflect more accurately and powerfully the intensity and fullness of the necessary community work. Authentic community engagement includes inclusivity, equity, and equality. It is a condition for transformational impact and therefore a condition for CI 3.0.

Robust authentic community engagement is back-breaking work. It takes time to map out and identify stakeholders to invite to the table; skill to create good opportunities to engage people at each stage of the change process; and confidence and humility to navigate the inevitable conflicts between participants who differ in their values, interests, and power. The Tamarack Institute has worked on the craft of community engagement for more than a decade. Some of that experience is captured in Born's books, *Community Conversations* (2012) and *Deepening Community* (2014). While useful, they merely scratch the surface.

The case for authentic and inclusive involvement of a broad spectrum of system stakeholders, especially those most affected by complex issues, is overwhelming. Such involvement can allow the CI initiative to draw on "360-degree insight" into the nature of the problems and their solutions. It creates a broader constituency for change which is so critical in any effort to disrupt and change systems. It cultivates broad ownership and long-term commitment to the change process which is essential after the initial excitement has run its course. Most importantly, it supports a key concept in community development that those most affected by an issue should participate fully in attempts to address it. Canadians often use the term "Nothing about us without us" to reflect this fundamental democratic and moral principle. Authentic community engagement lays the groundwork in the upgrade Five Conditions in CI 3.0.

Shared Aspiration Upgraded from Common Agenda

Connor quotes an exchange between a journalist and Francis Ford Coppola, famous as the director of the Academy Award winning movie, *The Godfather*. When asked to explain the difference between what made a good movie versus a bad one, Coppola responded, "In a good movie, everyone is making the same movie." Similarly, Kania and Kramer assert many participants professing to work on a common problem are, in fact, working from different perspectives on the nature and root causes of the problem and solutions. Therefore, the results generated are likely to be fragmented, not collective. A true common agenda requires leadership to bring a broad group of key community stakeholders together to review the key data which informs the problem or issue; to develop a shared vision for change; and to determine the core pathways and strategies that will drive the change forward. This is more than a simple planning exercise. It requires would-be collaborators to find (or create) common ground despite their very different values, interests, and positions.

A focus on a shared community aspiration can have an even more powerful impact when creating a broader movement for change. Shared aspiration requires participants to develop outcomes based on community values. The outcomes must be sufficiently ambitious to require the community to work together in ways it has not worked before. A solid community aspiration can also create the kind of "big tent" under which a wide range of participants can pursue the interdependent challenges underlying tough issues.

In a CI initiative, it is critical to see the interdependent, underlying challenges of each complex community problem. Focusing on one slice of a complex problem may make the challenge less overwhelming and improve the chances of developing a shared agenda. It may also have some perverse consequences.

Consider, for example, the efforts to reduce malaria and HIV, two leading causes of child mortality in the developing world. Spearheaded by the support and leadership of the Bill and Melinda Gates Foundation, international donors for the past decade have focused on developing and deploying high-impact vaccinations. While their efforts have saved millions of lives, they have created other problems. Funders, governments, and health organizations diverted many human and financial resources from other types of medical care, nutrition, and education to support that effort. As a result, there has been a sharp increase in more common ailments, such as birth sepsis, diarrhea, and asphyxia. One report described how some patients walked nine hours to clinics to get their HIV and malaria medications, only to regurgitate them due to hunger and fatigue. In some countries, malaria and HIV rates have begun to climb again.

In response, many international funders have adjusted their effort to focus on a bigger aspiration, "broader, integrated child survival," and have broadened their strategies to focus on prevention and treatment of diseases and on strengthening the entire health care delivery system.

Contrast this experience with the Hamilton (Ontario) Roundtable for Poverty Reduction. Formed in 2002, it drew members from the city's business, government and voluntary sectors, and community leaders with the lived experience of poverty. After extensive consultations in the broader community, Roundtable leaders concluded that "poverty reduction" would not mobilize the energies of a large and diverse network of people. Instead, they embraced a bolder aspiration: "Make Hamilton the Best Place to Raise a Child." Consequently, they organized a framework around five critical points of investment (from early learning and parenting to employment) that engaged dozens of networks and organizations.

The shared aspiration was contagious. In October 2005, Hamilton's main newspaper, the *Spectator*, announced that it would make poverty coverage a priority. It published a front page that was blank except for one statement: "The stories have been removed from this page to remind us that nearly 100,000 children, women and men live in poverty in Hamilton, people whose stories rarely make the front page. We're going to change that" (Pillar & Smith, 2017). Soon afterward city council embedded the words "Best Place to Raise a Child" in Hamilton's mission statement and a local marketing expert praised the aspiration for its ability to inspire community-wide action (Weaver & Makhoul, 2009). By 2011, a Nanos survey reported that 80 percent of respondents felt that municipal investment in poverty reduction should be the city's number one priority. This result startled the veteran pollster administering the survey, "There are very few issues that you get 80 percent of anybody to agree on" (Weaver & Makhoul, 2009).

Strategic Learning Upgraded from Shared Measurement

Among the original Five Conditions of Collective Impact, shared measures generate some of the most conversation and experimentation among CI initiatives. Since 2011, much has been learned about the mechanics of developing shared measurement systems, yet there is still much to be learned.

Developing a shared measurement system is essential to CI. Agreement on a common agenda is illusory without agreement on the ways success will be measured and reported. Collecting data and measuring results consistently on a short list of indicators at the community level and across all participating organizations not only ensures that all efforts remain aligned, it also enables the participants to hold each other accountable and learn from each other's successes and failures.

Developing Shared Measurement

One of the most significant insights gained over the past few years is that CI participants have more success with shared measurement if it is treated as one part of a larger system of learning and evaluation.

Consider, for instance, the different measurement approaches taken by General Motors and Toyota in the 1980s and 1990s. General Motors was a data-heavy and report-heavy organization. It employed sophisticated systems to gather, analyze, and develop thick reports for senior managers. Toyota, on the other hand, emphasized management practices that were data-light and learning-heavy. It chose to focus on a few select measures, real-time feedback loops, and floor-level decision making. While the performance gap between the companies has recently closed, researchers and business leaders credit the different evaluation and measurement processes for Toyota's consistently better outcomes in earlier years.

A robust learning and evaluation process is even more critical in community-wide change efforts. Unlike the relatively routinized nature of an automotive production line, social innovators try to change dynamic and complex systems underlying social problems. They want measurement systems which:

- can provide real-time feedback on the multiple outcomes expressed in their theory of change or strategy;
- are manageable;
- have robust processes for sense-making and decision-making; and,
- co-evolve with their ever-changing strategies.

CI initiatives may be tempted to rush into shared measurement with the question, "What should and could we measure together?" Unfortunately, without first having laid the foundations for strategic learning, they can find themselves wrapped up in messy, frustrating, chaotic, tail-chasing processes that offer little chance of producing useful data.

Many 10-year plans to end community homelessness in Canadian communities illustrate the point. These initiatives have employed relatively sophisticated homelessness management information systems (HMIS). This is due, in part, to a well-developed "Housing First" philosophy used to identify the key outcomes that deserve extra measurement and attention. Most of these groups have also developed effective processes and practices for using the data to inform decisions about overall strategy. Not only have these resulted in adaptations to the Housing First model, they have prompted many to recognize their need to develop entirely new models for the prevention of homelessness (Limitations of Housing, 2018). Community-based initiatives to end homelessness have become exemplars in strategic learning and data use.

A formal shift to a strategic learning approach, which includes shared measurement as a component rather than a central feature of the process, is straightforward. It has appealed to experienced community builders who know measures are only part of learning. Evaluators seeking to build measures for outcomes that matter also welcomed this approach. The outcomes matter most when social innovators use the feedback to improve their efforts, rather than write reports and consign them to a shelf.

Much of the groundwork for adopting a strategic learning stance in CI initiatives has already been laid. The Atlantic Philanthropies and the Center for Evaluation Innovation, pioneers of the approach, feature multiple tools and examples on their websites. FSG has produced a comprehensive, easy-to-use, and solid resource on building strategic learning systems. In CI 3.0, the next generation of CI practitioners would do well to adopt and adapt these frameworks.

Focus on High-Leverage Activities Upgraded from Mutually Reinforcing Activities

"Mutually reinforcing activities" has been especially important among the Five Conditions of CI because it captures the need of any CI initiative to be more than the sum of its parts. Yet, as elegant as it is, the focus on mutually reinforcing activities has two limitations. First, it may unintentionally encourage CI participants to focus on areas that offer great opportunities for cooperation rather than the greatest opportunities for results as explained in Boumgarden and Branch (2013). In "Collective Impact or Collective Blindness," they state: "While we do not doubt the benefits of collaboration, we argue that 'Collective Impact' over and above competition often results in coordinated but misdirected effort."

CI initiatives must see beyond collaboration to identify strategies focused on "high leverage" opportunities for change. They must commit to a systemic reading of the complex systems they are trying to change and to make a realistic assessment of where local stakeholders have the knowledge, networks, and resources to make a difference. Finding where this reading of the systems and realistic assessment intersect is not always easy.

Consider this illustration. Thousands of participants in CI initiatives work to replace fragmented programs for vulnerable families with more holistic, coordinated, and accessible services. The co-location of services and case management offer a typical promising approach as they are relatively easy to implement and "don't require co-locators to give up funds, authority or turf." However, this approach is also low leverage. That is, while families have benefited from having services in one place and an advocate willing to help them navigate them, the majority of these co-located programs have still operated with some of the usual problems. These have included inflexible eligibility criteria, "cookie-cutter" supports, and such poor coordination of services that clients find accessing them excessively time-consuming. Such strategies have rarely resulted in better outcomes for struggling families.

A higher leverage strategy would be for policy makers and funders to decentralize responsibility for program design to regional and local organizations and hold them accountable for broad—rather than discrete—outcomes. While these broader outcome measures are far more likely to lead to comprehensive, flexible and high-quality services with better results for families, they consistently meet with resistance from people within the systems because they are messier and require shifts in power and resources.

A second limitation resulting from a strong emphasis on mutually reinforcing activities is the risk of excluding the need to occasionally allow CI initiative stakeholders and partners to pursue independent—even competing—pathways to a common goal. In the case of Tillamook County, Oregon, for example, health organizations, education groups, and faith-based organizations settled on a common aspiration to eliminate teen pregnancy. However, they could not agree on a common strategy. Consequently, each pursued its own unique path. Public health advocates promoted safe sex. Educators focused on increasing literacy on sexuality. Faith-based organizations preached abstinence. The cumulative result of their efforts was a 75 percent reduction in teen pregnancy in 10 years. (Tillmock County, 2018) Why? Because different strategies triggered different outcomes for different groups of vulnerable families and teens.

Pursuing different pathways is especially productive when social innovators are unclear about the nature of the problem they are trying to address. In these situations, it makes good sense for people to try different approaches. In the case of Opportunities 2000, a pioneering CI effort to reduce poverty levels in the Waterloo (Ontario) region to the lowest in Canada, nonprofit organizations worked together to advocate the creation of a fund to invest in innovative ways to reduce poverty. Each applied to access the fund through competitive bidding, with many nonprofits participating in multiple proposals. This resulted in a range of innovative responses, including Canada's first head-hunting employment service for working poor immigrants and the country's first Individual Development Accounts. It also increased the monthly income of nearly 1,600 low-income families (McNair & Reid, 2002).

Zimmerman, an expert on managing complex systems, concluded that a key attribute of successful social innovators was the ability to know when and how to "mix cooperation with competition" (Zimmerman & Plsek, 2008). This is contrary to conventional wisdom which suggests collaboration is nearly always the best response. The conventional wisdom of mutually-reinforcing activities, therefore, may be a barrier to utilizing a critical condition of Collective Impact 3.0: focusing focus on high-leverage strategies and permission for partners in a CI initiative to work as loosely or tightly as the situation requires.

Container for Change Upgraded from Backbone Support

Backbone support, CI's fifth condition, was warmly received by many veteran community builders and change makers. "Creating and managing Collective Impact requires a separate organization and staff with a very specific set of skills to serve as the backbone for the entire initiative. Coordination takes time, and none of the participating organizations has any to spare. The expectation that collaboration can occur without a supporting infrastructure is one of the most frequent reasons why it fails" (Kania & Kramer, 2011).

This simple statement reaffirms what community builders have said since the 1960s: community change across organizational and sectoral boundaries needs to be front and center, not on the side. It warrants an investment of extra resources in an intermediary or coordinating body whose job it is to oversee and manage the day-to-day work of collaboration. Even its outspoken critics have acknowledged how the CI framework has encouraged practitioners and funders to invest more time, energy, and financial resources into ensuring backbone support is in place (Wolff, 2016).

The renewed emphasis on backbone support has also brought a much better understanding of the infrastructure required for community change. Backbone support refers simply to the appointment of one or more organizations to fulfill various essential day-to-day coordination and management functions for the CI initiative. In some cases, the backbone support may require extra financial resources to provide these services. The backbone support, for example, can guide the creation of a vision and strategy, mobilize funding, and advance policy as well as facilitate the development of leadership and governance structures and funding models required to support a CI initiative. These insights represent significant steps forward in the practice of backbone supports in five short years.

However, the concept of backbone support has also been misunderstood and confused by what backbone support actually involves. In some cases, it has been erroneously interpreted as a recommendation to create a designated "backbone organization" from scratch. This can result in the loss of time, energy, and resources as CI initiatives focus on building and managing a new legal entity. It also increases the risk that other groups and individuals in the CI initiative feel less ownership and responsibility for the change effort. Instead, they let the "backbone organization" run the show.

In other cases, well-meaning CI leaders working on different challenges (e.g., poverty, homelessness, early childhood development, etc.) have created their own "boutique" backbone groups. When this happens, the limited human and financial resources available for backbone work can be spread too thinly and be too little to help. The use of "boutique" backbone groups tends to strengthen silos and impede boundary-crossing and joint action.

The next generation of CI practitioners, instead of simply creating backbone supports, must create a strong container for change to assist CI participants in the task of growth at the inter-organizational and interpersonal levels. A strong container is a situation when social innovators can:

> . . . transform their understandings [of the system they are trying to change], the relationships [with others in the systems] and their intentions [to act]. The boundaries of this container are set so that the participants feel enough protection and safety, as well as enough pressure and friction, to be able to do their challenging work.

Building a strong container for change requires attention to a variety of dimensions of backbone work, including:

- The mobilization of a diverse group of funders, backbone sponsors, and stewardship arrangements that demonstrate cross-sectoral leadership on the issue.
- The facilitation of the participants' inner journey of change, including the discovery and letting go of their own mental models and cultural/emotional biases, required for them to be open to fundamentally new ways of doing things.
- Facilitation of processes to cultivate trust and empathy amongst participants so they can freely share perspectives, engage in fierce conversations, and navigate differences in power.
- Utilization of the dilemmas and paradoxes of community change – such as the need to achieve short-term wins while involved in the longer-term work of system change – as creative tensions to drive people to seek new approaches to addressing challenging and working together without overwhelming them.
- Provision of timely nudges to encourage self-care in the midst of change in order to sustain multiple cycles of learning and periodic drops in momentum and morale.

Creating a container for change is among the most important work done in a CI initiative by CI practitioners and backbone support. It may even be more important than "charismatic leadership, technical expertise, or even funding." The "soft stuff" of creating a container for change may be more difficult than managing the "hard stuff" of research, planning, and program design. Peter Senge wrote, "You cannot force commitment. What you can do is nudge a little here, inspire a little there, and provide a role model. Your primary influence is the environment you create" (Senge, 2015).

The Energy Futures Lab in Alberta has demonstrated the value of creating that environment. The Lab is an effort to help stakeholders in the province's export-oriented, oil- and gas-dominated energy sector to move toward a future less dependent on carbon-based fuels but economically vibrant, socially equitable, and environmentally sustainable. The design team invested significant time and energy laying the effort's foundations:

- A formal commitment to create a radical middle position in the polarized mainstream debate over the energy system (e.g., "economy versus the environment," "resource development versus community well-being").
- The creation of a backbone group comprising five diverse organizations—an energy company, a key government department, two well-respected environmental non-governmental organizations, and an outstanding leadership development institute with growing expertise in Aboriginal leadership.
- The recruitment of a "whole system team" of participants who are a microcosm of the diverse values, interests, and perspectives of the energy system's current stakeholders, and the engagement of their organizations, networks, and the broader public.

Using this foundation, the backbone group worked diligently to create space for Lab participants to learn more about the energy system, themselves, and other participants. They conducted in-depth interviews with stakeholders to surface their hopes, aspirations, and fears of energy transition. The backbone facilitated structured conversations about social and political narratives that shape people's perspectives on tough issues and how to empathize with alternative viewpoints. The group sponsored learning journeys to explore different parts of the energy system from a worm's-eye view, and systems-mapping sessions to examine the same systems from a bird's-eye view. Finally, the backbone facilitated dialogue that allowed people to have unspeakable conversations (e.g., can Albertans really maintain this standard of living in a carbon constrained future?).

The Lab's commitment to building a strong container has paid off. The participants signed their names to an op-ed piece, in a major newspaper, that advocated cross-sectoral leadership to shape, rather than merely endure, the energy transition already in progress. They designed a vision document with 11 "pathways to energy system innovation" that they plan to upgrade once it has been tested with scores of networks and organizations across the province. Nearly a dozen teams developed prototypes to test breakthrough technologies, policies, and business models within the Lab's portfolio of promising initiatives. As one veteran of sustainability activism commented: "The commitment and the progress of this diverse group have been simply remarkable."

Business leader Bill O'Brien noted: "The success of an intervention depends on the inner conditions of the intervener." In the same vein, the success of the next generation of CI initiatives depends on the ability of backbone teams to create the strong containers for change that support participants to dig deep when tackling stubborn social challenges.

Conclusion

Collective Impact is still young and its ability to generate deep, wide, and sustained impact on tough societal challenges is yet unknown. Researchers at the Aspen Institute's Roundtable on Community Change have studied comprehensive community change initiatives for 20 years. To date, they have found an impressive number of successful changes in policy and system changes, along with innovative programs. However, "few if any [initiatives] were able to demonstrate widespread changes in child and family well-being or reductions in the neighborhood poverty rate."

The CI framework breathed new life into the tired efforts of many long-standing community change initiatives. It also dramatically increased the number of new and aspiring change makers. Nonetheless, the exemplary stories of impact are still the exception rather than the rule.

The success of the next generation of community change efforts depends, in part, on the willingness of CI participants not to settle for minimal improvements to the original Five Conditions of the CI framework. Instead, they must take on the challenge of continuously upgrading the approach based on what they are learning in the quest to transform communities. The CI framework is—and always will be—unfinished business.

This chapter described the foundational elements of a CI 3.0 framework. Collective Impact efforts are likely to be more effective when their participants and stakeholders operate from a movement-building paradigm. It is impossible for a leadership group of 20 to 40 leaders—no matter how committed and influential—to tackle issues and make deep and durable change on their own. Successful change requires the engagement, commitment, and investment of an entire community striving to be the best it can be and willing to make whatever changes to community systems—and its own behaviors—that are necessary to build safe, prosperous, inclusive, and sustainable communities.

There is room for others to propose upgrades to Collective Impact and CI 3.0. There is no sure-fire recipe for community change, but there are patterns of effective ideas and practices that can improve the probabilities of success. In a world that seems a bit more fragile, disruptive, and anxious than normal, everyone working in community development is needed to help uncover, frame, and share those patterns.

Note

1   A previous version of this material was published by Tamarack. The authors have permission to reprint this revised and expanded version.

References

Boumgarden, Peter & John Branch. 2013. "Collective Impact or Coordinated Blindness." *Stanford Social Innovation Review*. Retrieved from: http://ssir.org/articles/entry/collective_impact_or_coordinated_blindness

Cabaj, Mark. *Shared Measurement: The How is Clear, the Why Continues to Develop Webinar, Tamarack Institute*. Accessed Jan. 7, 2018, www.tamarackcommunity.ca/library/shared-measurement-the-why-is-clear-the-how-continues-to-develop-webinar

Carson, Emmett. October 31, 2012. *Rethinking Collective Impact* [Blog Post]. Retrieved from: www.huffingtonpost.com/emmett-d-carson/rethinking-collective-imp_b_1847839.html

CBC Hamilton. More Hamilton Employers Pledge to Pay Workers $15 per Hour, *CBC Hamilton*, last update June 30, 2015, www.cbc.ca/news/canada/hamilton/economy/more-hamilton-employers-pledge-to-pay-workers-15-per-hour-1.3129929

Collaboration for Action. *Developing Shared Measurement, Collaboration for Action*. Accessed Jan. 8, 2018, www.collaborationforimpact.com/collective-impact/shared-measurement/

Connor, Jay. Retrieved from: http://tamarackcci.ca/blogs/larrygemmel/jay-connor-collective-impact-summit

Connor, Joseph A. & Stephanie Kadel-Taras. 2003. *Community Visions, Community Solutions: Grantmaking for Comprehensive Impact*. St. Paul, MN: Amherst Wilder Foundation.

Corcoran, Rob. 2010. *Trust Building: An Honest Conversation on Race, Reconciliation and Responsibility*. London: University of Virginia Press.

Developing Shared Measurement. www.collaborationforimpact.com/collective-impact.shared-measurement

Edmonton Movement. *Welcome to the End Poverty*. Retrieved from: www.endpovertyedmonton.ca/news–blog/2015/9/18/welcome-to-the-endpovertyedmonton-movement

Etmanski, Al. February 11, 2016. *Eight Questions for Thinking and Acting Like a Movement* [Blog Post]. Retrieved from: http://aletmanski.com/impact/eight-questions-for-thinking-and-acting-like-a-movement/

Farias, Chris. 2013. What is Hamilton's Brand? *Hamilton Spectator*.

FSG. *Collective Impact Approach Delivers Dramatic Results in New York's Juvenile Justice System, FSG*. Accessed Jan. 7, 2018, www.fsg.org/projects/collective-impact-approach-delivers-dramatic-results-new-yorks-juvenile-justice-system

Hanleybrown, Fay, John Kania, & Mark Kramer. 2012. Channelling Change: Making Collective Impact Work. January. *Stanford Social Innovation Review*. Retrieved from: http://ssir.org/articles/entry/channeling_change_making_collective_impact_work http://ssir.org/articles/entry/the_equity_imperative_in_collective_impact

Hanleybrown, Fay, John Kania, & Mark Kramer. 2012. Channeling change: Making collective impact work. *Stanford Social Innovation Review*. [Online] 1–8. Available from: www.ssireview.org

Harwood, Rich. 2014. Putting Community in Collective Impact: Five Characteristics of Civic Culture that Collective Impact Efforts Must Address. *Stanford Social Innovation Review*. [Online]. Available from: www.siireview.org

Holmgren, Mark. 2015. *Collective Impact: Watch Out for the Pendulum Swing and Other Challenges* [Blog]. Retrieved from: http://tamarackcci.ca/files/collective_impact_watch_out_for_the_pendulum_swing_and_other_challenges.pdf

Housing First. *What are the Limitations of Housing First, Homeless Hub*. Accessed Jan. 8, 2018, http://homelesshub.ca/blog/what-are-limitations-housing-first

Jolin, Michele, Paul Schmitz, & Will Seldon. 2010. *Needle-Moving Community Collaboratives: A Promising Approach to Addressing America's Biggest Challenges*. The Bridgespan Group.

Kahane, Adam. 2012. *Transformative Scenario Planning: Working Together to Change the Future.* San Francisco, CA: Berrett-Koehler.

Kania, John V. & Mark R. Kramer 2011. Collective Impact. *Stanford Social Innovation Review.* Retrieved from: http://ssir.org/articles/entry/collective_impact

Kania, John V. & Mark R. Kramer. 2013. Embracing emergence: How collective impact addresses complexity. *Stanford Social Innovation Review.* 1–7. Retrieved from www.ssireview.org

Kania, John V., Fay Hanleybrown, & Jennifer Splansky Juster, 2014. Essential mindset shifts for collective impact. *Stanford Social Innovation Review.* 2–5. Retrieved from www.ssireview.org

Kania, John V. & Mark Kramer. (2011) http://ssir.org/articles/entry/collective_impact

Kania, John V. and Mark Kramer. 2015. The Equity Imperative in Collective Impact. *Stanford Social Innovation Review.* Retrieved from: http://ssir.org/articles/entry/the_equity_imperative_in_collective_impact

Klaus, Tom & Liz Weaver. 2018. Progress, Challenges, and Next Steps in Collective Impact: CI as Disruptive Illumination, Chapter 7 in this volume.

Kubisch, Anne, Patricia Auspos, Prudence Brown, & Thomas Dewar. 2010. Community Change Initiatives from 1990–2010: Accomplishments and Implications for Future Work. Federal Reserve Bank of San Francisco. *Community Investments.* Spring. Volume 22, Issue 1: 8–12.

Limitations of Housing, 2018. What are the Limitations of Housing First? Homeless Hub. Accessed Jan. 8, 2018.

McNair, Don & Eric Leviten-Reid. 2002. Opportunities 2000: Creating Pathways out of Poverty. Waterloo, ON: Lutherwood Community Opportunities Development Assotion.

Murray, Robin. 1995. Well-known industrial economist and professor at the University of Sussex, explored during participation in a jury-assessment evaluation, facilitated by Mark Cabaj of the Community Opportunities Development Association, the organization that preceded the Tamarack Institute.

O'Brien, Bill. http://daindunston.com/the-success-of-the-intervention/

Piller, Charles & Doug Smith. 2007, Unintended Victims of Gates Foundation Generosity. Los Angeles Times. Retrieved from: http://articles.latimes.com/2007/dec/16/nation/la-na-gates16dec16

Pittman, Karen. Forum on Youth Investment. Retrieved from: http://collectiveimpactforum.org/blogs/51306/advancing-practice-collective-impact

Reilly, Emma. 2010. Voters Target Poverty, Not Stadium. *Hamilton Spectator.* Retrieved from: www.thespec.com/news-story/2112136-voters-target-city-poverty-not-stadium/

Robinson, Tynesia Boyea, [Blog post]. Retrieved from: www.gjcpp.org/en/resource.php?issue=21&resource=200

Schmitz, Paul. 2014. The Culture of Collective Impact [Blog]. Retrieved from: www.huffingtonpost.com/paul-schmitz/the-culture-of-collective_b_6025536.html

Schorr, Elizabeth. 1998. *Common Purpose: Strengthening Families and Neighborhoods to Rebuild America.* New York, NY: Anchor Books. p. 315.

Senge, Peter M. www.goodreads.com/author/quotes/21072.Peter_M_Senge

Senge, Peter, Hal Hamilton, & John Kania (2015). The dawn of system leadership. *Stanford Social Innovation Review.* 27–33. Retrieved from www.ssireview.org

Strive Cincinnati. 2014–15 Partnership Report. www.strivepartnership.org/sites/default/files/kw_partnership_rpt1014_v11_0.pdf

Stroh, David Peter. 2015. *Systems Thinking for Social Change: A Practical Guide for Solving Complex Problems, Avoiding Unintended Consequences, and Achieving Lasting Results.* White River Junction, Vermont: Chelsea Green Publishing.

Tamarack's Engage newsletter, 2016. The Fall and Rise of Shared Measurement.

Tillamook County, Oregon. A Successful "Turn the Curve" Strategy: How Tillamook County, Oregon Did It, Implementation Guide, Results Based Accountability, Accessed Jan. 7, 2018, http://raguide.org/a-successful-turn-the-curve-strategy-how-tillamook-county-oregon-did-it/

Turner, Shiloh, Kathy Merchant, John Kania, & Ellen Martin. 2012. Understanding the value of backbone organizations in collective impact. *Stanford Social Innovation Review*. [Online] 1–12. Available from: www.ssireview.org.

Weaver, Liz & Anne Makhoul. 2009. Making Hamilton the Best Place to Raise a Child. Ottawa, ON: The Caledon Institute. www.caledoninst.org/Publications/PDF/760ENG.pdf

Wolff, Tom. April 8, 2016. Ten Places Where Collective Impact Gets It Wrong [Blog Post]. Retrieved from: www.gjcpp.org/en/resource.php?issue=21&resource=200

Zimmerman, Brenda, Curt Lindberg, & Paul Plsek. 2008. Edgeware: Insights from Complexity Science for Health Care Leaders. VHA Incorporated.

Zimmerman, Brenda. Collective Impact Summit, Tamarack Institute, posted October 25, 2014, www.tamarackcommunity.ca/latest/brenda-zimmerman-at-the-collective-impact-summit

7

USING COLLECTIVE IMPACT TO MOVE THE NEEDLE ON POVERTY REDUCTION

Karen Schwartz, Liz Weaver, Natasha Pei, and Aaron Kozak

This chapter describes a unique Social Sciences and Humanities Research Council (SSHRC) funded project where a campus–community partnership is making progress in moving the needle on complex issues such as poverty. The goal of the broader project is to examine the impact on communities from involvement with universities. This involvement can include community service learning, community engaged research or other collaborative activities. By working together across municipal and provincial jurisdictions, as well as by collaborating to break down the implied barrier between community organizations and academic institutions, this project seeks to mobilize the strengths and resources of various partners to initiate a larger impact than could be possible without this network.

Collective Impact is defined as a cross-sectoral and disciplined approach to solving complex issues on a large scale (FSG: Social Impact Consultants 2011). Collective Impact has been used as a tool to document micro level outcomes of collaborations like higher reading scores of school children and lower teen pregnancy rates (Weaver 2016), which are elements that contribute to poverty reduction. However, there is little literature that documents macro level policy change as a result of Collective Impact. This chapter explores effective methods for creating policy change and measuring its impacts using a CI approach. In order to explore these methods, we will examine the case study of a locally based poverty reduction roundtable's living wage campaign and use its outputs and outcomes to discuss implications for practices that make real shifts in policy.

CFICE and the Poverty Reduction Hub

The Community First: Impacts of Community Engagement (CFICE) research project is structured to encompass five hubs of learning and exchange activity: poverty reduction, violence against women, community environmental sustainability,

Canadian food systems, and knowledge mobilization. It is funded by a grant from the Social Sciences and Humanities Research Council (SSHRC). Each hub is co-managed and co-chaired by a community-based partner and an academic partner. Through a series of local demonstration projects based in communities across Canada and the national hub network, the project seeks to uncover the levers required to ensure that campus–community partnerships lead to real impact for both partners. Each hub is tasked with responding to the following research question: how can community–campus engagement, including Community Service Learning (CSL) and Community-Based Research (CBR), be designed and implemented in ways that maximize the value created for nonprofit community-based organizations?

The Poverty Reduction Hub is co-chaired by Carleton University and Vibrant Communities Canada. Vibrant Communities is a Pan-Canadian initiative that started with a base of 13 communities and has grown to more than 47 local and provincial/territorial community partners (Weaver 2016) who have experimented with innovative approaches to poverty reduction. These approaches emphasize collaboration across sectors, comprehensive thinking and action, building on community assets and a long-term process of learning and change (Gamble 2010). Universities and colleges are among the collaborators who have been involved with the communities' initiatives to reduce poverty. During the initial engagement phase of the CFICE project, Vibrant Communities conducted an environmental scan of its Cities Reducing Poverty membership to determine which roundtable initiatives were already involved in campus–community partnerships (where "involvement" broadly encompasses CBR, CSL, student placements and/or other community projects involving students).

In addition to on-the-ground demonstration projects that further the community-based organization's poverty reduction program or policy goals, the Poverty Reduction Hub also studies the evolving design and impact of campus–community partnerships. Each local demonstration project has been selected

FIGURE 7.1 CFICE Hub Structure

based on its unique campus–community partnership approach. With Vibrant Communities Canada (VCC) acting as a co-lead, the Poverty Reduction Hub benefits from the Collective Impact work carried out by its organization and the networks it has developed through its trail-building initiatives.

As two key components of CI, project participants co-created the Hub's common agenda to conduct research on the elements of community–campus engagement (CCE) that allow poverty reduction work to succeed. Throughout the past four years, the Poverty Reduction Hub has used a theory of change method (shared measurement) to monitor, review, and evaluate its progress. With an established backbone infrastructure, Vibrant Communities Canada was relied upon during the course of the project to provide strong co-leadership by bringing links to other collaborative poverty reduction networks and strengths in evaluation. These strengths were verbalized by research leads at the beginning of the project as a predictor of community–campus engagement success as well as being echoed in the literature (Turner, Merchant, Kania, & Martin 2012).

Poverty reduction is a complex concept to tackle. The definition was put forward by Vibrant Communities Canada co-leads and adopted by Hub participants. It explores six key concepts:

- *It is difficult to frame*—Is poverty just a lack of income or does it also include poor education, jobs with meager benefits, insufficient education, hopelessness, and self-esteem?
- *It has multiple joined up root causes*—Income is affected by decent housing and the ability to obtain good housing depends on income.
- *It involves multiple stakeholders*—No single organization or sector has authority, resources or leverage to address the causes of poverty on its own.
- *It has unique manifestations*—There are different levels of poverty (e.g. homelessness to working poor), demographics (e.g. youth, senior, immigrants) and local contexts (e.g., Fort McMurray in Alberta, Regent Park in Toronto).
- *It evolves*—As demographics, economies, policies, and other aspects change, the manifestations of poverty and possible solutions also change.
- *It is not clear when poverty is reduced*—When is someone considered to be out of poverty?

Vibrant Communities Canada has pioneered a tool called the Poverty Matrix (Cabaj 2004), which, when completed, provides a comprehensive picture of the number of individuals in a community experiencing poverty and the depth of that experience for different socio-economic groups. This analysis provides an evidence-based foundation from which communities can build strategies and action plans.

The Poverty Matrix (Cabaj 2004) also identifies multiple ways to look at poverty across a continuum. The elements of the Poverty Matrix include six broad (interrelated and overlapping) categories of poverty that people may experience. The following case study discusses policy initiatives that primarily target improvements for people experiencing poverty in the first two categories of the continuum:

- *At-Risk*—People who are currently not poor but are vulnerable to experiencing poverty in the near-to-medium future. Demographic groups that often fit into this category are young people struggling financially in school, people approaching retirement with little-to-modest savings or pension plans, people with mental disabilities and persons working in struggling industries, businesses, sectors, or jobs (e.g., commercial fishery, downsizing corporations, etc.).
- *Working Poor (or Waged Poor)*—People who work in full or part-time or seasonal jobs with few, if any, benefits and receive inadequate wages or job stability to maintain themselves in a decent standard of living. Demographic groups that tend to fall into the category of working poor more often than others include youth, persons with high school education, lone parents, older workers, seasonal workers, and immigrants.
- *Temporarily Unemployed*—People who are normally gainfully employed, often at good wages and income, but are temporarily unemployed due to a lay-off or firing or because they have left a job voluntarily. Demographic groups with a higher than normal incidence of temporary unemployment include people returning to school from the workforce, older workers transitioning to new employment due to a lay-off, seasonal workers, and women on maternity leave.
- *Persistently Unemployed*—People who have trouble securing and maintaining paid work and often find themselves unemployed and frequently, though not always, receiving social assistance. Demographic groups that experience higher than average rates of persistent unemployment include youth entering into the job market, people involved in the criminal justice system, people with physical disabilities, people experiencing mental illness, Aboriginal people, and people without a high school education.
- *Dependent Poor*—People unable to work and whose major source of income is from savings or government income support. There are several demographic groups more likely to be dependent poor, including retired persons living on a fixed income, persons on long-term disability pensions, single parents, Aboriginal people, immigrants, and students.
- *Homeless*—People with sporadic income that is often insufficient to pay for basic food, shelter and clothing, due to a combination of factors. Historically, persons with mental illness and youth have a higher than average risk of homelessness. More recently, however, there are instances of fully employed persons in communities with high rents and low vacancy rates (e.g., Calgary, Victoria, Vancouver) spending extended periods looking for accommodation.

Annually, the Poverty Reduction Hub announced a call for proposals for CCE projects that addressed poverty, according to the above definitions, from the communities that are part of VCC. Funded projects funded included large-scale projects working at a macro level, for example one team is convening federal, provincial, and municipal stakeholders to address poverty in a comprehensive manner in one Canadian city so that the six key concepts above are addressed.

Another project explored the hesitancy of small businesses to employ a living wage. The first project is ongoing and involved locating multiple new resources (library, health clinic, grocery store, etc.) into one section of a city, where historically people at the various levels of poverty lived. They are in the process of measuring whether this targeted infusion of resources has made an impact on the rate of poverty in that neighborhood.

The second project has been completed, and discussions with small business owners about how to remove the barriers they have identified to employing a living wage are proceeding. Because these discussions are underway, the feeling was that using the latter project as a case study for this paper was most appropriate and starts with the background on what is a living wage and the living wage movement.

Literature Review on the Living Wage

The living wage movement seeks to provide workers and their families with incomes that are sufficient to make ends meet in their region. There are several ways to determine a living wage. The Canadian Living Wage Framework provides a useful definition:

> A living wage is not the same as the minimum wage, which is the legal minimum all employers must pay. The living wage sets a higher test—a living wage reflects what earners in a family need to bring home, based on the actual costs of living in a specific community. The living wage is a call to private and public sector employers to pay wages to both direct and contract employees sufficient to provide the basics to families with children (2013).

Furthermore, the Canadian Centre for Policy Alternatives (CCPA) has determined how the living wage is calculated in 25 communities across Canada (Ivanova & Klein 2013):

> The living wage is calculated as the hourly rate at which a household can meet its basic needs, once government transfers have been added to the family's income (such as the Universal Child Care Benefit) and deductions have been subtracted (such as income taxes and Employment Insurance premiums).
>
> Ivanova & Klein 2013: 2

Some definitions bring slightly different twists to each calculation, such as focusing on an hourly wage that provides for a family of four, based on the assumption that there are two wage-earners or basing the wage calculation on a set number of hours per week (i.e., 70) that can be split between the household's income-earners (Graces 2011).

There are numerous limitations to these calculations, with some of the biggest criticisms in the literature pointing to what items the family's budget is not structured to incorporate. The calculations rely on a limited household budget that does not allow for extras such as entertainment (Ivanova & Klein 2013), subtracts government transfers such as childcare, and does not provide room for payments of any family debt (Graces 2011). The calculation also does not automatically increase, so communities need to continually update their living wage calculations.

The current case study explores the barriers to implementing a living wage. One barrier identified in the literature is that there is no legal obligation for an employer to provide one, unlike the minimum wage (Graces 2011). Living wage campaigns attempt to engage employers in the movement by convincing them of the benefits of providing a living wage through advocacy and documentation.

Advocates of the living wage cite research that says employers see an increase in the quality of life for employees (Graces 2011), an increase in productivity, and decreases in employee absenteeism and turnover rates (Graces 2011; Brenner 2005). White (2012) explains that the benefits to the employees and employer are reduced stress of employees and increased productivity. Zeng and Honig (2016) empirically show that there is a significant difference between living wage workers and minimum wage workers. Living wage workers have a higher affective commitment, increased organizational citizenship behaviors, and lower employee turnover.

In order to encourage employers to adopt living wage policies, living wage advocates work closely with the business community to build collaborative relationships which will facilitate their understanding of the potential benefits of employing a living wage (White 2012). As stated by Loewen (2008) the purpose of the resource *Collaborating with Business for Social Transformation* is:

to identify how collaborating with business can enhance social change outcomes, provide some tips on meeting the challenges that such collaboration creates, offer inspiring stories about contributions businesses have made (and are still making) toward the achievement of social justice initiatives and supply some practical tools for planning the engagement with the business sector.

In addition, White (2012) argues that the Corporate Social Responsibility (CSR) model, which proposes that implementation of a living wage is socially responsible, is a benefit to employers that has not been adequately utilized. During the past 20 years, living wage campaigns have emerged as one of the most important endorsements of labor justice across the world (Reynolds & Kern 2001). The Corporate Social Responsibility (CSR) benefits include highlighting a more humanistic, positive brand for the employer and associating that employer with human rights issues.

Further, Cornish (2012) makes the case for implementing living wages to counter the effects of historical discriminatory practices, including pay gaps, among governments and employers. Low wages can be viewed as bad public policy, and lead to negative health and social outcomes (Cornish 2012). Historically, women and people who face racism make significantly less money than those who have not been marginalized (Cornish 2012). In addition, a country that does not implement a living wage will not be able to compete in a global economy because low wages devalue the skill of vulnerable workers, especially during a time when the economy requires highly skilled workers (Cornish 2012).

Ivanova & Klein (2013) claimed that any discussion of a living wage should start with the assumption that a living wage is an effective means to address a broad range of social issues such as child poverty, health coverage, housing and more. This is consistent with the definition used in this chapter. It is important that a living wage would allow children to grow up to lead more fulfilling and successful lives. One minimum wage worker in Hamilton, Ontario, described her situation in the following manner:

> By earning a minimum wage, I can only feed myself and my kids. I don't have enough money to go to a dentist. I don't have enough money to bring my kids to the cinema and watch movies. I don't have enough money to do my laundry. And I cannot even invite my friends to have a simple dinner with me in my house. I feel that I am isolated from others because I cannot afford things besides basic food.
>
> Living Wage, Hamilton, 2014

In their study of advocates working on living wage campaigns, Pei et al. (2015) recommend best practices for implementing a living wage policy including: i) developing a core group of individuals; ii) engaging champions to extend the buy-in of companies; iii) a positive framework for the campaign; and iv) dedicating more resources to research and knowledge. These best practices are linked to Collective Impact in that the first and second recommendations relate to choosing a strong backbone organization. The third recommendation is linked to establishing a common agenda and the final recommendation is linked to establishing shared measurement. The synergies between good practice in implementing a living wage and the Collective Impact approach will become clearer in the next section on Collective Impact, beginning with theories about policy change.

Factors Involved with Policy Change

A key outcome of the Collective Impact framework is the ability for collaborative groups to leverage their resources, uncover the root cause of the problem or issue, and mobilize to identify the appropriate policy implications that will result in significant and lasting change.

In Pathways *for Change: Ten Theories to Inform Advocacy and Policy Change Efforts*, Stachowiak (2013) identifies ten separate theories about how communities, collaborative planning groups and organizations might influence the policy agenda. These theories are described in the following ways:

- large leaps or punctuated equilibrium theory;
- a coalition approach;

- walking through an open policy window;
- working through power politics;
- regime theory;
- focusing on messaging and frameworks;
- media influence;
- grassroots organizing;
- group or collaborative formulation around the policy agenda; and
- diffusion theory or engaging public opinion.

Five of these theories (large leaps, coalition building, power politics, policy windows, and engagement of policy makers) are characterized as global theories, while another five (messaging and frameworks, media influence, grassroots organizing, group formation, and large-scale engagement) are characterized as advocacy strategies and tactics.

Pursuing a global policy change theory requires many particular conditions to be in place. These approaches to change policy and influence often take time in order to establish a deep understanding of the opportunity and build a policy approach and/or a coalition of partners. The approaches use advocacy strategies and tactics, including developing messaging or frameworks, pursuing power politics and grassroots organizing, focusing on key decision makers, key strategic connections, and the ability of large groups or networks to influence the decision-making process. As Stachowiak (2009) writes, "[k]nowing about existing theories may sharpen your own thinking, provide new ways of looking at the policy world, and give you a leg up on developing your own theory of change."

At the same time that Stachowiak wrote about ten theories of policy change, the Caledon Institute of Social Policy convened a community of practice in Canada to identify the key elements of how the community and government can collaborate on policy change and influence. The net result of this community of practice is *Collaboration on Policy: A Manual Developed by the Community –Government Collaboration on Policy* (Caledon Institute on Social Policy 2009). The community of practice was established to develop an effective policy monitoring process and to identify those strategies used by community partners and government to influence the policy agenda. The members of the community of practice shared their policy influence approaches (both the successes and challenges they faced) and identified the key elements required to support policy change.

The *Collaboration on Policy* manual (2009) identifies core skills for collaborative groups to build into the policy influence process:

- building a strong collaborative;
- focusing on policy work;
- creating an enabling environment both internally to the collaborative and externally with policy makers; and
- ensuring evaluation and debriefing.

Ensuring evaluation inevitably includes discussion of shared measurement—a common set of measures to be in the evaluation—which will be discussed more in the next section. Similar to Stachowiak, the manual describes the process of collaboration and policy change. The process of building a collaborative approach to influencing policy change can have significant impact.

The *Collaboration on Policy* manual (2009) advises community groups to understand and determine both the costs and benefits of collaboration. The costs and benefits could include partners determining up-front the amount of time, money, responsibility and accountability required to move a policy change forward. Collaborative partners also have to navigate different points of view that partners might have about the policy agenda and build agreement around risk management and key messaging.

In developing a policy approach, the *Collaboration on Policy* manual (2009) identifies nine key strategies for policy work that are possible once agreement is reached on shared measurement, including:

- monitoring policy developments;
- building an evidence base;
- ensuring access to programs;
- improving existing measures;
- creating new measures;
- reducing costs;
- designing appropriate environments;
- ensuring compatibility of policy measures; and
- assessing policy impacts

In addition to policy work, the manual identifies components to creating an enabling environment, including:

- developing key principles for working collaboratively;
- securing funding to enable the policy change effort;
- ensuring sufficient and appropriate timeframes for the policy influence process;
- learning from past processes and from peers; and
- developing evaluation frameworks

Implementing a policy change strategy must include securing, developing and supporting partners as well as focusing on the policy process and the opportunities that may or may not be accessible through the policy process. These two resources provide useful strategies for organizations and groups considering policy change as their goal. As the Caledon Institute on Social Policy (2009) states, many possibilities for intervention at the level of public policy are possible: public policy does not follow a straight line and there are often interruptions in the process.

Collective Impact and Policy Change

Collective Impact is a framework for community and systems change that is built on five core conditions: "building a common agenda; engaging in shared measurement; supporting the collaborative work through mutually reinforcing activities; keeping partners and the community engaged through continuous communication; and ensuring that the collective effort is supported by a back bone infrastructure" (Weaver 2016: 274). Three of these components facilitate measuring policy impact: common agenda, shared measurement and continuous communication. Parkhurst & Preskill (2014) state that changing the way that the various stakeholders in any Collective Impact process interact with each other, unite around a common agenda, encourage discussion and continuous communication is vitally important in achieving policy outcomes. For example, they coincidently use a quote from our community partners, ". . . an evaluation of Vibrant Communities, a pan-Canadian anti-poverty initiative, found that the 'multi-sectoral nature of Vibrant Communities helps government move on [policy] change because proposals are already vetted from multiple interests in the community' " (Parkhurst & Preskill 2014: 18).

Some authors believe that having a common agenda does not lead to change unless there is agreement on how success will be measured (Kania & Kramer 2011).

In Collective Impact terms, this agreement means 'shared measurement.' Shared measurement is defined as "the use of a common set of measures to monitor performance, track progress towards outcomes and learn what is and is not working in the group's collective approach" whose purpose is to allow a Collective Impact initiative to "improve data quality, track progress toward a shared goal, enable coordination and collaboration, learn and correct course and catalyze action" (Caledon Institute on Social Policy 2009). Figure 7.2 illustrates this process[1].

There are many challenges in measuring policy impact. Poverty reduction is a complex problem ". . . with multiple root causes, unclear solutions, and requires orchestrated action by diverse stakeholders, who do not agree on how it should be addressed" (Cabaj 2014), often due to very different ideological ideas about the root causes (Holmgren, 2015). The professional literature contains many views on what shared measurement should look like. Cabaj (2014) claims the best way to address such complex problems is by building in an evaluation that does not focus on delivering results on a fixed schedule but by employing a flexible framework rooted in developmental evaluation.

Parkhurst & Preskill (2014) describe a similar flexible framework of taking a snapshot at one or more points in time. While this kind of evaluation may not address the complexity of the issue, it can tell a story of the effectiveness of an intervention over time. Vibrant Communities' poverty reduction roundtable trailbuilders developed shared measurement frameworks that:

> varied from community to community, [but] all tended to have the following elements: (a) a working definition of poverty, (b) an analysis of the leverage

points for change in their community, (c) a pool of strategies to achieve, (d) a set of 'stretch targets' for reducing poverty, (e) principles to guide their efforts, and (f) a plan for evaluating their efforts.

Cabaj 2014: 111

This perspective allows one to measure intended and unintended outcomes, document failures (from which one can learn a great deal) in addition to successes, evaluate efforts that are in progress and document the shifting context of the complex problem (Cabaj 2014).

Finally (and a priority for Collective Impact partners), Cabaj (2014:17) says one of the strengths of a developmental evaluation model is to be able to "embed evaluation in their DNA":

Rather than use performance measurement and evaluation to determine success or failure, Collective Impact partners should use the information

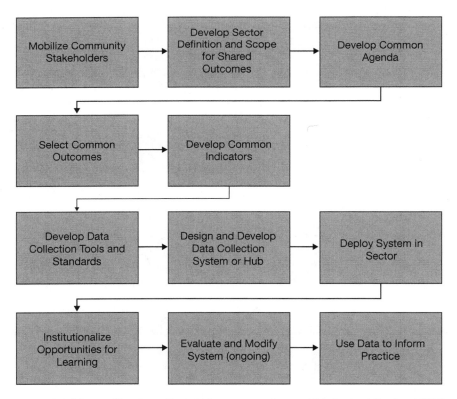

FIGURE 7.2 How to Develop a Shared Measurement System (E:\sshrc\publications\CDS book chapter\Developing Shared Measurement _ Collaboration for Impact. htm) [Accessed May 9 2016]

they provide to make decisions about adapting and improving their initiative. To that end, Collective Impact partners should embed evaluation and learning into their initiative's DNA, rather than treating it as an annual (or quarterly) exercise. Embracing this comprehensive, adaptive approach to evaluating Collective Impact requires leaders to do three things differently. . . . they should "ask what," "ask why," and "ask often."

There are also critiques of shared measurement. For some authors, shared measurement seems like a one size fits all approach that does not allow for a diversity of stakeholders (Holmgren 2015). There is a concern that adhering to a shared measurement regime can limit creative and strategic thinking in the interest of consensus.

Many veterans in the field of poverty reduction argue that employer wages and the benefit levels in government income support programs can have a far greater impact on poverty than innovations in front line social services, where the case for aligning measures across organizations may be quite strong. By pre-determining the indicators to be measured, the group is inherently limiting the scope of their observations. Collective Impact participants should focus on strategies with the highest opportunities for impact, not ones that offer greater prospects for shared measurement (Cabaj 2014: 115).

Another way to view this process is that measures can also become barriers (Holmgren 2015). For example, one of the goals of Collective Impact is social action. Some authors feel that building consensus around shared measurement limits social action.

A talented and hardworking network of Collective Impact participants in the greater Toronto area have elected to keep their strategy "in first gear," while they sort out their outcomes and measures, and have been spinning their wheels for years trying to land on the right ones. Collective Impact initiatives should avoid trying to design large and perfect measurement systems up front, opting instead for "simple and roughly right" versions that drive—not distract—from strategic thinking and action (Cabaj 2014: 115).

Methodology

The current project is a summative evaluation and employed a case study methodology. Summative evaluation was appropriate because as the poverty reduction project wound down, participants were ready to ask the questions about the impact, merit, value, or significance of the work accomplished (Parkhurst & Preskill 2014).

Qualitative interviews were conducted with three key informants selected based on their involvement with poverty reduction efforts in Hamilton, Ontario. Efforts were made to ensure variegated perspectives, so each of the key informants had roles in poverty reduction projects that were dissimilar. Twelve questions were developed, but key informants were asked only a subset of relevant to each of their roles. For example, one of the key informants was asked ten questions, another was asked five questions, and the other was asked four questions. Key informants participated in phone interviews of approximately 30 minutes each.

A content analysis was conducted from the interviews with the data distilled into the following case study format. The results were then presented to a group of stakeholders who had participated in the community–campus poverty reduction research since the start of the project to see if the themes identified resonated with their experiences in the community–campus partnership and the policy change achieved. The Carleton University Research Ethics Board approved this project as part of an omnibus clearance for the evaluation of the Poverty Reduction Hub's work.

Case Study: History of Hamilton Living Wage Initiatives

A leading proponent of living wage policy in Hamilton, Ontario, is the Hamilton Roundtable for Poverty Reduction (HRPR). The Roundtable was formed in 2005 with the goal to brand Hamilton as the Best Place to Raise a Child and in order to help curb poverty rates (Hamilton Roundtable for Poverty Reduction 2011) and many of these partners remain in continuous communication. These member organizations include community-funded organizations such as the Social Planning and Research Council, Wesley Urban Ministries, the City of Hamilton, Hamilton Community Foundation, and private sector partners. It was quickly established that Collective Impact would guide their work and that the common agenda focused on attempts to implement a living wage in Hamilton.

In 2011, the Roundtable issued calculated costs to live in Hamilton that generated a community dialogue and planted the seed with employers for living wage discussions (Interview 1). In partnership with the Roundtable, advocates from various sectors collaborated on Hamilton's living wage initiative, and Living Wage Hamilton created a living wage employer recognition program where businesses can apply for certification (Hamilton Roundtable for Poverty Reduction 2011).

In Hamilton, 30,000 people (total population in 2011 of 520,000) who live below the low-income cut-off (LICO) are employed (Hamilton Roundtable for Poverty Reduction 2011). Hamilton's living wage calculations are based on four-person families with both parents working 37.5 hours per week (Hamilton Poverty Roundtable). When creating a living wage calculation, incorporating costs that could apply to children of various ages is challenging: there is no all-encompassing family structure, but the family structure must be standardized because it would be impossible to implement wages according to all possible combinations (Interview 2).

The living wage calculation also includes an implicit narrative: a wage is abstract but attaching the wage to a family helps people relate to it (Interview 2). Although the current family structure that the living wage calculation uses is a traditional nuclear family, it associates the costs with an image. Furthermore, it is important that the image contains children because living wage is about being able to raise families (Interview 2). In addition to promoting higher wages, then, the living wage initiative illuminates issues surrounding child care.

In 2014, Hamilton's living wage calculation was $14.95/hour (Hamilton Roundtable for Poverty Reduction 2014). Living wage calculations do not consider debt or savings, but they do consider community living expenses: citizens need to engage in social activities in order to create healthy communities (Hamilton Roundtable for Poverty Reduction), and a goal of living wage is social inclusion (Pei et al. 2015). This calculation is important because it became the basis of shared measurement and the knowledge of how many people are brought out of poverty because they made a living wage.

The living wage initiative is especially important in Hamilton because 25% of Hamilton children live in poverty, and in some neighborhoods, the rate is as high as 40% (Interview 2). Recently, there has been signs of recovery (from the 2008 recession) in Hamilton, especially parts of retail and food services. The irony is that it is smaller businesses that have been more likely to adopt living wages in Hamilton, despite these businesses' lower profit margins. In part due to a stronger sense of community among smaller businesses and owners (Interview 2). For service-based businesses, it is very difficult to adopt a living wage because they depend on low-wage labor for a significant percent of their expenditures (Interview 3).

Collective Impact and Measuring Policy Change

Within the living wage initiative, involving dynamic partners spurs Collective Impact (Interview 1). One benefit of a CI approach is that it ensures that community members are knowledgeable about and are comfortable with the approach (Interview 1). Hamilton's living wage initiative started with four key partners: the Hamilton Roundtable for Poverty Reduction, the Social Planning and Research Council, the Workforce Planning Table and the McMaster Community Poverty Initiative. Each of these groups brings strengths and contacts to contribute to the initiative's Collective Impact goals (Interview 1).

Collective Impact can be on a local or broader scale. For example, if several cities adopt a living wage, the Province of Ontario is much more likely to adopt a living wage as its minimum wage standard (Interview 2). Although these cities might implement their strategies individually, their collective efforts can have an impact outside the jurisdiction in which they operate. Furthermore, municipalities frequently look to each other when developing best practices, so the work done in one municipality begins a conversation with representatives in other areas.

Communities across Canada adapt the National Living Wage Framework to their local context so that their calculations and employee wages reflect the actual cost of living in their regions. Living wage campaigns across the country are community-based because of costs of living This localization can make it difficult to engage and certify employers who are based in multiple localities and thus must subscribe to multiple living wage rates (Pei et al. 2015). Hamilton achieved early success with the living wage initiative, and since then Ontario has developed a living wage network where 25 communities are developing local living wage campaigns (Interview 1). These communities are at different stages—some have engaged employers, while others have recently started living wage calculations—but they work together as part of this mutually-supportive movement and exchange best practices (Interview 1).

It is difficult to mandate living wage at the provincial level because these calculations can differ significantly among communities. For example, rural locations often have lower living wage calculations than cities because of lower housing costs. Furthermore, the Fight for 15 across Ontario might constitute a living wage in some parts of the province, but in many cities $15/hour is already too low. If adopted by many communities, the living wage would be a base towards a provincial minimum wage, which is currently happening in New York and California. Most recently there have been increases in the minimum wage in Ontario in January 2018 and January 2019 to $15 (Interview 2).

Currently, living wages are calculated based on municipal costs of living data (Interview 2), though there is a provincial recognition program underway so businesses operating in multiple jurisdictions can join the initiative (Interview 1). Having a standard living wage framework across Ontario would provide companies a sense of cost, which would help them plan for incremental steps towards becoming a living wage (Interview 2). First, it might be necessary to develop regional frameworks across Ontario, such as different ones for Northern Ontario, Southwestern Ontario, rural Ontario, and other locations. So far, the bulk of the work has been done in urban centers (Interview 2).

When advocating to municipal governments to become living wage employers, noting that hundreds of municipalities in the United States have already adopted living wage has an impact (Interview 2). Since popular support for the initiative exists, early adopters and champions are important to bring more partners on board. However, many people are still unfamiliar with the concept (Interview 2). Recently, the Bernie Sanders Presidential campaign in the United States and the failure of the New Democratic Party (NDP) in the 2015 Canadian election mark two important intersecting political moments regarding a restructuring of the possibilities for policy development (Interview 2). A key aspect of these moments is the relationship between the generational shift and precarious employment: this issue is not exclusive to millennials, but it is more concentrated among them (Interview 2), which makes the wage gap an increasingly prevalent discussion and one that is unlikely to taper off.

Economically, the living wage has a ripple effect throughout the community by acting as a local stimulus for buying power with a multiplier effect (Interview 2). In addition to an individual bringing home a living wage, this capital then circulates back into the local economy as people can afford to purchase food, clothing, rent, and other goods (Interview 2). When wages are raised for low-income earners, the vast majority of this money is spent because these individuals use much of their wages buying items to meet basic needs. Unfortunately, the multiplier effect is difficult to measure, since people paying and earning a living wage are not the only beneficiaries, which is referred to as the free rider problem (Interview 2). Because employers who do not support the living wage initiative benefit from other employers paying their employees living wages (since those employees will have more income to contribute to the community's economy), the free rider problem can serve as a disincentive for some employers to support the living wage initiative.

In addition to economic benefits, higher wages also catalyze social engagement, which is very important for community development. If nobody can afford to engage in the community, people do not spend money in the local culture, making it difficult for the community to prosper (Interview 3).

Impact on Living Wage Policy

Hamilton's living wage initiative has had a critical impact on policy change: 30 employers had officially signed on as Living Wage employers as of April 2016 (Interview 1). The Hamilton Roundtable for Poverty Reduction and other groups have helped make issues of precarious and low-paid work talking points throughout the city (Interview 1). The Roundtable's collaborative approach, which includes representatives from diverse backgrounds, has been essential to illuminate different perspectives (Interview 2). Since this initiative began, nearly 30 living wage employers have come on board in Hamilton (Interview 1). Comprising these employers is a mixture of smaller businesses in the private sector, nonprofit organizations, and some faith groups (Interview 1). The largest living wage employer is currently the Hamilton–Wentworth District School Board, which was also the first school board in Ontario to sign on to the initiative (Interview 1).

The living wage model promotes progressive employers, but it is not about shaming those who are not at living wage: it is about promoting good business practices (Interview 1). However, employer recognition programs offer incentives in terms of branding. The certification process has been successful in Hamilton because employers like having documentation of their commitment, and implicit within this commitment is the aspect of championing ideas: stores can put up a sticker on their door that can act as a conversation generator for staff and customers (Interview 1). The certificate encourages employers, employees, and the community to feel good about participating in the living wage initiative (Interview 1).

Since many employers have difficulty offering all employees a living wage right away, the phase-in component, allowing employers to begin with a commitment of pay living wages to full-time workers and working towards raising the wage levels of part-time employees, students, and contract positions is a helpful aspect of the certification program (Interview 2). Many of these employers have also committed to pay part-time and/or contract workers a living wage (Interview 1).

One of the recent living wage employers (LWE) in Hamilton, Cake and Loaf Bakery, signed on in December 2015. Since that sector is typically lower paid, they have received significant attention as a local living wage success story, including an article in *The Globe and Mail*. Declaring themselves a living wage employer has improved business: community members want to shop where employees are treated well. Not all living wage employers can expect this much publicity, but the living wage initiative tries to profile employers who step up (Interview 1).

The Best Place to Raise a Child initiative branding provided the intersection that helped incentivize the public school board to sign on as a living wage employer (Interview 1). Their mandate was to address child poverty, so making their organization a LWE reinforced that mandate (Interview 1). Since institutions such as the City of Hamilton (currently in the process of becoming a LWE) and the Hamilton–Wentworth District School Board (the first elected body in Ontario to become a LWE) have responsibility for the community and its children, the impact of LWE branding is significant. As more major institutions in Hamilton take this position, paying living wages can be part of what it means to be a Hamilton company (Interview 2).

Some major companies with many people working at low wages have not been part of these conversations (Interview 2). For example, although supermarkets are unionized, they do not pay all their employees living wages (Interview 2), and though construction companies often pay full-time workers a living wage, most workers on–site are temporary (Interview 3). Owners of service-based businesses often are hesitant to talk about living wage policies because they want to look good to the public, but they do not believe they can afford these wages (Interview 3). The lack of dialogue halts the communication and educational components of the initiative (Interview 3).

When chain stores adopt a living wage, they run into a ripple effect problem—when low-income workers receive a living wage, this causes other people already at a living wage to also want a wage increase (Interview 3). Thus, if a chain store makes the decision to increase wages in one place, they have to increase wages for workers in all places (Interview 3).

The groups with the larger proportion of workers earning close to a minimum wage, such as major companies, need increased concentration and are where the living wage initiative has been less successful (Interview 2). Going forward, the Hamilton initiative plans to concentrate on engaging institutions whose missions identify with the branding and entwining of Hamilton's civic identity with living wage (Interview 2). Other cities can build on that kind of community pride as well (Interview 2).

An Analysis of the Case Study: Hamilton Living Wage Work

Parkhurst and Preskill (2014) identify two types of change related to policy: change in systems and change in behaviors. The elements are essential to achieving a high level of impact that can be sustained over time. They view changes in systems, (large-scale change), as influencing cultural norms, public policies, and funding flows. Change in behaviors include changes in professional practices or

TABLE 7.1 Analysis of the Changes in Systems and the Changes in Behaviors
Demonstrated in Our Hamilton Living Wage Work Case Study

Large Scale Change*	Change documented in the case study	Elements of Collective Impact that facilitate change
Changes in systems (influencing cultural norms, public policies, funding flows)	Paper documenting costs of raising a child in Hamilton	Common agenda
	Creating a definition of a living wage in Hamilton and agreeing on the interpretation	Common agenda/Shared measurement
	Issues of precarious and low-paid work have circulated as talking-points throughout the city and among stakeholders	Continuous communication across a variety of stakeholders
	Hamilton Roundtable for Poverty Reduction, formed in 2005, that meets regularly	Continuous communication across a variety of stakeholders
	CCE research to identify barriers small businesses experience to implementing a living wage	Shared measurement
Changes in behaviors (professional practices or changes in individual behavior)	Living Wage Employer Recognition and Certification Program	Shared measurement
	30 living wage employers have come on board in Hamilton and become advocates in their sectors	Shared measurement

* This analysis is based on principles in Parkhurst & Preskill, 2014

changes in individual behavior. The analysis of the Hamilton case study is
approached by identifying these types of policy-informed changes, the activities
associated with these changes in the case study and how these changes and activities
relate to Collective Impact.

Conclusion

The Hamilton living wage initiative reinforces several of the main components
of the Collective Impact literature. The CI approach involves a diverse group of
relevant stakeholders that engage in mutually-reinforcing activities. One of the

benefits of these activities, as shown in the case study, is that actors or community members in each sector are more comfortable with an initiative when an established, credible figure can speak the same language and vouch for the initiative. It can help communicate to policy makers that the ideas and proposals have been vetted and critiqued by stakeholders who share similar goals and values, which allows for quicker acceptance, communication, and uptake of policies such as living wage. However, mutually-reinforcing activities must occur in tandem with the other aspects of Collective Impact documented such as a common agenda, continuous communication, and shared measurement practices, to lead to policy changes in broad systems and organizational behaviors.

By collaboratively identifying common goals, living wage campaigns engage allies and partners and can mobilize their unique contacts to grow the conversation through each network. As the conversation proliferates simultaneously through different channels, it builds and helps sustain the campaign's momentum such as by creating the space for the community to host ongoing dialogue and by getting buy-in from employers and the community as they continually re-calculate living wage rates that reflect local costs of living.

Some recommendations specific to the case study can be made that would help other jurisdictions create policy change.

- Utilizing a roundtable format where key stakeholders meet regularly (common agenda/continuous communication) to discuss a specific issue and incorporate Collective Impact principals is very important for policy change. The Hamilton Roundtable for Poverty Reduction has worked together since 2005 with a broad poverty reduction agenda that included a living wage campaign as part of its strategies.
- Having various reports circulate in the community that educate the public about the identified problem was very important in setting the stage for policy change. This approach also extended the conversation about shared measurement, for example, beyond the Roundtable.
- Engaging with a university partner to conduct research (CCE) on living wage practices added to the information available about the issues and pointed to ways to have a policy impact. Community organizations often have neither the expertise nor the resources to engage in research that, in this case, led to a plan for how to overcome barriers identified by small businesses.
- Establishing a recognition program was an important step in supporting businesses who took the risk of adopting a living wage program and showed the community the benefits of adopting this shared measurement.

The living wage initiative in Hamilton has extended its scope beyond organizational wage policies. Using the living wage data and language as a starting point, together with living wage champions they are connecting to broader systemic issues such as precarious employment, low-paid work, and affordability that impact the economic security of individuals and families. By bringing together a diversity of actors whose values or goals intersect under living wage, the collaborative poverty reduction initiative built popular support for living wage policies to the extent that they are now aiming to associate Hamilton business owners' civic identity with ethical employer practices.

Note

1   Figure 7.2: How to Develop a Shared Measurement System (E:\sshrc\publications\ CDS book chapter\Developing Shared Measurement _ Collaboration for Impact.htm) [Accessed May 9 2016]

References

Brenner, M. D. (2005). The Economic Impact of the Boston Living wage Ordinance. *Industrial Relations*, 44(1), pp. 59–83.

Cabaj, M. (2014). Evaluating Collective Impact: Five Simple Rules. *The Philanthropist*, 26(1), pp. 109–124.

Cabaj, M. (2004). Making the Case: Clarifying Ways Businesses Benefit from Poverty Reduction Strategies a Tool for Vibrant Communities. Toronto: Tamarack: An Institute for Community Engagement.

Cabaj, M. (2004). *Poverty Matrix: Understanding Poverty in Your Community*, [online]. Available at: http://tamarackcommunity.ca/downloads/tools/poverty_matrix2e.pdf

Caledon Institute on Social Policy (2009). Collaboration on Policy: A Manual Developed by the Community–Government Collaboration on Policy, [online]. Available at: www. caledoninst.org/Publications/PDF/772ENG.pdf

Cornish, M. (2012). *A Living Wage as a Human Right*. Toronto: Canadian Centre for Policy Alternatives.

FSG: Social Impact Consultants (2011). Collective Impact, [online]. Available at: www.fsg. org/publications/collective-impact

Gamble, J. (2010). *Evaluating Vibrant Communities 2000–2010*. Toronto: Tamarack: An Institute for Community Engagement.

Graces, M. L. (2011). *Living Wage: An Introduction*. Guelph: The Research Shop.

Hamilton Roundtable for Poverty Reduction, [online]. Available at: hamiltonpoverty.ca.

Holmgren, M. (2015). What Does 'Living' Mean in a 'Living Wage'? *Vibrant Communities Canada*, [online]. Available at: http://vibrantcanada.ca/blogs/mark-holmgren/what-does -%E2%80%9Cliving%E2%80%9D-mean-living-wage

Ivanova, I., and Klein, S. (2013). Working for a Living Wage Making Paid Work Meet Basic Family Needs in Metro Vancouver 2013 Update. Toronto: Canadian Centre for Policy Alternatives.

Kania, J., and Kramer, M. (2011). Collective Impact. *Stanford Social Innovation Review* [online]. Available at: http://ssir.org/articles/entry/collective_impact

Kozak, A. Interview 1 (Apr 22, 2016). *Hamilton's living wage initiative*.

Kozak, A. Interview 2 (Apr 23, 2016). *Hamilton's living wage initiative*.

Kozak, A. Interview 3 (Apr 23, 2016). *Hamilton's living wage initiative*.

Kozak, A. Interview 4 (Dec 18, 2015). *Hamilton's living wage initiative*.

Living Wage Canada (2013). Canadian Living Wage Framework, [online]. Available at: http://livingwagecanada.ca/files/3913/8382/4524/Living_Wage_Full_Document_Nov.pdf

Living Wage Hamilton (2014). Isabella Challenges Us to Think about Making Hamilton a Living Wage Community, [online]. Available at: http://livingwagehamilton.ca/wp/

Loewen, G. (2008). *Collaborating with Business for Social Transformation.* Toronto: Tamarack: An Institute for Community Engagement.

Parkhurst, M. and Preskill, H. (2014). Learning in Action: Evaluating Collective Impact. *Stanford Social Innovation Review,* [online]. Available at: http://ssir.org/articles/entry/learning_in_action_evaluating_collective_impact

Pei, N., Feltman, J., Ford, I. and Schwartz, K. (2015). Best Practices for Implementing a Living Wage Policy in Canada: Using Community–campus Partnerships To Further the Community's Goal. *The Engaged Scholar Journal,* 1(1), pp. 87–106.

Reynolds, D., and Kern, J. (2001). Labour and the Living-Wage Movement. *The Journal of Labour & Society,* 5(3), pp. 17–45.

Stachowiak, S. (2009). Pathways for Change: 6 Theories about How Policy Change Happens. *Organizational Research Services,* [online]. Available at: http://bistandstorget.no/files/docs/pathways_for_change_6_theories_about_how_policy_change_happens.pdf

Stachowiak, S. (2013). Pathways for Change: 10 Theories to Inform Advocacy and Policy Change Efforts. *Center for Evaluation Innovation,* [online]. Available at: http://orsimpact.com/wp-content/uploads/2013/11/Center_Pathways_FINAL.pdf

Turner, S., Merchant, K., Kania, J., and Martin, E. (2012). Understanding the Value of Backbone Organizations in Collective Impact: Part 2. *Stanford Social Innovation Review,* [online]. Available at: http://ssir.org/articles/entry/understanding_the_value_of_backbone_organizations_in_collective_impact_2

Weaver, L. (2016). Possible: Transformational Change in Collective Impact. *Community Development,* 47(2), pp. 274–283.

White, R. G. (2012). *Corporate Social Responsibility and a Living wage.* Toronto: Canadian Centre for Policy Alternatives.

Zeng, Z., and Honig, B. (2016). A Study of Living Wage Effects on Employees' Performance Related Attitudes and Behaviour. *Canadian Journal of Administrative Sciences,* Early View, [online]. Available at: http://onlinelibrary.wiley.com/doi/10.1002/cjas.1375/abstract

8

healthTIDE

Utilizing Aspects of Collective Impact and Other Models of Coordinated Action to Drive Statewide Obesity Prevention in Wisconsin

Amy Korth and Amy Meinen

Contributing Authors: Amy Hilgendorf, Catherine Breuer, and Brian Christens

Obesity Prevention

Obesity is among the most pressing of current public health challenges in many industrialized countries, including the United States. Rates of overweight and obesity in the United States have surged since the 1990s. Nationally, nearly 38% of adults are now obese (up from around 12% in 1990), and there are significant racial, ethnic, and socioeconomic inequities in rates of obesity (Ogden 2014). Reasons for the steadily increasing rates of obesity range from changes in food environments, local built environments and transportation systems, to commercial messaging (Huang 2009).

Obesity increases the risk of chronic diseases, including heart disease, stroke, diabetes, and cancer (Wang 2011). It poses risks to psychological well-being (Halfon 2013; Pulgarón 2013). It lowers life expectancy and disability-free life expectancy and creates strain on national economies and health care systems (Economos 2014). Due to these negative effects, there have been many calls to reduce rates of obesity (ODPHP 2014).

In the state of Wisconsin, current estimates are that only 26.1% of adults are in the normal weight range, while 33.4% are overweight and 39.4% are obese (1.2% are underweight), (Eggers 2016). This represents a nearly quadrupled rate of adult obesity over the last several decades—in 1990, Wisconsin's adult obesity rate was estimated at 11.8% (The State of Obesity 2016). Excess body mass currently accounts for between 20% and 86% of population attributable risk for a range of comorbidities among Wisconsin adults, including stress, anxiety, depression, asthma, hypertension, sleep apnea, and diabetes (Eggers 2016).

Childhood obesity is highly predictive of adult obesity so many efforts have focused on preventing childhood weight gains (Reed 2014). Preventing obesity is complex. Individual interventions—from changes in clinical to educational practices—have proven inadequate for addressing population weight gains (Story 2008; Swinburn 2011). The systemic factors that have led to increases in obesity make it necessary to change multiple policies, systems, and environments (PSE) within local communities and at broader scales (Huang 2009; Spahr 2016). Most of these types of changes cannot be imposed from the outside and must instead be accomplished through local community-driven efforts and often require coordination across localities. Food and transportation systems are examples.

The necessary changes to PSE can be costly and controversial. Current approaches recognize that many social, economic, and physical factors in the community environment can work against a person's intent and ability to pursue a healthier lifestyle (Centers for Disease Control and Prevention, Communities Putting Prevention to Work). Conversely, those with vested interests in the status quo will often resist attempts to make changes that could reduce obesity (Mialon 2015).

Obesity Prevention Efforts in Wisconsin

In Wisconsin, efforts to address obesity started in the late 1990s under the leadership of the Wisconsin Department of Health Services (DHS). In 2003, DHS received the first five-year cooperative agreement from the Centers for Disease Control and Prevention (CDC) to work on obesity prevention statewide. DHS convened partners to create a state plan for addressing obesity resulting in new state policies related to Farm to School and Complete Streets. This plan provided partners with experiences of working on public policy to support healthy eating and physical activity (Wisconsin Legislative Council Study 2008).

In 2010, DHS was awarded three grants focused on nutrition and physical activity as part of the American Recovery and Reinvestment Act (Communities Putting Prevention to Work). The goals of these grants included: fostering statewide farm to school efforts, increasing physical activity opportunities within schools and early childhood, and piloting multi-setting, PSE interventions in two counties with local and state-level infrastructure. These initiatives enabled some public health leaders to form deeper relationships and undertake collaborative action with organizations that they had not worked with previously. As this work was underway, however, a change in Wisconsin's political leadership and administration initiated a need to reconsider the role that the public sector would play in primary prevention.

Formation of healthTIDE and Utilization of the Collective Impact Framework

The concept of healthTIDE began through discussions about obesity prevention, healthy eating and physical activity PSE work, and creating a more coordinated statewide effort. A grant proposal early in the formation of healthTIDE was funded by the Wisconsin Partnership Program (WPP) to explore increased statewide coordination, and one model that especially resonated with partners was Collective Impact (Kania 2011).

With the initial WPP funds, the healthTIDE "backbone staff" was hired at the University of Wisconsin–Madison and attended national trainings on Collective Impact provided by the Foundation Strategy Group (FSG) and the Tamarack Institute. During this time, staff began determining healthTIDE's applicability to the pre-conditions of CI and initiated one-to-one meetings with partners to collect perspectives on statewide coordination. From these meetings, there was consistency with the preconditions of CI by having clearly identified champions, resources, and the need to "do something," have "a united front," and be purposeful about "equity in voices."

The backbone staff also began convening a group of local and state advisors, "champions," to discuss using the Collective Impact framework and forming a common agenda. This group of more than 40 advisors came from multiple sectors including government (local and state-level), nonprofit organizations, advocacy organizations, university-research institutions, funders, health systems, and businesses. The advisors agreed to implement the CI framework for healthTIDE and drafted a common agenda around preventing obesity in children and adolescents through implementing policy, systems, and environmental changes. During this time, backbone staff helped lead an effort to secure a new, five-year, targeted grant for obesity prevention from the WPP. This effort was later called the Wisconsin Obesity Prevention Initiative, which has further supported the infrastructure for healthTIDE and allowed backbone staff an opportunity for additional CI training and technical assistance provided by the Tamarack Institute. In addition, once the WPP funds were secured, the Wisconsin State Alliance of YMCAs, the University of Wisconsin-Extension, Cooperative Extension, and DHS supported backbone staff through monetary co-investments. Currently, the healthTIDE backbone staff has grown to seven full-time equivalents.

As healthTIDE grew in both partner involvement and backbone staff, four teams were established and have utilized the Collective Impact framework by creating the five conditions for CI to address obesity. The teams are: early childhood (Healthy Early), schools, active communities, and healthy food retail. Each team works together to implement the CI conditions at its own pace, and healthTIDE backbone staff provide opportunities for strategic convening and facilitation, connection and alignment of mutually–reinforcing activities, and support for coordinated communications and shared metrics. Figure 8.1 visualizes a timeline of the obesity prevention and coordination efforts in Wisconsin.

Broadly, all four teams have collectively identified a common agenda (common priorities) and defined mutually reinforcing activities to advance the team's common agenda. Examples of these priorities are highlighted in Figure 8.2. They also have established continuous communication techniques and processes. Through working with the teams, backbone staff have found shared measurement efforts to be more difficult to implement, including the determination of indicators and collaborative data sharing.

Due to the complex nature of obesity, there is a need for shorter-term progress indicators rather than solely measuring body mass index (BMI). Specifically, the

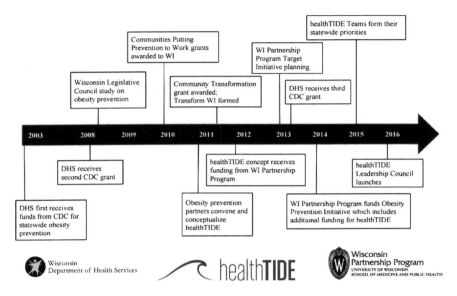

FIGURE 8.1 History of Obesity Prevention and Coordination Efforts in Wisconsin

Schools Team	Active Communities Team	Healthy Food Retail Team	Early Childhood Team
Coordinating School Health: CDC's Whole school, whole community, whole child model	Community design Active transportation Safe places to play	Increase consumer demand for healthier foods and beverages in: Restaurants	Caregiver education Childcare licensing standards Wisconsin's YoungStar criteria
Healthy school meals		Grocery and convenience stores	Family engagement
Shared metrics/data			
Physical activity in schools			
Quality physical education			

FIGURE 8.2 healthTIDE Team Priorities

measurement of PSE change is difficult with few established metrics in the literature. The processes for implementing these five conditions of CI has varied for each team, though there have also been illuminating similarities. Each team has experienced progress toward and/or success achieving a PSE change. An example of a PSE "win" from the early childhood team centered on the team's desire to influence existing regulatory and quality rating and improvement systems for child care centers and providers. Through the common agenda setting process, the team decided to strengthen the quality rating and improvement system (YoungStar) for Wisconsin childcare centers. Accomplishing this change resulted from: strategic alignment of early childhood and public health partners and opportunities; utilizing shared data, resources, and technical assistance; providing formal recommendations; and outlining an evidence–based rationale for including nutrition and physical activity criteria to strengthen YoungStar. Additional successes and challenges related to implementation of the Collective Impact conditions are discussed further in the results section.

Since 2011 when Kania and Kramer published their piece on "Collective Impact," this approach to coalition action has been particularly pervasive in practice in a variety of fields, including public health and obesity prevention efforts (Christens 2016). Collective Impact has meanwhile been criticized as a top-down approach, and it has as of yet been subject to few rigorous empirical investigations or evaluations (Wolff 2016). As its critics have pointed out, the widespread adoption of CI by funders and practitioners has caused many to lose sight of longer standing and more rigorously evaluated approaches to coalition action (Butterfoss 2008).

For these reasons, healthTIDE began to look for ways to augment the model including paying closer attention to power and community engagement within healthTIDE's work and framing health equity as a guiding principle. healthTIDE also determined that the discussion around shared metrics had to occur earlier in the priority setting process and that a more defined theory of change could assist in determining process and outcome evaluation indicators. Staff experimented with technology (e.g., social media, peer-to-peer networking platforms) to enhance continuous communication techniques.

Furthermore, healthTIDE sought to learn about and incorporate additional community change approaches while working to implement Collective Impact. Specifically, staff examined grassroots community organizing (Christens 2015) approaches to collaborative action that prioritize equity and justice (Wolff 2016) and adoption of the CI approach by practitioners (Weaver 2016). Collective Impact was the primary guiding framework of healthTIDE during the time of this study, and backbone staff and partners involved received many types of training on the implementation of this model and have adopted the goals and terminology of the model in their day-to-day work. Because CI remains a relatively untested model—for instance, there has not yet been a study of the application of this model to statewide coordinated work on obesity prevention—the central research question for this chapter is: what are the strengths and weaknesses of Collective Impact as a guiding framework for statewide coordinated action to prevent obesity?

Methods

The analysis and findings presented here are drawn from an ongoing mixed methods descriptive study and a developmental evaluation (Gamble 2008; Patton 2011) of the efforts of healthTIDE to achieve policy, systems, and environmental changes to prevent childhood obesity in Wisconsin. This work has been conducted collaboratively between healthTIDE leaders (Korth and Meinen) and partners at the University of Wisconsin–Madison (Hilgendorf, Breuer, and Christens).

Quantitative data are drawn from a web–based network survey conducted in 2015. healthTIDE leaders identified known stakeholders in obesity prevention efforts in Wisconsin to complete the survey, including government staff, nonprofit leaders, local and state public health staff, clinicians, and academic researchers, among others. The questions in the survey tried to gather information about characteristics of stakeholders, their perceptions about the issue of obesity and priorities for action, and their perceptions of the progress and impacts of healthTIDE efforts to date, including progress in setting the five conditions of Collective Impact for each of the teams convened by healthTIDE (Kania 2011). The survey had 281 stakeholder respondents, a 23% response rate. For the survey items concerning progress in the conditions of Collective Impact, 83 respondents completed these items for one or more of the teams (30% of respondents) for a total of 107 responses for all teams.

Qualitative data for this study are drawn from several sources, including quarterly interviews with healthTIDE leaders since 2014; observations of healthTIDE team meetings; reviews of archival records of healthTIDE teams, especially meeting minutes; and interviews conducted with core partners of the healthTIDE early childhood team (Healthy Early) in a previous, related study (Meinen 2016). Documentation of one-to-one connections made by healthTIDE leaders with stakeholders in obesity prevention to build the network or advance initiatives was also reviewed and analyzed. As part of the ongoing developmental evaluation activities for healthTIDE's work, healthTIDE leaders serving as co-authors on this paper (Korth and Meinen) have documented and drawn on their own observations of utilizing Collective Impact as a source of qualitative data.

The concept of CI offered by Kania and Kramer was used as an initial framework for analysis. Both quantitative and qualitative data were used to examine each of the five conditions of Collective Impact and the process of seeking to implement them within healthTIDE. Items from the network survey concerning CI concepts were analyzed using descriptive statistics. Qualitative data were first coded and analyzed deductively around the five conditions of Collective Impact. After the initial analysis, qualitative data were further analyzed through an inductive process to examine the work of healthTIDE beyond what the CI framework afforded.

The next section presents results and ways in which CI helped the efforts of healthTIDE as well as challenges experienced in trying to achieve the conditions of CI. Drawing on this analysis, a description is provided of healthTIDE's response to these challenges in identifying the potential limitations of the Collective Impact model and the modifications, augmentations, and other adjustments that may be necessary to achieve collaborative progress toward complex issues like obesity.

Results

Table 8.1 presents results from the 2015 network survey by summarizing the percentage of respondents who "agreed" with statements regarding progress on achieving the conditions for Collective Impact for each healthTIDE team and overall. These findings are described further below in concert with the qualitative findings for each of the five CI conditions.

TABLE 8.1 Level of Agreement for Progress in Each Collective Impact Condition by healthTIDE Team and All

	Early Childhood (n = 26)	Schools (n = 30)	Active Communities (n = 33)	Food Retail (n = 18)	All (n = 107)
The convened group is committed to a common agenda.	88%	90%	79%	56%	80%
The convened group has the structural support (backbone) to ensure effective collective work.	69%	50%	45%	44%	52%
The convened group engages in continuous and effective communication.	65%	50%	45%	28%	49%
The convened group uses shared measures to document and examine progress.	62%	23%	30%	6%	32%
The convened group engages in mutually reinforcing and complementary activities.	65%	70%	52%	17%	54%

Backbone Support

Seeing unmet needs for coordination around obesity prevention efforts in Wisconsin and promise in the Collective Impact approach, healthTIDE was formed as backbone support staff. But staff soon realized that it is challenging and perhaps not best practice to self–identify as the backbone. Doing so presented some degree of role confusion and difficulty determining what the added value of healthTIDE was among established organizations. This process continues to take time and considerable trust–building to resolve, including discussions to explore and define the roles and expectations of backbone staff in relationship to organizations that already exist. Upon reflection, a process of nomination, identification of potential needs and gaps, determination of specific value added by a backbone staff, and vetting amongst partners to select a backbone may be preferable.

healthTIDE staff provides backbone support for the statewide scope of the network including convening the healthTIDE leadership council whose role is to provide guidance on the direction of the healthTIDE network with shared input and leadership from the backbone. The leadership council has assisted the backbone in creating a governance structure led by a "theory of change" specific to the healthTIDE network to showcase the value of the network and the staff as a whole. Ingrained in this theory of change are staff roles to: connect with people and organizations to build and maintain diverse partnerships; convene and facilitate meetings of healthTIDE teams; and catalyze and identify resources with an eye toward taking collective action. See Figure 8.3 for roles of healthTIDE backbone staff.

One interviewed team member commented, "[backbone staff] are providing us with the tools and the resources and the plans as to how to move forward." Figure 8.4 presents results for items in the 2015 network survey specific to healthTIDE backbone staff functionality. Backbone staff often identifies and leverages funding opportunities while facilitating processes to support collaboration among partners and organizations rather than duplicative or competitive grant

---

Connect: Build and maintain partnerships; Provide updates on progress of priorities, status of evaluation tools/techniques/data, and process improvement ideas; Seek and find technical assistance providers and content expertise as capacity building resources

Convene: Leverage existing knowledge and relationships to link similar efforts together; Set-up leadership council meetings; Convene and facilitate healthTIDE team meetings

Catalyze: Develop communication strategies including website and social media assets; Provide recommendations to and take strategic direction from the leadership council

Collective Action: Provide management of priority, collective projects; Actively seek funding to support healthTIDE priorities and infrastructure

---

FIGURE 8.3 Roles of healthTIDE Backbone Staff

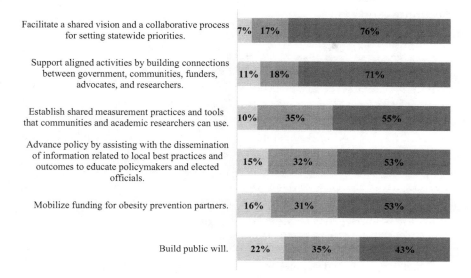

Facilitate a shared vision and a collaborative process for setting statewide priorities. — 7% | 17% | 76%

Support aligned activities by building connections between government, communities, funders, advocates, and researchers. — 11% | 18% | 71%

Establish shared measurement practices and tools that communities and academic researchers can use. — 10% | 35% | 55%

Advance policy by assisting with the dissemination of information related to local best practices and outcomes to educate policymakers and elected officials. — 15% | 32% | 53%

Mobilize funding for obesity prevention partners. — 16% | 31% | 53%

Build public will. — 22% | 35% | 43%

■ Very Ineffective/Ineffective   ■ Neither Ineffective nor Effective   ■ Effective/Very Effective

FIGURE 8.4 Effectiveness of healthTIDE in Performing Backbone Functions

writing. Over time, backbone staff has also taken the lead on communication activities to use mainstream and social media to build public will for obesity prevention. In addition, backbone staff has worked to support advancing public policy through work related to aligning health advocacy organizations with each other hoping to work together to advance statewide policies.

A series of reflective meetings among healthTIDE staff and key partners in 2015, identified and discussed several issues related to the work of backbone staff. healthTIDE staff felt that many participants in the network did not fully recognize or remember the importance of backbone work in successfully aligning activities and achieving outcomes—especially the many hours spent in behind-the-scenes relationship development and coordination. Nor did they recognize the staff time and skill this work required.

Furthermore, partners often saw the backbone staff as "implementers of the common agenda" versus working to connect and align efforts and resources to achieve the agenda. Since healthTIDE staff soon found their capacity exceeded, it has been difficult to get healthTIDE participants to provide for or to assist in funding for additional backbone staff. Even though a majority of interviewed and surveyed healthTIDE team members value the work of the backbone and find it effective (see Figure 8.4), it has been difficult to adequately staff the backbone with a statewide scope. healthTIDE also has found that the work of backbone staff must vary and evolve over time given the dynamics of specific teams, political context, and progress; all of which further complicate effective staffing.

Common Agenda

Leading up to the formation of healthTIDE, stakeholders in obesity prevention (from diverse fields) had noted a desire for "a united front" and better coordination of efforts. healthTIDE has found that a process of defining a common agenda can help "ground" the work and make the efforts and the individual roles within them more concrete for stakeholders. However, not finding many resources or published accounts of how to come to a common agenda in the collective impact model, healthTIDE staff developed and then refined its own process as it was implemented within the four teams.

This process began with mapping of key stakeholders in a given obesity–related area (e.g., schools, healthy food retail) including state and local government professionals, nonprofit and advocacy organization staff, academic researchers, business executives, and community leaders. healthTIDE staff then pursued concerted relationship building with these stakeholders. Borrowing from the community organizing practice of "one-to-ones" (Christens 2010), healthTIDE staff met individually with stakeholders to gain better understanding of their interests and priorities for obesity prevention, as well as their potential resources (e.g., knowledge, materials, funding, staffing, relationships) and constraints. In 2015, for instance, healthTIDE staff engaged in over 100 one-to-one meetings with stakeholders. healthTIDE staff then planned a convening of those stakeholders with shared or intersecting interests that could move obesity prevention forward in a particular area.

Over the course of two or three convened meetings, healthTIDE staff then led stakeholders in discussion and activities to understand the challenges of obesity in a specific area and the possibilities for intervention. They sought to develop a shared vocabulary and identify positive work already happening. From there, healthTIDE staff guided stakeholders to consider possible actions by reviewing the evidence base for interventions while also openly discussing strategy feasibility for various stakeholders (i.e., what they are comfortable and willing to put their resources and names behind).

With this list of potential priority actions, healthTIDE staff then facilitated a group consensus process to select three to five top priorities to pursue, ideally incorporating a mix of policy, systems, and environmental changes and a range of interventions and required resources. Each team succeeded in defining priorities that outlined the policy, systems, and/or environmental changes they wanted to see move forward collectively. The process of agreeing on these top priorities took approximately one year for each of the four teams. The early childhood team noticed its efforts shift over time due to changing factors (e.g., organizational staffing, grant opportunities, partnerships); however, intentionally revisiting the defined priorities helped guide their efforts and keep them on track. Though the agenda-setting process was time intensive, the early childhood team members viewed it as a smooth and worthwhile process (Meinen 2016).

healthTIDE partners who were interviewed and surveyed agreed that their teams had identified and committed to a common agenda (see Table 8.1), yet some challenges still remained. healthTIDE staff observed strong and positive initial commitment from partners in this process, but often noted less active involvement in implementing plans to advance priorities. Teams often formed small working groups, but these groups seemed to need the convening and facilitation support of healthTIDE staff in order to achieve the desired productivity. Large meetings of the teams often ended with lists of "to-dos" and suggested follow-up activities with few volunteers to work on them. Often it seemed that partners assumed the facilitators (or backbone staff) would implement next steps or follow through on these activities. This dynamic added to the workload and sense of overwhelm often felt by backbone staff.

To combat this expectation, healthTIDE staff began to intentionally shift its support. One key shift was within the facilitation technique to better coordinate task delegation. This was done in a collaborative manner by engaging team participants in discussions around what had to be done and who would do it. This process naturally identified additional team leaders to take on tasks associated with the common agenda. healthTIDE's communication strategies had to shift to better explain how the backbone staff are not the implementers of the team priorities, utilizing technology to have web-based "team hubs" to keep the work organized, and provide regular feedback on progress toward priorities.

healthTIDE also struggled with engaging specific types of stakeholders in the common agenda process and the ongoing work. The staff values the experiences and contributions of community members—especially those most directly affected by obesity-related issues and who are most likely to be excluded from community decision-making. However, they found it particularly difficult to effectively reach out to community members and to address barriers and power dynamics to enable authentic engagement. Moreover, stakeholders from the private sector have been reluctant to engage fully in the common agenda process, expressing opinions that the process was too "time-consuming" and "drawn out."

Mutually-Reinforcing Activities

healthTIDE teams identified priorities that aligned with the overarching common agenda of obesity prevention, and for each priority, developed action plans and volunteer groups to move them forward. The plans attempted to leverage the strengths and capacities of partner organizations and enhance their impact through strategic coordination. healthTIDE staff has observed high interest among stakeholders in partnering broadly, but in many cases, waning interest as the work proceeds to design plans to advance the priorities and taking action on these plans. As described above, this dynamic can burden the backbone staff and can tend to undermine the sustainability of the teams. In some teams, movement from prioritization to planning to implementation has worked well. In these cases, backbone staff often support the ongoing conversation and hold partners accountable for the deliverables outlined in the plan. Survey responses (see Table 8.1) appear to reflect this variation in experiences with establishing mutually-reinforcing activities.

Interviewees have identified how increased activity alignment seemed to create opportunities that were previously out of reach because of the constraints within which individual agencies and organizations operate. For instance, some grants are available only to nonprofit organizations, while others are available only to government agencies and researchers. Yet coordination and alignment discussions have helped healthTIDE partners identify lead applicants and coordinate activities in successful grant applications that fit the requirements of grant opportunities while also embedding support of partners and activities that leverage the capacity of the broader team.

In fact, several persons interviewed mentioned joint grant writing and implementation as being critical to their efforts in developing mutually-reinforcing activities. The process of grant writing, interviewees noted, often spurred discussions about related and overlapping activities that they felt would not likely happen otherwise, including sometimes challenging conversations around "turf."

Collaborative grant writing also brought partners to the table in a joint effort who previously would have seen each other as "competition" for the same pool of resources. Complementary grants received and implemented helped to further sort out partner roles and actualized specific activities for particular partners who work in concert with others. An interviewed member of the early childhood team said the grant writing process "allowed [them] to figure out where [the] roles and strengths are of different people and organizations." Grants also provide incentives for partners to stay engaged in collaborative work, for both the added funds they provide as well as the accountability required (i.e., reporting progress to funders).

Continued one-to-one meetings by healthTIDE staff helped retain partners and ensure accountability and support in the teams. One-to-ones with additional stakeholders can bring new partners into the teams and boost work on the priorities. For example, one-to-one meetings created an opportunity to showcase short videos created by University of Wisconsin-Madison Athletics in partnership with healthTIDE. These videos were designed to increase physical activity for children and adolescents and are now available for use by teachers in Wisconsin schools.

healthTIDE staff also makes connections with timely opportunities to align the work of statewide and national efforts external to the teams. These connections have had promising results including forming partnerships and leveraging grant opportunities that led to policy and system changes. For example, bringing interested food system and early childhood partners together around the concept of farm to early childhood education (Farm to ECE) resulted in applying for and receiving a grant from the Kellogg Foundation. This grant focused on state-level policy change to support increasing access to local fresh fruits and vegetables in group and family child care centers.

Continuous Communication

Continuous communication efforts of healthTIDE vary in scope. They include activities: internal to the teams, across the teams, between the teams and healthTIDE staff, across all partners and stakeholders engaged with the healthTIDE network, and with the public in general. Regular and effective communication informs partners of healthTIDE and the teams' current activities, supports timely progress in advancing teams' plans, and encourages cross-promotion of ideas and strategies. Communication efforts support consistent messaging among partners on issues related to childhood obesity and can inform stakeholders about new resources or new opportunities (e.g., grant announcements, public policy commenting periods) to leverage the work.

Continuous communication has been difficult to fully implement due to the multiple layers of communication needed for the statewide work of healthTIDE. The diverse audiences and potential communication platforms complicate these efforts further. Therefore, healthTIDE has had to prioritize communication practices based on urgent needs and current resources. Many of the teams have succeeded by focusing first on internal communication practices by developing a team-based informative "one–pager" outlining team priorities, contact lists, shared folders for team resources and working documents, and improved orientation practices for new members. These approaches naturally shifted to discussions on how to better engage more distant or less involved members through platforms such as conference lines, team websites, and online social media.

Though these attempts at improving external communication succeeded in some regard, many teams still struggle with knowing how to best engage members from around Wisconsin. As an example, team members have noted their struggles to determine the "best" type of communication to use with different stakeholders and when. One team found emails and text messages to be very effective in supporting the communication regarding their leadership; however, they have struggled with effectively engaging other members of the team. While this team has tried to use distance technology (i.e., conference calls and webinar programs) to engage team members in their meetings, the limitations of this technology may aggravate rather than resolve feelings of lacking buy-in. The statewide reach of healthTIDE teams challenges communication efforts further.

Given the variety of audiences and interests, it has been difficult for healthTIDE to meet all of its communication needs while also building healthTIDE's backbone and network infrastructure. As such, the healthTIDE website and social media platforms have been the primary tools for external communications. Survey responses (see Table 8.1) further suggest a mix of experiences with healthTIDE communication practices.

Shared Measurement

As with the communication efforts, many healthTIDE teams have delayed work around establishing shared measurement until after other Collective Impact conditions were implemented and efforts to define and structure their collective work felt more secure. Survey respondents (see Table 8.1) as well as interviewees typically noted the least progress in their shared measurement efforts. One member stated,

> There certainly are [success] stories,. . . but I wouldn't say we have [an] evaluation plan and that these are our indicators and this is how we're collecting information to find out if we've met our objectives with these indicators. We haven't done a lot there. We need some dedicated time and expertise.

When healthTIDE teams invested time into shared measurement work, success has been found most frequently by determining some potential sources of data that support the priorities determined by the team. Some teams found that agreement around a few shared measures can be more difficult than anticipated, as each partnering member or organization collects different measures and may have differing views around their meaningfulness. Teams have also come across situations when metrics for identified priorities do not currently exist especially regarding policy, systems, and environmental change strategies. Teams also sometimes find the process of sharing measures more difficult than expected, given data sharing procedures and restrictions, as well as varying time lags for data uploads and cleaning.

Discussion

This study examined healthTIDE, a statewide network for obesity prevention in Wisconsin that has sought to achieve and utilize Collective Impact. While most applications of the CI model have been at the level of a municipality or county, this may be the first study to examine CI on obesity prevention at the state level. This study presents a unique opportunity to examine potential strengths and weaknesses of the Collective Impact model for catalyzing and guiding efforts addressing complex issues, such as obesity, on a large, geographic scale. The findings from this study have practical implications for other groups seeking to work with the CI model as well as scholarly implications for those who study CI and other models for community change.

The Collective Impact model has been valuable to the work of healthTIDE in some ways but found lacking in others. The model has offered guidance to healthTIDE in orienting itself as a backbone organization, including the roles and functions it should perform. Having funding for specified and skilled backbone staff has been especially valuable for developing a common agenda and priorities within the teams, supporting alignment planning, and mobilizing funding.

A study of the application of the Collective Impact model by the Tenderloin Healthy Corner Store Coalition (Flood 2015) similarly recognized the importance of dedicated and funded backbone staff for convening partners and facilitating diverse partners through collaborative processes. Indeed, the value of an intentional infrastructure built and supported by dedicated staff that is made possible by a "backbone" organization may receive renewed attention in collaborative health promotion efforts because of its prominence in the CI model (Friesen 2015; Grumbach 2017; Rudolph 2013).

However, at least in the case of healthTIDE, a backbone organization seeking to operate across an entire state is complex and time-consuming and involves considerable skill and energy to build and maintain productive inter-organizational relationships across sectors and issue areas. Despite being relatively "well-funded" and having a staff of seven full-time equivalents, healthTIDE staff have been under-resourced and pressed for time to accomplish their goals. The implications of this finding may be especially significant to those working collaboratively on many other social issues and/or with a statewide scope where less funding is available.

The successes that healthTIDE has experienced, however, are also owed to other ideas beyond the Collective Impact model and often sought to compensate for the limitations of the model. Several useful practices emerged as healthTIDE experienced the limitations of the CI model and tried to respond. Strategies of grassroots organizing have been especially valuable to healthTIDE, especially the practice of one-to-ones (Speer 1995; Speer 2014). Indeed, many healthTIDE successes depended on intentional relationship development, an aspect of coalition work that is sometimes overlooked or underemphasized, as it is in the Collective Impact model (Gillam 2016). healthTIDE therefore learned about and practiced relational community organizing techniques—like one-to-ones, and have engaged in these meetings with partners throughout its work. healthTIDE found this practice to be crucial for bringing diverse partners to the teams, keeping them engaged, and shaping priorities and strategies based on partners' interests and capacities.

Other valuable strategies for healthTIDE have been rooted not in specific models, but rather pieced together from prior experience, insights, and trial-and-error. The common agenda setting process that healthTIDE staff developed was a result of not finding enough practical guidance for how to achieve a common agenda, especially when bringing together partners who had not interacted with one another before and may initially see little common ground. Based on group facilitation processes, Appreciative Inquiry techniques, "Theory U" ideas about change management (Scharmer 2007), and iterative refinements as they applied this process within the teams, healthTIDE developed its own common agenda setting process. This process, when applied, helped all healthTIDE teams define a shared vision for their work together and set the stage for detailed planning and coordinated action.

Through experience, healthTIDE staff also found it valuable to keep "an ear to the ground" for emerging opportunities and to maintain a degree of nimbleness to pursue especially promising opportunities. Whether these opportunities become apparent through one-to-one meetings or from scanning grant announcements—and though they do not always bear fruit—healthTIDE found that some of its greatest accomplishments came from connections outside the four teams, including leveraged dollars and opened windows for influencing state-level policies.

However important and valuable, this "dot-connecting" work takes time, depends on relationships and systems-thinking skills, is hard to teach others, and can be difficult to justify to funders especially when many efforts are not guaranteed to pay off. If others engaged in collective action efforts pursue connectivity, this may be an area ripe for peer-to-peer learning or scholarly study to identify best practices and assess outcomes.

Experience has also shown healthTIDE that grant proposals can sometimes help teams coalesce around mutually-reinforcing activities, as the proposal writing process can encourage conversations about roles that cut through territoriality and can formalize some accountability for follow through. This is certainly a promising strategy for other collaborative efforts, although it may be less relevant to coalitions working on issues that are not health-related since there are fewer funding opportunities in the health field.

Some aspects of the Collective Impact model are challenging for healthTIDE, and effective solutions remain elusive. Continuous communication continues to challenge healthTIDE teams. Given the statewide scope of its work, comparisons with other CI efforts that typically have a more local focus, have had limited value. Indeed, some CI implementers have found regular in–person meetings essential for effective continuous communication (Flood 2015). However, the same practice in the statewide work of healthTIDE can aggravate feelings of division and isolation among partners who do not reside in the region of the state capitol. While healthTIDE is working with various communication technologies to spur additional ongoing and two-way engagement, geographic distance and connecting with partners in more rural areas continue to be challenging.

Little progress in shared measurement has been made in the healthTIDE teams, most often due to feelings of overwhelm in trying to establish some other conditions of Collective Impact. Uncertainties also exist as to what measurement techniques to use for something as complex as obesity and its related policy, systems, and environmental changes in ways that will be meaningful to a diverse set of partners. One idea of possible use to others applying the CI model is to develop and implement one central data collection effort rather than try to choose or merge existing partner data. The Tenderloin Healthy Corner Store Coalition anchored its shared measurement in a corner store survey designed specifically around strategies the coalition was pursuing toward its common agenda. The Coalition found this process valuable for assessing progress and adapting strategies, as well as for spurring continuous communication (Flood 2015).

Given the challenges of evaluating policy and advocacy efforts, especially for complex issues influenced by many systems, healthTIDE is still uncertain how the work to establish shared measurement will progress. The identified issues are related to obtaining sufficiently comprehensive, reliable, inexpensive, and disaggregated data that are collected with enough frequency to measure progress in a timely manner.

Some difficulties experienced by healthTIDE, however, may speak less to the uniqueness of the effort and more to weaknesses in the concept of Collective Impact as well as the resources available for training and technical assistance. For example, healthTIDE has struggled to engage residents who are not representing organizational constituencies. Others have pointed to this weakness of the Collective Impact approach (Klaus 2016; Raderstrong 2016).

Furthermore, it is possible that organizational representatives in the CI effort either have vested interests in the status quo or disincentives for challenging the interests of powerful actors in the state (e.g., parts of the food industry). As a model, Collective Impact has been critiqued for lack of an analysis of power (Christens 2015) and as such, dynamics like these may undermine the overall effort while providing no tools to address these issues (LeChasseur 2016).

Conclusion

In summary, healthTIDE has made important strides toward achieving policy, systems, and environmental changes to prevent obesity in Wisconsin. Some successes have been supported by the use of the Collective Impact approach. For example, the concept of backbone infrastructure and the functions that the backbone staff provides in guiding efforts have been important to the initiative's progress.

Other elements of the CI framework, however, have proven difficult to implement in healthTIDE's work. Continuous communication, for example, has been more elusive. This may be partially due to the particular context and topical focus of healthTIDE. Finally, through its attempt to adhere as closely as possible to the CI framework, healthTIDE became aware of some weaknesses and omissions in the model as originally conceived. Many of these have been simultaneously described in critiques (Wolff 2016) and updates (e.g., Collective Impact 3.0) to the framework.

Coalitions and collaboratives seeking to truly transform systems must therefore not only learn from the Collective Impact model, but also from other approaches and tactics for achieving policy, systems, and environmental change. For example, Wolff and colleagues present an alternative set of principles that can guide efforts aiming for systemic transformation and draw insights from longer-standing models of community change, such as Community Coalition Action Theory (Butterfoss 2008) and grassroots community organizing (Speer 1995; Speer 2014). Changing systems and policies is complicated and difficult work and unfortunately there does not seem to be a single set of simple conditions or a single framework that can be applied in all cases. It is therefore important that researchers and practitioners continue to experiment with and learn from a variety of strategies and approaches rather than coalesce around a single model of collaboration in order to advance community change.

References

Butterfoss, F. D., Kegler, M. C., & Francisco, V. T. (2008) "Mobilizing organizations for health promotion: Theories of organizational change," in K. Glanz, B. K. Rimer, & K. Viswanath (eds.) *Health behavior and health education: Theory, research and practice (4th ed.)*, San Francisco, CA: Jossey-Bass.

Christens, B. D. (2010) Public relationship building in grassroots community organizing: Relational intervention for individual and systems change. *Journal of Community Psychology*, *38*(7), 886–900. doi:10.1002/jcop.20403

Christens, B. D. & Inzeo, P. T. (2015) Widening the view: Situating collective impact among frameworks for community-led change. *Community Development*, *46*(4), 420–435. doi:10.1080/15575330.2015.1061680

Christens, B. D., Inzeo, P. T., Meinen, A., Hilgendorf, A. E., Berns, R., Korth, A., Pollard, E. C., McCall, A., Adams, A., & Stedman, J. (2016) Community-led collaborative action to prevent obesity. *Wisconsin Medical Journal*, *115*(5), 259–263.

Economos, C. & Blondin, S. (2014) Obesity interventions in the community. *Current Obesity Reports*, *3*(2), 199–205. doi:10.1007/s13679-014-0102-2

Eggers, S., Remington, P. L., Ryan, K., Nieto, J., Peppard, P., & Malecki, K. M. (2016) Obesity prevalence and health consequences: Findings from the Survey of the Health of Wisconsin 2008–2013. *Wisconsin Medical Journal*, *115*(5), 228–232.

Flood, J., Minkler, M., Hennessey Lavery, S., Estrada, J., & Falbe, J. (2015) The collective impact model and its potential for health promotion: Overview and case study of a healthy retail initiative in San Francisco. *Health Education & Behavior*, *42*(5), 654–668.

Friesen, C.A., Hormuth, L.J., & Cardarelli, T.L. (2015) Community-based participatory initiatives to increase breastfeeding rates in Indiana. *Journal of Human Lactation*, *31*(4), 600–606.

Gamble, J. A. (2008) *A developmental evaluation primer*. Montreal: JW McConnell Family Foundation.

Grumbach, K., Vargas, R.A., Fleisher, P., Aragon, T.J., Chung, L., Chawla, C., Yant, A., Garcia, E.R., Santiago, A., Lang, P.L., Jones, P., Liu, W., & Schmidt, L.A. (2017) Achieving health equity through community engagement in translating evidence to policy: The San Francisco Health Improvement Partnership, 2010–2016. *Preventing Chronic Disease*, *14*(E27).

Halfon, N., Larson, K., & Slusser, W. (2013) Associations between obesity and comorbid mental health, developmental, and physical health conditions in a nationally representative sample of US children aged 10 to 17. *Academic Pediatrics*, *13*(1), 6–13.

Huang, T. T., Drewnowski, A., Kumanyika, S. K., & Glass, T. A. (2009) A systems-oriented multilevel framework for addressing obesity in the 21st century. *Preventing Chronic Disease*, *6*(3).

Kania, J. & Kramer, M. (2011) Collective impact. *Stanford Social Innovation Review*, *2011*(Winter), 36–41.

Klaus, T. W. & Saunders, E. (2016) Using collective impact in support of communitywide teen pregnancy prevention initiatives. *Community Development*, *47*(2), 241–258. doi:10.1080/15575330.2015.1131172

LeChasseur, K. (2016) Re-examining power and privilege in collective impact. *Community Development*, *47*(2), 225–240. doi:10.1080/15575330.2016.1140664

Mialon, M., Swinburn, B., & Sacks, G. (2015) A proposed approach to systematically identify and monitor the corporate political activity of the food industry with respect to public health using publicly available information. *Obesity Reviews*, *16*(7), 519–530. doi:10.1111/obr.12289

Office of Disease Prevention and Health Promotion (ODPHP) (2014) *Healthy People 2020.* www.healthypeople.gov. Accessed March 15, 2016.

Ogden, C. L., Carroll, M. D., Kit, B. K., & Flegal, K. M. (2014) Prevalence of childhood and adult obesity in the united states, 2011–2012. *JAMA: The Journal of the American Medical Association, 311*(8), 806–814. doi:10.1001/jama.2014.732

Patton, M. Q. (2011) Developmental evaluation: Applying complexity concepts to enhance innovation and use. Hove, UK: Guilford Press.

Pulgarón, E. R. (2013) Childhood obesity: A review of increased risk for physical and psychological comorbidities. *Clinical Therapeutics, 35*(1), A18–A32. doi:10.1016/j.clinthera.2012.12.014

Raderstrong, J. & Boyea-Robinson, T. (2016) The why and how of working with communities through collective impact. *Community Development, 47*(2), 181–193. doi:10.1080/15575330.2015.1130072

Reed, S. F., Viola, J. J., & Lynch, K. (2014) School and community-based childhood obesity: Implications for policy and practice. *Journal of Prevention & Intervention in the Community, 42*(2), 87–94. doi:10.1080/10852352.2014.881172

Rudolph, L., Caplan, J., Mitchell, C., Ben-Moshe, K., & Dillon, L. (2013) Health in all policies: Improving health through intersectoral collaboration. Washington DC: National Academy of Sciences.

Scharmer, C. (2007) Theory U: Leading from the Future as it Emerges. Cambridge, MA: The Society for Organizational Learning.

Spahr, C., Wells, A., Christens, B. D., Pollard, E., LaGro, J., Morales, A., Dennis, S., Hilgendorf, A. E., Meinen, A., Korth, A., Gaddis, J., Schoeller, D., Carrel, A., & Adams, A. K. (2016) Developing a strategy menu for community-level obesity prevention. *Wisconsin Medical Journal, 115*(5) 264–268.

Speer, P. W. & Hughey, J. (1995) Community organizing: An ecological route to empowerment and power. *American Journal of Community Psychology, 23*(5), 729–748. doi:10.1007/BF02506989

Speer, P. W. & Christens, B. D. (2014) Community organizing. In V. Chien & S. Wolfe (Eds.), *Foundations of community psychology practice.* (pp. 220–36). Thousand Oaks, CA: Sage Publications.

The State of Obesity (2016) Adult obesity in the United States. Retrieved from: http://stateofobesity.org/adult-obesity/

Story, M., Kaphingst, K. M., Robinson-O'Brien, R., & Glanz, K. (2008) Creating healthy food and eating environments: Policy and environmental approaches. *Annual Review of Public Health, 29*, 253–72. doi:10.1146/annurev.publhealth.29.020907.090926

Swinburn, B. A., Sacks, G., Hall, K. D., McPherson, K., Finegood, D. T., Moodie, M. L., & Gortmaker, S. L. (2011) The global obesity pandemic: Shaped by global drivers and local environments. *The Lancet, 378*(9793), 804–814.

Wang, Y. C., McPherson, K., Marsh, T., Gortmaker, S. L., & Brown, M. (2011) Health and economic burden of the projected obesity trends in the USA and the UK. *The Lancet, 378*(9793), 815–825.

Weaver, L. (2016) Possible: Transformational change in collective impact. *Community Development, 47*(2), 274–283. doi:10.1080/15575330.2016.1138977

Wolff, T. (2016) Voices from the field: 10 places where collective impact gets it wrong. *The Nonprofit Quarterly*, April 28, 2016. nonprofitquarterly.org/2016/04/28/voices-from-the-field-10-places-where-collective-impact-gets-it-wrong/

Wolff, T., Minkler, M., Wolfe, S. M., Berkowitz, B., Bowen, L., Butterfoss, F. D., Christens, B. D., Francisco, V. T., Himmelman, A. T., & Lee, K. S. (2016) Collaborating for equity and justice: Moving beyond collective impact. *The Nonprofit Quarterly, 23*(4), 42–53.

9

WHEN CULTURAL DIFFERENCES MAKE A DIFFERENCE

The Case of Community Change in an Arab Community in Israel

Smadar Somekh, Yehonatan Almog, and Fida Nijim-Ektelat

Introduction

This chapter addresses the challenges involved in implementing a Collective Impact approach in cultural contexts that diverge from the majority culture. More specifically, it addresses the role of backbone organizations in addressing the challenges posed by cultural diversity and the need to adapt form and substance to the cultural norms of minority groups.

The importance of backbones is examined in the context of the Better Together comprehensive community change initiative in Israel, which has been implemented in a wide range of diverse communities. The focus is on the implementation of the program in the Arab community of Arrabe in northern Israel. The Arab population represents 21% of the population of the State of Israel, and while a portion of this population lives in mixed Jewish–Arab cities, the majority lives in cities where the population is fully or predominantly Arab.

Subsequent analyses build on the literature on cultural adaptation in general and in the context of CI initiatives. The case study adds to the rather limited variety of examples in the literature of successful efforts to address cultural barriers. It makes a unique contribution in illustrating how addressing these barriers requires both determination and willingness to compromise. It emphasizes a need for a multiyear perspective regarding challenges and for an openness to engage in an ongoing learning process. The study clearly illustrates the important role of the backbone organization in overcoming the obstacles to the meaningful engagement and involvement of the community, from the outset and as challenges arise along the way.

Literature Review

Collective Impact is the commitment of a group of important actors from different sectors to a common agenda for solving a specific social problem. The concept of CI hinges on the idea that in order to address large-scale social problems, stakeholders must coordinate their efforts and work together around clearly defined goals (Kania and Kramer 2011).

CI efforts are geared towards change at the system level. They can be a framework for addressing change and are congruent with holistic approaches to comprehensive community change (Chaskin 2001b; Kubisch et al. 2010; Weaver 2014).

The CI framework suggests a useful set of five conditions that provide simple rules for complex interventions: a common agenda driving collective action, shared measurement to assure progress is being achieved, mutually reinforcing activities that ensure alignment and contribute to the goals, continuous communications, and a backbone infrastructure that coordinates and supports the collective efforts (Hanleybrown, Kania, & Kramer 2012).

A major critique of the initial article by Kania and Kramer (2011) is that it does not explicitly stress the central role of meaningfully engaging community members, especially those in the community most affected by the issues, in the success of CI efforts (Wolff 2016). However, both the authors and other scholars have since addressed the issue and emphasized that community engagement is an essential part of the CI approach (Kania & Kramer 2016; Weaver 2014; Harwood 2014).

Backbone Support

Backbone organizations seek to improve social outcomes by organizing cross–sector groups of partners to transform an often inefficient, fragmented system (Turner et al. 2012). While there are many backbone models and variations, backbone organizations essentially pursue six common activities to support and facilitate CI over the lifecycle of an initiative (Turner et al. 2012):

- Guide vision and strategy;
- Support aligned activities;
- Establish shared measurement practices;
- Build public will;
- Advance policy; and
- Mobilize funding.

Backbone organizations support fidelity by the various cross-sector players to both the common agenda and the rules for interaction. They help CI efforts move forward by monitoring the overall vision and by understanding and tracking the strategies employed. They can bring partners to the table around shared measurement strategies and mutually reinforcing activities. The backbone infrastructure can also facilitate the development of the collective voice needed to identify and advocate for potential policy shifts and for additional funding (Kania & Kramer 2013; Weaver 2014).

Research shows that each backbone organization engages in these activities to different degrees and in different ways, depending on the context and capacity of the organization and the scope and maturity of the initiative (Turner et al. 2012).

Finally, it is important to note that a central role of a backbone organization is to help build and sustain relationships of trust among the various groups in the community and the key stakeholders to enable them to work well together. This is an essential condition for success. This is often very challenging, and depends to a great extent on the characteristics of the community (Chaskin 2001a; Turner et al. 2012; Weaver 2014).

Cultural Competence and Cultural Adaptation

Cultural adaptation is based on the need to adapt interventions, programs and social services to the cultural characteristics of minority groups in order to enable their effective participation in the process. The professional literature on Collective Impact contains a range of overlapping and parallel concepts of cultural adaptation, including "cultural sensitivity," "cultural awareness," and "cultural competence."

The present chapter relates to two concepts—"cultural competence," and "cultural adaptation." The term "cultural competence" refers to the acquisition of relevant cultural insights regarding issues characterizing minority groups (Lum 1999). The term "cultural adaptation" deals with developing and implementing intervention strategies that are culturally adapted to an individual or to a group, including attitudes, behaviors, and policies that enable effective work with the minority group (Corin-Langer & Nadan 2012; Cross et al. 1989).

Cultural adaptation of a program or intervention will take into account differences in language, knowledge, values, customs, religion and religiosity, the characteristics of family ties, collective vs. individual emphasis, and lifestyles (Brown et al. 2002). The current literature shows that various professional disciplines are making changes in their procedures, codes and standards in order to adapt them culturally to various ethnic groups (Hasnain et al. 2009; Fortier & Bishop 2003).

Cultural Adaptation in Collective Impact

The literature on comprehensive community change and, increasingly, the literature on CI, stress the importance of applying an equity lens to community engagement and CI work. This approach emphasizes, among other things, that instead of trying to "plug and play" a standard solution, the cultural context in which people implement that solution should be considered (Barnes & Schmitz 2016; Kubisch et al. 2010).

Thus, a deep understanding of the community context, a meaningful connection to the community and efforts to accommodate its cultural uniqueness are essential for the success of backbone organizations and CI efforts. A top priority is to ensure that programs and practices are meaningful within the framework of the racial and ethnic context of the community (Kubisch et al. 2010; Stone & Butler 2000).

One challenge, according to Stone and Butler (2000), is that community coordinators often come from the dominant culture and not the local minority culture, which creates a cultural bias—especially if they bring answers instead of questions. Considerations of skin color, background, and cultural awareness are relevant to the choice of community coordinators because of the distance that residents might feel from those who work in the community. Alternatively, intensive preparation of community workers who are not from a similar background can mitigate the feeling of distance between residents and others who work in the community (Stone & Butler 2000). However, having a community coordinator who comes from local culture, but is culturally detached from his own culture, is even worse. It creates a set of expectations from him that can be difficult for him to meet or to adhere to (Stone & Butler 2000).

Another challenge, according to the authors, is that

> Ethnic and racial groups will tend to have their own leadership structure, some deeply embedded in cultural traditions, presenting enormous challenges for Comprehensive Community Initiative (CCI) coordinators who may be both ideologically inclined and required by the directives of an initiative to promote and achieve inclusiveness and equal representation in the local effort.
>
> Stone & Butler 2000

In some cases, they may develop a competitive relationship with the indigenous leadership that can impede cooperation.

In addition, when working in minority or other disadvantaged communities, it is important to take into consideration that ethnic, racial and other characteristics may impede mutually beneficial relationships between the community and the public and private sectors due to societal power arrangements. To overcome the obstacles, actors must invest significant resources (time, and political, social, and economic capital) to broker relationships and create new habits of thinking, acting, and collaborating to enable alignment to occur more naturally (Kubisch et al. 2010).

Finally, the literature on comprehensive community change stresses the need for adaptive leadership in these complex situations, one that can address adaptive challenges that require changes in people's priorities, beliefs, habits, and loyalties, rather than technical problems that can be resolved through the application of authoritative expertise and current structures, and procedures (Barnes & Schmitz 2016; Heifetz, Grashow, & Linsky 2009).

Cultural Competence and Cultural Adaptation Regarding Arab Society in Israel

The Arab population in the State of Israel is a national minority group characterized by unique cultural and social norms, holding traditional values and emphasizing collectivism, family values and a hierarchical-patriarchal social structure (Haj-Yahia 2004). Planning and implementing intervention programs in Arab society in Israel require a deep knowledge of its sociocultural values and practices.

The Family in Arab Society

Political, social and economic processes in Western countries have led to the growth of individualism and decreased individuals' dependency on their family. These processes have not fully occurred in Arab societies and countries, where the preferred social organization still revolves around family ties (Dwairy 2006a; Zeidan 2005; Haj-Yahia 2004), and the family collective remains highly significant in the life of the individual (Erez & Earley 1993).

The most prominent broad affiliation group in Arab society is the clan [*hamula*], an extended family comprising families of relatives of more than three generations, and it is the most prevalent traditional social structure among Arabs in Israel and the Middle East. Despite Arab society's exposure to Western culture and individualism, the extended family continues to play a traditional role in economic and social spheres (Kimmerling 2004) with great influence in local politics (Hamdallah 2013).

Position of Women and Teenage Girls in Traditional Arab Society

The nuclear family occupies central place in Arab society. It has a patriarchal, hierarchal structure, where the father is the supreme authority in everything relating to the household, the domestic budget, and politics (Zoabi 2010; Manna 2001; El-Saadawi 1995), and the mother is responsible for all aspects of childcare (Zeidan 2005; Haj-Yahia 2004).

Despite their seemingly inferior standing in traditional Arab society, women play a cardinal role in maintaining the family's integrity and stability, and therefore, any change in their role is perceived as undermining the family and a threat to the entire social structure (Read & Oselin 2008; Brown 2006). The women's role in maintaining the family's integrity begins in their teenage years. Values and norms in Arab society situate teenage girls at home and impose on them full responsibility for the family's honor (Naber 2005). Traditional Arab society connects a girl's modesty with family honor, therefore Arab girls are prohibited from going out on their own after dark, visiting unsanctioned places, and associating with girls who have a bad reputation (Naber 2005; Zoabi 2010).

Volunteerism in Arab Society

Arab society encourages volunteerism and providing help, though this is mainly within extended family (clan) circles. Volunteerism is considered one of the basic roles that family members assume (Al-Krenawi 2000; Zoabi 2010; Zeidan 2005; Lapidot-Lafler & Bishara 2010), and thus Arab society does not see the importance of organized volunteerism in formal organizations (Zeidan 2005). This characteristic of Arab society creates difficulty for many social and community programs that rely on volunteers as a vital aspect of their operation (Lahad, Cohen, & Leikin 2015).

Residential Patterns and Public Spaces in Arab Society

Most community initiatives include activities conducted in public spaces and efforts to improve them for the benefit and use of residents. However, Arab localities in Israel contain almost no public spaces. Most of them are characterized by a "selective urban" residential pattern, meaning that they are a hybrid of village and city. Although they encompass broad geographic areas, they are mostly a collection of villages with a small public urban center (Haj-Yahia 2004; Dwairy 2006a). This unique residential pattern was developed in keeping with the conservative Arab values and norms regarding traditional use of public spaces (Khamaisy 2000, 2005).

The shortage of public spaces stems also from the separatism dictated by clan affiliation. The division of land in Arab localities is clan related and most of it is privately owned. Any encroachment on privately owned land and any attempt to change its designation for public use meets with fierce resistance and is liable to provoke tension and conflict (Khamaisy 2007). Ultimately, both of these characteristics of Arab society in Israel have led to the expansion of large urban villages with limited public spaces.

The Cultural Identity of the Professionals

A widely held assumption in the practice of cultural adaptation is that employing a professional who belongs to the culture to which the intervention is directed is an effective way to achieve cultural competence and cultural adaptation. Familiarity with the cultural codes and knowledge of the language contribute to a professional's ability to understand the unique difficulties of the minority group and to identify the accepted ways of contending with them (Asael-Eyal 2012). When cultural identity exists between the professional and the participants, the latter perceive the professional as someone who understands their ways, boosting their confidence in him and in the program.

However, membership in the same society does not always guarantee that a professional will uphold the principle of cultural sensitivity, especially in cases where the society is a traditional one, such as Arab society in Israel (Haj-Yahia

2004; Zoabi 2010). Many Arab professionals were educated at Israeli or Western universities and have undergone professional socialization with a modern and Western orientation. The dissonance between the Western set of values and social conventions and those of Arab society often creates a dilemma for Arab professionals when they return to work with their own population (Dwairy 2006b). The dilemmas and conflicts that derive from the dissonance between the assumptions and approach of the intervention program and the sociocultural context of the particular community should be taken into account when planning and implementing interventions (Manna 2001).

Methodology

The current study is part of a broader, five-year (2012–2017) evaluation of the national Better Together program. The broader study is assessing the implementation of the program and the extent to which the goals and expected outcomes have been achieved.

The present analysis seeks to understand the role of backbone organizations in addressing the challenges posed by cultural diversity. Studies on cultural adaptation of the CI approach to Arab culture are very few. Therefore, an explorative approach was chosen as a means to understand these complex and multidimensional issues (Lieblich, Tuval-Mashiach, & Zilber 1998), and to investigate the intricate integration of the CI approach in diverse cultural contexts. The study relies mainly on in-depth interviews with backbone staff and key neighborhood stakeholders, designed to reveal hidden knowledge by giving a voice to those involved in the process.

All interviews were analyzed through qualitative content analysis to find common patterns and themes, which were later divided into the subthemes presented here. Finally, the themes were presented to backbone staff and neighborhood stakeholders, for further interpretation and validation.

Background: The Better Together Initiative

Better Together is a neighborhood change program that promotes community-wide collective action on behalf of children and youth in disadvantaged communities in Israel. The program's goal is to improve the well-being of children and youth and reduce their exposure to risk situations.

The program has been ongoing since 2006 in 35 communities of a broad range of ethnic backgrounds throughout the country. A national organization (JDC-Ashalim) serves as the backbone organization in each community and promotes an organized process of sharing and learning. The program aims to create effective community–based systems in which professionals and residents can work together. In the belief that it does indeed take a village to raise a child, the program emphasizes three levers of change:

Voice and partnership of the residents. This approach includes the broad mobilization of residents to support the process and to be involved in multiple ways. One important focus is on creating a core group of volunteer leaders along with a broader group of activists. They are frequently recruited from among members of the existing community leadership who are active in various forums such as the neighborhood council, housing committees, school parent committees and other existing frameworks. One strategy is to engage in activities that create extensive awareness of the program and thus encourage broad participation and support. Thus, there are several activities that use central community space open to the whole community.

Integrated multidisciplinary and multi-organizational mechanisms. Creating mechanisms to promote coordination, cooperation and partnerships among key communal organizations and the leaders and professionals from the various organizations is vital to success. Much importance is given to including key people from the municipality in these mechanisms. One of the key functions of these mechanisms is to mobilize external support, both financial and organizational, from a broad range of external sources and organizations.

Responses for children and youth. Creating a continuum of responses appropriate to the needs of children of all ages, boys and girls alike, throughout the day; and to the needs of their families and both parents is important. The program serves as a platform for a wide spectrum of interventions and activities selected according to the specific needs of each neighborhood. Activities include one-time special events to increase awareness of the program and mobilize support and engagement of the residents (such as large community events) as well as ongoing programs and initiatives that address the needs of the community (such as after-school learning centers, recreational activities, and improvement of public spaces).

This chapter focuses on a case study of one specific community that participated in the program. Since the end of 2011, the program has been implemented in the Assale-Cnaane neighborhood in the Arab town of Arrabe. The neighborhood has approximately 4,500 residents who belong to two clans: the Assale and the Cnaane. It is one of the oldest, most physically neglected, and densely populated neighborhoods in Arrabe. Its population is poor with a low level of education. Prior to the introduction of the program, the number and range of programs and services for children and youth in the neighborhood were very limited.

Research Findings

From the early planning stage of the program, the backbone staff understood that the general model required adaptation to local cultural codes; however, only basic adaptations were implemented at that stage. Later, in the course of the program's ongoing operation in the neighborhood, further challenges arose, due to the disparity between the local cultural codes and those of the program's activities. The study findings demonstrate that the backbone endeavored to address this disparity, adapting and changing the program to make the codes and activities more compatible. These adjustments solved many of the difficulties that emerged during the implementation of the program. The disparities were identified by the backbone staff in various stages of the program implementation and the actions taken to address them are described below.

Cultural Adaptation of the General Model in the Early Planning Stage

From the start, the Better Together backbone staff was fully aware of the need for cultural adaptation of the model. Indeed, a basic principle of the national program is to adapt the program to correspond with each neighborhood's characteristics and needs as a first step. However, the backbone did not see a need for extensive adaptation aside from translating all the relevant documents into Arabic and choosing a neighborhood coordinator from within the local culture. A key member of the backbone staff relates:

> The principle of adaptation – according to population, sector, Arab or ultra-Orthodox society etc. – is the basis of the program . . . The program comes with a framework and when it is introduced into a neighborhood, it absorbs the cultural emphases that arise within the groups themselves. Each group emphasizes its own needs and, as a result, the mechanisms are adapted to local specifications. Therefore, there was no initial need for a very specific adaptation for Arrabe. Thus, the basic steps that we took involved translating the questionnaire into Arabic and taking the clan factor into account.

Interviews also revealed that the neighborhood's local leadership and partners on the local council did not feel that any special adaptation was necessary. Another member of the backbone staff relates:

> Actually, in Arrabe no one came out and said, "in our society it works this way or that way." Sometimes, in some of our other localities, I'm told, "it won't work here, because our social conventions are such and such . . ." In Arrabe we didn't hear any [complaint] . . . We came with the standard model and all were in agreement that first of all it's important to hear what the residents had to say. They reviewed the planned residents' questionnaire. There was not even one sentence that they had any comments on. They said: Wow – it's really gotten a good reception here. Let's get it translated into Arabic and get it under way . . . We didn't make any adaptations beyond the language issue, and also when we went door to door we made sure that the husband was at home so that the wife wouldn't be alone [with the professional].

A key neighborhood worker, a local Arab woman, also assumed the model needed no special adaptation:

You adapt the model to the need; it [the model] is appropriate for anywhere.

However, during the implementation and in the course of the daily activity, dilemmas, and difficulties arose. The next section includes prominent examples and describes the way in which the program dealt with them.

Difficulty recruiting men and teenage girls to the program. During the first two years of Better Together's implementation in the Arab neighborhood, the participants included mainly adult women and male teens. Men and teenage girls were almost completely unrepresented in the program's activities, despite the fact that many of the needs articulated by the neighborhood involved these groups. The literature emphasizes the difficulty that exists in Arab society in recruiting men to participate in social and community programs, as well as the fear by many families of allowing girls to participate in activities outside the home without supervision (Asael-Eval, 2012; Rasner and Zeira, 2014). The interviews with backbone staff in the neighborhood show that these aspects played an important part in this neighborhood too.

Difficulty recruiting men. As noted, in the traditional division of family roles in Arab society, the man is responsible for the family's livelihood and for discipline, while the woman is responsible for providing for the family and children in all other areas. Participant interviews emphasized that this division of responsibility played an important role in the lack of participation of the men since the program focused on content areas not in their purview. One of the community workers related:

> We work less with the men. The men's perception of these things [the Better Together activities] is that they pertain more to women and children. But we try to get them to come too. A year ago, there were no men at all.

According to Asael (2012) and Shemer (2010), in order to include men from traditional societies in social and community programs, their honor and place in the social and family hierarchy must be preserved, and the program content must be framed using terms from their spheres of responsibility. The authors further emphasize the importance that program professionals contact the men directly rather than through their wives, and that they conduct house calls that allow them to view the family as a whole in its natural environment. In this way, they can seek to create an alliance with them and demonstrate respect for the father and his family.

Accordingly, one of the key neighborhood workers visited many neighborhood homes and gathered community leaders to provide program details. Similarly, they made an effort to frame the activities using terms from the spheres of the men's responsibility. One community worker relates:

> We reached them [the men] through the Fathers and Sons project. Its [the project's] objective is to allow fathers and sons to bond through a soccer game. This project [Better Together] had more than one objective: One was

to nurture the father-son relationship and encourage closeness, and the second was to inform the fathers about the program and encourage them to become an active member of the group.

In an interview conducted about a year later, one of the key neighborhood workers described the change that occurred in the wake of the efforts that had been made:

> We have already recorded a success and we want to expand on that. For example, we now have a demand to start a Fathers and Sons bicycle group.

Difficulty recruiting teenage girls. The women and teenage girls in Arab society are perceived as responsible for the security and stability of the family. Arab society sees a direct link between a teenage girl's modesty and morality, and her family's honor. Therefore, she is very closely supervised and behavioral restrictions and safeguards include prohibitions against leaving the home unaccompanied after dark, associating with girls whose moral conduct is perceived as dubious, and visiting unfamiliar locations.

As noted, during the first two years of Better Together in Arrabe, the girls were almost entirely absent from the program's activities and their parents resisted their participation in the program's evening activities at the Better Together clubhouse, where most of the youth activities were held.

Several measures were introduced to contend with these difficulties. According to Rasner and Zeira (2014), successful work with teenage girls in Arab society requires confidence-building with her family. A girl cannot decide on her own to attend the activities outside her home, without her father giving his consent to her and to the program professionals. One key step was to invite the parents to the program clubhouse, making sure to approach the fathers first, to allow them to inspect and view the activities and win their trust. A neighborhood worker relates:

> Look, the girls' participation began with a visit by a number of fathers to the clubhouse one evening. One of them said, "My son comes here and I don't know what they do here." He came and knocked at the door, came up to the clubhouse, saw the activities there and observed that the community worker and I were present.

An additional step was to invite the girls' mothers to participate in an activity at the Better Together clubhouse. To facilitate this, they shifted some of the activity to hours in which the mothers would find it easier to attend. A community worker relates:

> We invited the mothers to the workshop. I also wanted the mothers to feel comfortable and to continue to persuade their husbands that they were in a good place and in good hands.

An additional confidence-building measure was taken when program professionals came to the girls' homes to explain the content and nature of the clubhouse, and to obtain the father's direct consent for his daughter to participate. A clubhouse employee states:

> Regarding girls who would come without their parents' authorization – immediately after my shift at the clubhouse was over I would visit their homes . . . [tell them] that their daughter had attended that day and ask if they permitted her participation in such and such activities. I would say that I wanted her participation to be authorized by them, and if not then I would not allow her to participate. I would also ask for their phone number so that I could notify them when she was leaving.

These steps proved successful in dispelling the parents' uncertainty regarding their daughters' participation in the activities.

Clan influence over the program's activities in Arrabe. As explained previously, two extended families live in the Assale-Cnaane neighborhood: the Assale and the Cnaane clans (after whom the neighborhood is named). The clan's closed structure dictates traditional social conventions that shape behavior in public spaces. This greatly affects the operational leeway of social and community programs. An official in the local council underscored the sizeable influence that the clans wield over the ability to implement the program in their area:

> The social structure [of] traditional society can be articulated in two contradictory ways – positive and negative. Let us start with the positive. If they are part of the clan or relatives, they can cooperate and be one group. In other words, if the leaders are convinced that it is indeed beneficial to everyone, then it will be possible to implement the program in the neighborhood. On the other hand, if one or more of the leaders are not convinced, or question the need, all the rest will go along with their view and then it will be difficult to implement the program in the neighborhood. It's not like in the Jewish sector where there are small families.

The backbone staff said that from the start, the separation of the population into two separate clans was recognized as a factor that had to be addressed. Indeed, there were consultations from the outset with the local council on how to address this issue. The council assisted in the selection of a neighborhood coordinator who could operate without generating tension between the clans. A key member of the backbone organization reports:

> We took the clan issue into consideration. It was a factor in the choice of the neighborhood coordinator. One person was considered but after we discussed it with the local council, we went with someone else who the council felt would raise less tension.

Despite the careful selection of the neighborhood coordinator during the first three years of the program's implementation in the neighborhood, most of the activities took place in an area that was home to one of the clans (Assale). The closed clan structure sharply reduced the possibility for joint activities. Another backbone staff member reports:

> The first time that we encountered it close up was when we tried to organize a get-together for youth from both clans, and one father told me: My daughter will never come to the clubhouse because we don't socialize with them.

Similarly, in an interview about two years later, a key neighborhood worker described the significant challenge that the program faced regarding the inclusion of Cnaane clan members in the program's activities:

> In Cnaane, there are many areas where we have yet to see success. We have only succeeded in the Debka group and in the project led by the school in which we are partners. Aside from that, the Cnaane members don't even come to the clubhouse because they consider themselves superior to members of the Assale clan.

Only toward the end of the third year of the program's implementation in the neighborhood did its directors realize that in order to include the Cnaane clan members in the program they had to develop parallel interventions in both sections of the neighborhood, including an additional youth club. A key neighborhood worker explains:

> This year we opened an extension of the youth club in Cnaane, in order to bring them into the program.

The establishment of the separate club promoted a higher level of confidence on the part of the Cnaane clan in the program's leaders and in the program itself, and many members of the family began to take advantage of various activities offered by the program on a separate basis.

In the wake of this, at the end of the fourth year, it was possible to attempt some shared activities with participation by both clans. One of the backbone staff members reports:

> We established two clubs and currently there are attempts—some successful— to bring the clans together, but it has taken almost four years.

Volunteerism. In general, in the community development framework, an effort is made to establish an infrastructure of activists and volunteers from among the residents who would take responsibility for community life. These are the program's change agents in the neighborhood, and their contribution to its implementation is significant.

However, the establishment of a circle of activists and volunteers in the Assale-Cnaane neighborhood represented an especially complex challenge. Behavioral conventions encouraged volunteerism and assistance within the clan, while concurrently limiting the importance of organized volunteerism outside of the clan. Moreover, unlike Jewish communities, which have resident committees and neighborhood committees around which local leadership and a nucleus of volunteers can be developed, Arab communities do not commonly have such committees.

An analysis of the interviews shows that during the first two years of the program's implementation, the backbone staff managed to recruit and retain a small group of only about 30 volunteers who were residents of the neighborhood. They were unsuccessful in expanding the group, and even its retention proved difficult. In an interview, a community worker describes the challenges:

> There is indifference toward the wider society. Everyone is in his own home and maintains contact only with family or with people he personally knows.

A key neighborhood worker elaborated mainly on the difficulty in creating a group of proactive volunteers:

> Another thing that was missing was the value of volunteerism . . . they don't initiate. Perhaps it is because they don't yet know how to do things. But when someone plans something or says "let's do things," then everyone tries to help in whatever way they can. However, I would like them to internalize the value of initiating.

In order to change the situation, the neighborhood worker decided to adopt a strategy of setting a personal example, by volunteering in various ways beyond the duties that her position entailed. Since the community and neighborhood workers are greatly appreciated among neighborhood residents, it influenced other residents to volunteer. A neighborhood worker reports:

> What helped the volunteers succeed is that I begin working before them. I begin planning, assigning, getting down to work. And if, for example, bars are being painted, I take a brush and I paint with my own hand. Then, I am also a role model for them. When I came, they were surprised to see me lifting a pail of sand and pouring it out, and that I was wearing work clothes. Despite the fact that it was a workday, I did not come in a suit. So they see that I don't come only in order for them to work and serve.

In the wake of this activity, the number of adult activists grew to 50 activists from both clans (Assale and Cnaane), including women, men and another approximately 35 active teenagers, both girls and boys. This was a significant increase compared with the numbers before 2014.

One of the community workers reported that after three years of program activities, a larger number of residents were ready to join activities organized within the program:

> For example, a project that was in the month of Ramadan, when we fast from dawn to dusk. We have families here with poverty and economic hardships. There was a recruitment of volunteers and a recruitment of people who would donate meals to these families, as well as packages with all kinds of food. And we even recruited people whose economic situation is very good in terms of money, while we gave funds to those in need – who are from the neighborhood and whose situation is difficult. It was done through our group of activists who helped us. We also prepared packages containing holiday cookies and we distributed them to the elderly in the neighborhood. It was very moving, because for the most part the older people do not come to Better Together.

Public spaces. Like many social and community programs, many elements in the Better Together model stem from the assumption that there are public spaces where it is possible to assemble residents and hold community events. As was noted, in the Assale-Cnaane neighborhood there is a significant shortage of public spaces, posing a major challenge to the program. In the words of a key neighborhood worker: "There are differences [between us and Jewish communities] . . . [Jewish communities have] gardens or areas that are public for the entire neighborhood – there is nothing like that [in the Arab sector]."

In an interview conducted about two years later, the neighborhood worker illustrated the adaptations that she made in the model, including conducting community activities in available spaces outside the neighborhood:

> Changes that we made in the model of the activity during the program in order to adapt it . . . for example, we took them on the study day to the mother and baby center [outside the neighborhood].

Over time, the neighborhood and community workers did succeed in creating public space in the neighborhood. In early 2015, a community park was established—the Peace Park. It was created on the southern edge of the neighborhood, in an abandoned area that does not belong to any of the clans. The neighborhood workers and a committee of residents (women and youth), worked to make this possible and to renew the area. One of the neighborhood workers says:

> At first, [the area] was like a dump. Later, we cleaned it up and planted and put in flowers and everything. The place had been a [meeting place] for

groups of people who get drugs and things like that, because there was no one to watch over the place, so it became a real environmental hazard . . . Besides getting the garbage removed, which the municipality takes care of, everything is maintained by [the residents who volunteer in the framework of] Better Together. We water, we weed, we do activities—it is unbelievable when you think about what it once was.

However, the park is located near the section in which the Assale clan members live. Thus, the park is used mainly by members of the Assale clan. However, in the wake of the success, the residents who are members of the Cnaane clan identified a similar space in the area where they live, and currently a parallel park is being planned. One of the backbone staff members explains:

A group of residents [who are members of the Cnaane family], the moment they saw the residents getting organized in the big park, said wow, we also have an idea . . . It was as a result of a study day with professionals and residents, and we identified additional places in the neighborhood. The residents themselves pointed them out. And one of the places was a very neglected river bed located at the edge of the Cnaane neighborhood . . . The Peace Park's success gave great hope to people, that it is possible to make changes.

To conclude, the case of implementing the Better Together program in Arrabe underscores that despite the initial efforts to contend with and adapt the program culturally, significant cultural barriers arose over time. There was a range of barriers and they influenced various components of the program as well as the various groups in the community. As the barriers were identified, the backbone staff initiated efforts to address them. While some of the barriers took only a short time to overcome, others took much longer until a solution was developed and successfully implemented.

Discussion

The current study sheds new light on the role of backbone organizations in addressing cultural barriers in the context of CI initiatives and reiterates the importance of meaningful community engagement in such efforts.

The literature addressing intervention strategies in distinct cultural settings emphasizes the need for adaptation to the local culture, and stresses the central role of engaging community members. The current study adds to that discussion by pointing to the important role of backbone organizations in identifying cultural barriers and in developing culturally appropriate strategies to address them. In such contexts, these approaches are an essential part of the backbone organization's broader role in guiding the vision and the strategy, and aligning community efforts.

In line with the recent literature on cultural adaptation in the context of CI (Kania & Kramer 2016; Weaver 2014; Harwood 2014), the current study also suggests that integrating staff from within the residents' culture is significant. These individuals help to identify cultural barriers and ways to address them and contribute to efforts to build trust and effective dialogue with the residents. Indeed, choosing staff from within the community proved to be necessary in order to address cultural adaptation challenges successfully, although this on its own was not enough, and the findings suggest that success is also dependent on adaptive leadership.

Finally, the study found that it is necessary to devote time and resources early in the process to gain an understanding of the local culture and the adaptations that may be required. At the same time, the study shows it is important to be aware that additional cultural issues may emerge over time, and pose additional challenges that the backbone organization must address. Cultural adaptation is an ongoing process that requires ongoing learning by those involved.

In summary, this case study is a demonstration of successful cultural adaptation. Responding to cultural issues as they arise and involving the community in this process proved to be key strategies for the backbone organization.

Notes

1 Including the national and regional managers, the neighborhood coordinator and the community worker, the head of the local municipality, the director of the local social services department and community activists.
2 Fathers and Sons is a project designed to strengthen the relationship between fathers and their sons, and among neighborhood residents, through soccer games.

References

Al-Krenawi, A. & Graham, J. R. (2000). "Culturally Sensitive Social Work Practice with Arab Clients in Mental Health Setting," *Health and Social Work* 25 9–22.

Asael-Eyal, V. (2012) "Culturally Sensitive Intervention based on a Human–Diversity Approach to Treating Violence in Israeli-Ethiopian families of 'Beta Israel'," in Grisaro, N. (ed): *Socially, Culturally, and Clinical Aspects to Ethiopian Immigrants in Israel* (pp. 1–25). Beer Sheva: Ben–Gurion University of the Negev (Hebrew).

Barnes, M. & Schmitz, P. (2016) "Community Engagement Matters (Now More than Ever)," *Stanford Social Innovation Review*, Spring: 32–39.

Brown, K. (2006) "Releasing Muslim Women's Rights: The Role of Islamic Identity among British Muslim Women," *Women's Studies International Forum* 29 417–430.

Brown, S., Garcia, A., Kouzekanani, K., & Hanis, C. (2002) "Culturally Competent Diabetes Self–Management Education for Mexican-Americans: The Starr County Border Health Initiative," *Diabetes Care* 25(2) 259–268.

Chaskin, R. J. (2001a) "Organizational Infrastructure and Community Capacity: The Role of Broker Organizations," The Organizational Response to Social Problems (Research in Social Problems and Public Policy, Volume 8), Emerald Group Publishing Limited 8: 143–166.

Chaskin, R. J. (2001b) "Building Community Capacity a Definitional Framework and Case Studies from a Comprehensive Community Initiative," *Urban Affairs Review* 36(3) 291–323.

Corin-Langer, N. & Naden, Y. (2012) "Social Work in a Diverse, Multi-Cultural Society," in: Hovav, M., Levental, A., & Katan, Y. (eds) *Social Work in Israel*, Tel-Aviv: Hakibbutz Hameuchad (pp. 506–526) (Hebrew).

Cross, T. L., Bazron, B.J., Dennis, K. W., & Issacs, M. R. (1989) Toward a Culturally Competent System of Care, Washington, DC: Georgetown University Child Development Center.

Dwairy, M. (2006a) "Introduction to Three Cross-Regional Research Studies on Parenting Styles, Individuation, and Mental Health in the Arab Societies, *Journal of Cross-Cultural Psychology* 37(3) 221–229.

Dwairy, M. (2006b) "Issues in Psychological Evaluation of Patients of Collective Societies: The Arab Case," *Sichot* 21(1) 26–32. (Hebrew).

El-Saadawi, N. (1995) "Gender, Islam, and Orientalism: Dissidence and Creativity," *Women: A Cultural Review* 6 1–18.

Erez, M., & Earley, P.C. (1993) *Culture, Self-Identity, and Work*, New York: Oxford University Press.

Fortier J.P., & Bishop, D. (2003) *Setting the Agenda for Research on Cultural Competence in Health Care: Final Report*. Edited by C. Brach. Rockville, MD: U.S. Department of Health and Human Services Office of Minority Health and Agency for Healthcare Research and Quality. www.imiaweb.org/uploads/docs/Setting_the_Agenda_for_Cultural_Competence_in_Health_Care_AHRQ.pdf (Accessed: January 2015).

Haj-Yahia, M. (2004) "The Arab Family in Israel: Its Cultural Values in Relation to Social Work," *Society and Welfare: Quarterly for Social Work* 34 249–264. (Hebrew).

Hamdallah, R. (2013) "The Influence of the Hamulla in Appointing School Principals in Arab Settlements in Israel," *Jammi'ah* 17, 1–20 (Arabic).

Hanleybrown, F., Kania, J. & Kramer, M. (2012) "Channeling Change: Making Collective Impact Work," *Stanford Social Innovation Review*.

Harwood, R. C. (2014) "Putting Community in Collective Impact. The Collective Impact Forum," www.fsg.org

Hasnain, R., Kondratowicz, D.M., Portillo, N., Borokhovski, E., Balcazar, F., Johnson, T., et al. (2009) The Use of Culturally Adapted Competency Interventions to Improve Rehabilitation Service Outcomes for Culturally Diverse Individuals with Disabilities. Submitted to the Campbell Collaboration, Education Coordinating Group.

Heifetz, R., Grashow, A. & Linsky, M. (2009) The Practice of Adaptive Leadership: Tools and Tactics for Changing Your Organization and the World, Boston (MA): Harvard Business Press.

Kania, J. & Kramer, M. (2011) "Collective Impact," *Stanford Social Innovation Review* 9 (1) 36–41.

Kania, J. & Kramer, M. (2013) "Embracing Emergence: How Collective Impact Addresses Complexity." *Stanford Social Innovation Review*.

Kania, J. & Kramer, M. (2016) "Advancing the Practice of Collective Impact," The Collective Impact Forum.

Khamaisy, R. (2000) "Something was Disrupted on the Way to the City," *Panim: Journal of Culture, Society, and Education* 13 78–83 (Hebrew).

Khamaisy, R. (2005) "Urbanization and Urbanism in Arab Settlements in Israel," *Horizons in Geography* 64–65 293–310 (Hebrew).

Khamaisy, R. (2007) Between Customs and Law: Urban Planning and Management of Land in Arab Settlements in Israel, Jerusalem: The Floersheimer Institute for Policy Studies.

Kimmerling, B. (2004) Immigrants, Settlers, and Natives: State and Society in Israel – between Multiculturalism and Culture Wars, Tel–Aviv: Am Oved Publishers (Hebrew).

Kubisch, A. C., Auspos P., Brown, P. & Dewar, T. (2010) Voices from the Field III: Lessons and Challenges from Two Decades of Community Change Efforts, Washington, DC: The Aspen Institute.

Lahad, M., Cohen, R., & Leikin, D. (2015) *The Field of Volunteering in the Ministry of Social Affairs and Social Services.* Jerusalem: The Division of Planning Research and Training, and the Division of Community Resources, Ministry of Social Affairs and Social Services (Hebrew).

Lapidot-Lafler, N., & Bishara, A. (2010) "Volunteering in the Arab Society in Israel, as a Means to Improve the Quality of Life," *Et Hasadeh: Quarterly Journal for Children and Youth in Situations of Risk & their Families* 4 30–35 (Hebrew).

Lieblich, A., Tuval-Mashiach, R. & Zilber, T. (1998) *Narrative Research: Reading, Analysis and Interpretation.* London: SAGE Publications.

Lum, D. (1999) (ed.) Culturally Competent Practice: A Framework for Understanding Diverse Groups and Justice Issues, Pacific Groove, CA: Brooks/Cole.

Manna, A. (2001) "Adapting ETGAR and TAF Programs to the Arab Sector," in Dayan, Y. (ed): *Educating-Caring of Preschoolers based on an Ecological-Developmental Approach* (pp. 1–19). Jerusalem: Schwartz Program, the Hebrew University of Jerusalem (Hebrew).

Naber, N. (2005) "Muslim First, Arab Second: A Strategic Politics of Race and Gender," *The Muslim World* 95(4) 479–495.

Rasner, N., & Zeira, A. (2014) Adolescent Girls in Severe Situations of Distress (Literature Review), Jerusalem: The Haruv Institute.

Read, J. & Oselin, S. (2008) "Gender and the Education-Employment Paradox in Ethnic and Religious Contexts: The Case of Arab Americans," *American Sociological Review* 73 296–313.

Shemer, O. (2010) *A Guide for "Fathers Program": A Social Program for Israeli–Ethiopian Fathers in a Cultural Transition.* Jerusalem: Ministry of Social Affairs and Social Services and Gvanim Center (Hebrew).

Stone, R. & Butler, B. (2000) *Core Issues in Comprehensive Community–Building Initiatives: Exploring Power and Race*, Chicago, IL: Chapin Hall Center for Children at the University of Chicago.

Turner, S., Merchant, K., Kania, J., & Martin, E. (2012) *Understanding the Value of Backbone Organizations in Collective Impact.* Stanford Social Innovation Review.

Weaver, L. (2014) "The Promise and Peril of Collective Impact," *The Philanthropist* 26(1) 11–19.

Wolff, T. (2016) "Ten Places where Collective Impact Gets it Wrong," *Global Journal of Community Psychology Practice*, 7(1).

Zeidan, A. (2005) *Volunteering, Donations, and Attitudes towards Organizations in the Arab–Palestinian Society in Israel: A Revisit.* Beer-Sheva: Israeli Center for Third Sector Research (ICTR), Ben–Gurion University of the Negev (Hebrew).

Zoabi, H. (2010) Culturally Biased Intervention Strategies: Identification and Conceptualization. *Mifgash: Journal of Social–Educational Work, 32*, 53–73. (Hebrew).

10

PROGRESS, CHALLENGES, AND NEXT STEPS IN COLLECTIVE IMPACT

Collective Impact as Disruptive Illumination

Tom Klaus and Liz Weaver

Introduction

Now, more than five years after its introduction, how are we to make sense of Collective Impact within the field of community development? For the authors, this single question has fueled email exchanges, conversations, interviews, and a search of the limited but growing body of literature on CI for more than a year. The discussions have finally come together sufficiently to inform a response to this question. It is not the first, nor should it be the only and final, response. Cullen-Lester and Yammarino (2016), writing about collective and network approaches to leadership, caution "as with any new and emerging area of research, theory is ahead of data" (p. 177). The same can be said of Collective Impact.

Three methods were used to explore the question—how are we to make sense of Collective Impact within the field of community development now? The first was a review of the literature on CI with special attention paid to the academic and peer-reviewed literature. Only recently has the topic of CI begun to appear in academic writing and peer-reviewed articles. *Community Development*, in fact, is one of the first peer-reviewed journals to solicit and feature articles specifically on the topic of Collective Impact (Walzer, Weaver, & McGuire 2016).

A simple search for the term "Collective Impact" in the ProQuest Dissertation & Theses Full Text database (the Humanities and Social Sciences Collection on Dec. 26, 2017) provided some indication of interest in the topic in academia. From 2011–2015 there was a steady annual increase in the number of dissertations submitted to ProQuest[1] that contained the term "Collective Impact." In 2011, there were 96 such dissertations and by 2015 that number had reached 188, which appears to have been a peak year. In 2016 the number fell to 155 and in 2017 it was at 107. However, not all of these papers used the term "Collective Impact" to refer to the specific collaboration phenomenon, but only as a descriptive term.

The second method used to address the question was key informant interviews. Interviews were conducted with nine individuals who were identified and selected because of their deep engagement in the world of CI. While the nine interviews are not, nor are they intended to be, representative of all involved in Collective Impact, they are not insignificant. Each person has closely worked with, researching and studying, or been thinking and writing about CI nearly since its introduction in 2011. Seven of the interviews occurred between July 5, 2016 and Oct. 13, 2016.

Each was a semi-structured interview, conducted by phone, using an interview protocol of five main questions. Follow–up questions were generated in the context of the interview in discussions about participant responses to the main questions. Each interview was recorded and the authors also took notes during the interviews. One interview was a follow-up to an earlier interview with another participant. One participant was unable to provide an interview but responded in writing to each of the main questions.

Finally, both authors have also been very involved with Collective Impact as early adopters, and as facilitators of community and social change throughout their careers. They employed a dialogue technique, via email, phone, and Skype, to think together and more clearly about what they have learned and experienced with CI, change, and community development. Their dialogue included comparisons and discussion of what they found in the literature search. In addition, the exercise included a review and discussion of each key informant interview. This chapter, in fact, began as an email exchange between the authors which turned into a full-on dialogue over several weeks about the nature of Collective Impact. That dialogue led to the additional inquiry methods described above and the development of this chapter.

The following pages examine some of the progress by the authors and others in understanding and using the CI approach. They consider some of the challenges that are before the field of community development, especially regarding the questions that need to be addressed to provide a fuller understanding of the approach. The authors also attempt to identify some next steps, and even new directions, for Collective Impact, especially as they relate to community development and social change. Finally, the term "disruptive illumination" is proposed to offer a new perspective on CI which can be useful to help make sense of it in community development at this moment in time.

A Question of Research

In the months leading up to the completion of this chapter a conversation surfaced in the *Collective Impact Forum* questioning the quality of research underlying the CI framework (Wolff 2016[2]; Kania & Kramer 2016[3]). This conversation gave voice to a similar concern the authors heard expressed among academics and researchers from the time of its introduction and earliest widespread adoption. Therefore, to make sense of Collective Impact within the field of community development now, it was important to explore questions about the research undergirding its framework that seem to persist. To this end, it is useful to first understand the context and intention behind Kania and Kramer's seminal 2011 Collective Impact article.

The 2011 article introducing Collective Impact resonated deeply among those working in social change initiatives and it was immediately embraced. One key informant, in an obvious understatement, said its adoption "has been exceeding expectations." In fact, the terminology and the framework has been embraced and adopted by many different sectors in all parts of the globe at an extraordinary speed. Recently, for example, one of the authors had a student in a doctoral course whose work involved facilitating a CI initiative in a rural area of his native Malawi.

The seminal article seemed to speak directly to many practitioners and funders eager for immediate, profound, and long-term social change. Consequently, they quickly adopted the CI five conditions framework. In their eagerness, though, many embraced it as a formula with, it seems, a limited understanding of the framework. However, the 2011 article did not offer a formula, but a theoretical framework based on observations made over nearly a decade of work with a broad scope of FSG clients around the world.

It was the first time FSG had attempted to cohesively and publicly describe their observations under the name "Collective Impact." Kania and Kramer concluded, "our research shows that successful Collective Impact initiatives typically have five conditions that together produce true alignment and lead to powerful results" (2011: p. 39). More recently, John Kania described the framework as the minimum specifications needed for social change, not as a formula. Kania and Kramer elaborated on this point in their *Collective Impact Forum* posting on May 4, 2016[4]:

> Unfortunately, some people have interpreted the five conditions of Collective Impact as a recipe or formula that is sufficient to engage in the deep and nuanced work of collaborative change. As we and many others have written since the initial article was published, while the five conditions are important foundational elements of collaborative change, they do not, in and of themselves, provide a complete and comprehensive playbook for achieving collaborative, collective change at scale.
>
> Paragraph 5

The insights in the 2011 CI article offered possibilities that were taken as a theory by some and as clear-cut solutions in a formula to others. Perhaps its misidentification as a formula rather than a theory partially explains the remarkable response to Collective Impact in so many fields and sectors. This misidentification may have been an unintended consequence of the language Kania and Kramer used to explain the origins of their framework. From their vantage point, the CI framework emerged from what they described as "research" (Kania & Kramer 2011: p. 30).

In 2011, the quest for evidence-based formulas and recipes was at a fever pitch, though today the case for "evidence-based" solutions to social problems is being reconsidered (e.g., Klaus 2015[5]; Gopal & Schorr 2016; Schorr 2016). Therefore, simply reading there was "research" behind CI seems to have fueled its unquestioning acceptance as a new evidence-based formula for social change that had been tried and tested. The authors' experience with a variety of CI implementers and initiatives suggests this interpretation is more accurate than not. Both have observed Collective Impact supporters and implementers fervently argue that it is an evidence-based approach supported by considerable research.

The use of the term "research," in the 2011 article, also caught the attention of academics and researchers. To this audience the use of the term "research" begged additional questions, often related to knowing more about the research methods used to ascertain the validity of the findings. These were among the questions raised by Wolff (2016) in a critique of Collective Impact, first published in the *Global Journal of Community Psychology Practice* and then reprinted in the *Collective Impact Forum*. He argued the 2011 CI article, "cites a few successful examples of community coalitions and draws their Collective Impact generalizations from them" (Wolff 2016). He adds that the 2011 article oversimplified the process of community collaboration and is not grounded in the existing literature on collaboration (Wolff 2016). Key informants interviewed for this chapter also raised questions about the number of cases that informed the development of the framework.

So, it appears some confusion has been generated by the use of the term "research" in their seminal 2011 article and because of Kania and Kramer's failing to explain what they meant by it or describing, even briefly, the research process and method. This left the term "research" open to interpretation and exposed the CI framework to criticism by other researchers. Inquiries for this chapter led the authors to conclude there has been a gap in knowledge related to the research on CI and that it is time to fill it, especially since, Collective Impact continues to generate additional scholarly research and scrutiny.

As part of the research for this chapter, the authors discussed this gap in knowledge with key CI leaders at FSG. This discussion may have prompted the publication of a blog on the FSG website (FSG 2016, November 29[6]) that attempted to answer questions about the research methods. In addition, the authors received a personal communication (2016, February 3) responding to that discussion and which further addressed the gap in knowledge about the research supporting CI:

> Kania and Kramer did not ground their work in deep academic research or a formalized research methodology. The framework they developed was derived from a combination of direct experience working with clients, interviews, and research to identify and understand other similar collective

efforts, an approach like the action research spiral (Kemmis & McTaggart 2005). Their intent was to offer inspiration and practical guidance to those engaged in funding and leading social change. They assumed that the concept would continue to evolve through practice, and were not proposing a final and comprehensive theoretical framework that met the rigorous standards of academic scholarship.

In the exploration to learn more about the research undergirding the collective impact framework, the authors gained two useful insights for understanding collective impact regarding community development. First, the findings were not intended as an evidence-based theoretical framework and formula for creating social change. The "research" referred to in the 2011 collective impact article aligns most closely with action research, which is a valid, intuitive, naturalistic research method, though others may challenge it on the grounds of rigor. Patton (2002) described action research:

> Action research aims at solving specific problems within a program, organ-ization, or community. Action research explicitly and purposefully becomes part of the change process by engaging the people in the program or organization in studying their own problems to solve those problems. As a result, the distinction between research and action becomes quite blurred and the research methods tend to be less systematic, more informal, and quite specific to the problem, people, and organization for which the research is undertaken. Both formative evaluation and action research focus on specific programs at specific points in time. There is no intention, typically, to generalize beyond those specific settings.
>
> p. 221

The 2011 CI article was intended to inspire, guide, and suggest collaborative principles and action, but not provide an evidence-based, rigorously developed theoretical framework or formula for community change. FSG intuitively utilized an approach like action research and began to observe the pattern of collective action emerge, which was renamed to "Collective Impact" prior to the publication of the 2011 article. Despite some criticism, key informants have credited FGS for being particularly adept at such pattern recognition.

Second, while some, perhaps even many, in the field of community develop-ment have adopted the CI framework it was not developed within or specifically for the field. This is an important distinction to make. Kemmis and McTaggart (2005) describe the family of action research and differentiate its members. One of those is *industrial action research* which is a consultant driven model frequently used in organizational development that tends to focus on improving organizational effectiveness (Kemmis & McTaggart 2005:p. 562).

More common in community development is the use of *participatory action research* that values shared ownership of research projects with the community,

community–based analysis of social problems and solutions, and community action (Kemmis & McTaggart 2005:p. 560). The action research behind Collective Impact has more in common with industrial action research than participatory action research. This may explain, in part, the claims by Wolff (2016), Le (2015[7]), and others that neither the CI framework nor its implementers have given as much attention to community participation, and other core principles of community development, as needed.

Collective Impact was not developed within or for the community development field. Consequently, it has sometimes been implemented in community change efforts in ways that appear to further marginalize the community it purports to serve. Le (2015), for example, writing on his experience with CI, describes nine ways that this can happen. As community development researchers and practitioners have begun to investigate and even use the CI framework, the critique that Collective Impact has the potential to do more harm than good to communities has been repeatedly raised and it has been heard.

As a result, several new directions for CI have emerged which attempt to address the model's perceived deficits in community participation, shared decision making, and equity. Some of these new directions are briefly described in this chapter.

Still, CI has become an integral part of the collaboration and community development world, a fact that is not disputed, even by the most ardent critics of Collective Impact. Already, community development practitioners and researchers have made significant contributions to the framework. As more community development researchers and practitioners extend the original research and work of Kania and Kramer, Collective Impact and community development will likely find more synergies that contribute to a better understanding of both frameworks as well as more effective, long-term community change. The contributors in this book are among those who are marking some noticeable progress in understanding CI through the community development lens.

Progress toward Understanding Collective Impact

During the past five years, an increasing number of coalitions and collaborative efforts around the world have attempted to utilize the CI framework. Community development researchers have increasingly turned their attention to CI seeking to more deeply understand it.

This volume captures some of the most recent efforts. Gillam and Counts studied implementation of Collective Impact in their organization and found that a work culture, in which relationships, curiosity, and accountability are key, is essential to successful deployment of the framework. Somekh and Yehonatan depict the challenges of implementing a CI approach in the culturally different settings of Arab and Jewish communities in Israel. Schwartz, Weaver, Pei, and Kozak described campus–community partnerships attempting to reduce poverty using a CI approach, led by Vibrant Communities, place–based community round-tables throughout Canada.

Considered individually and together, the chapters in this volume add to an understanding of Collective Impact and how it contributes to sense-making. This book follows contributions from various authors in Community Development, in 2015 and 2016. In 2015, Christens & Inzeo describes how CI compares to other community-led change initiatives. In 2016, a special CI issue of *Community Development* was published featuring a variety of authors on a range of topics related to Collective Impact and community development (see Vol. 47, No. 2).

In addition to these direct contributions from the Community Development Society's publications, others have explored CI through the lens of community development. Flood, Minkler, Lavery, Estrada, and Falbe (2015) compared and discussed the use of CI augmented by community coalition action theory for health promotion. Francis Dunn Butterfoss who, along with Michelle Kegler, is a developer of community coalition action theory, has also considered ways to integrate Collective Impact into coalition work (Butterfoss 2013).

The Community Tool Box[8], an online resource for community development practitioners, created and managed by the Work Group for Community Health and Development at the University of Kansas, has a section on Collective Impact and its use in community development settings contributed by Splansky Juster of FSG. Wolff, et al. (2017) introduced six principles for collaborating for equity and justice that are intended to move groups beyond the core ideas of CI. These principles resulted in the development of the Collaborating for Equity and Justice Toolkit also found in the Community Tool Box.

Several key informants remarked about the progress made in understanding CollectiveImpact in the previous five years. For example, it was recognized that CI offered a frame for a process already known under other names, yet which made the work of community development and social change more accessible to others:

> I didn't learn about Collective Impact from FSG necessarily . . . but I appreciated what it offered the field, particularly in the early days. The way it has been framed has opened a lot more people to come into this field. But I also find . . . the practice is limited by that framing, which is very accessible and tight, but does not really capture some of the other core pieces of the work.

In addition, the framing of Collective Impact, though it may not be well-understood by practitioners, has still resulted in progress in addressing important problems. One key informant described CI as being most effective when it pushes people to adopt a results orientation in the work of community change. "Collective Impact gives people language they need to feel comfortable with in the hard work of results-driven work."

While the enthusiasm for CI and its potential has been largely unbridled, increased understanding has also exposed some shortcomings. Vu Le (2015) indicated he has gained a greater understanding of how Collective Impact has affected communities of color, though much of what he has come to understand has not been encouraging. Another key informant acknowledges CI has "succeeded enormously in bringing coalition building back to the forefront" yet feels it did this in a way that has been damaging to communities. "It has come across as glib, as easy, as top down."

In 2014, during the Tamarack Institute's *Collective Impact Summit*, Cabaj introduced the perspective of *Collective Impact 3.0* (CI 3.0) as a useful lens through which to view and understand CI. Two years later, Cabaj and Weaver (2016) published a refined and expanded version of Collective Impact 3.0. Though only briefly described here, a fuller and updated explanation of Collective Impact 3.0 is found in Cabaj and Weaver's article in this volume. They suggest that CI has moved through two previous stages.

Collective Impact 1.0 refers to a time before the introduction of the term and framework in 2011. This period could arguably extend back several decades in coalition, collaboration, and community development work and research. It was a period of discovery, experimentation and prototyping in which diverse groups used elements of the Collective Impact framework without the language offered by the five conditions.

Collective Impact 2.0 includes the five years since the introduction of the framework. During that time, many coalition and collaborative efforts either adopted the Collective Impact framework from the outset or rebranded existing efforts with the term. Both critics and proponents, including those interviewed, recognize that not all efforts bearing the name of "Collective Impact" really fit the framework.

One key informant observed that in Collective Impact 2.0, "some folks do not understand the distinctions around Collective Impact and really use the term in a very loose way and that's not particularly helpful." This is true whether they have been newly-formed around the framework or whether existing initiatives have been "retrofitted" with the name. During this period, practitioners and researchers, including FSG, attempted to study and more clearly grasp the strengths and deficits of the framework as well as to learn more fully "how to do" CI. These efforts may have played a significant role in the rise of the next and current generation of CI initiatives, Collective Impact 3.0.

Currently, practitioners, researchers, proponents, and critics are trying to apply the lessons learned from the previous period to "deepen, broaden and adapt CI based on yet another generation of initiatives" (Cabaj & Weaver 2016: p. 3). These lessons also define some of the challenges that lie ahead.

Challenges of Collective Impact in Community Development

The latter part of the 2.0 period brought several critiques of the process regarding equity, inclusivity, and community engagement (e.g., Klaus 2013[9]; Le 2015; McAfee, Glover Blackwell, & Bell 2015; Raderstrong & Boyea-Robinson 2016;

Wolff 2016). Each area of critique continues to offer a prominent challenge. They were highlighted again in the key informant interviews in this chapter. One observed that the original Collective Impact framework failed to put sufficient focus on equity and the role of community voice. Another identified the need to include authentic community engagement in the work of CI

The Oxford English Dictionary (2016) defines "equity" as "the quality of being fair and impartial." It is sometimes linked to "inclusivity" by those speaking or writing about Collective Impact. McAfee, Glover Blackwell, and Bell define equity as the "just and fair inclusion into a society in which all can participate, prosper, and reach their full potential" (2015:p. 1).

The current authors see equity and inclusivity as two complementary, yet distinct, ideas and prefer to keep them separate in these discussions. In this context, "equity" is seen as valuing fair and impartial access to participation in the process. As such, equity refers to an ethic held by those leading a CI initiative rather than an action. "Inclusivity" is seen as a focused, intentional action to facilitate the fair and impartial participation of those who might otherwise be excluded; especially those most affected by the issue being addressed in the initiative (see "inclusivity," Oxford English Dictionary 2016).

The authors' experience in the field has been that equity, as an ethic or value, does not necessarily lead to the action of inclusivity. For example, a recent study of teen pregnancy prevention community initiatives showed that the value of equity alone in community coalitions was not sufficient to result in the act of including those most affected by the issue (Klaus & Saunders 2016). However, the act of inclusivity can lead to the development of the value of equity. Further, it is argued that inclusivity is a requirement of genuine equity.

Community engagement, when it occurs at all levels and sectors of the community, is viewed as the tactical driver of inclusivity. It is through community engagement that inclusivity and equity can be realized in a Collective Impact initiative. This is not, however, "trickle down community engagement" which is when "we bypass the people who are most affected by issues, engage and fund larger organizations to tackle these issues, and hope that miraculously the people most affected will help out in the effort, usually for free" (Le 2015). Unless the individuals and groups in the community most directly affected by the issue being addressed are first engaged, and engaged first in an authentic relational manner, their eventual participation risks being mere manipulation, decoration, or tokenism (Shier 2001).

Challenges related to equity, inclusivity, and community engagement are all areas in which community development practitioners and researchers can contribute. At the most basic level, the Community Development Society offers five core Principles of Good Practice (Community Development Society 2016[10]):

- Promote active and representative participation toward enabling all community members to meaningfully influence the decisions that affect their lives.

- Engage community members in learning about and understanding community issues, and the economic, social, environmental, political, psychological, and other impacts associated with alternative courses of action.
- Incorporate the diverse interests and cultures of the community in the community development process; and disengage from support of any effort that is likely to adversely affect the disadvantaged members of a community.
- Work actively to enhance the leadership capacity of community members, leaders, and groups within the community.
- Be open to using the full range of action strategies to work toward the long-term sustainability and well-being of the community.

Each area—equity, inclusivity, and community engagement—is explicitly or implicitly cited as essential elements of these core principles of practice. Minimally, the use of the Collective Impact framework in community change efforts should be informed by and animate these principles.

There has been a growing chorus of voices for Collective Impact to be placed more squarely in the broader tradition of community change and development. Thus, an opening exists for community development practitioners and researchers to contribute to an expanded understanding of the CI framework. Possible research and practice questions suggested by key informants included:

- How do we effectively integrate both the "grass tops" and the "grassroots" in a Collective Impact initiative in a meaningful way that is mindful of the power dynamics at play?
- What is it going to take to get those most affected by an issue involved in a Collective Impact effort to address it?
- How do you help those most affected by an issue learn, understand, and utilize the data in decision making for change?
- How do we do CI in a rural or a tribal context?
- How do we do CI with immigrant communities?
- What is the role of a coalition in CI?
- How do we grow a Collective Impact initiative out of a coalition—rather than tack one on after the initiative has already begun its work?
- What does it take for people with formal authority in CI initiatives to adopt a servant leadership style?
- Which inclusive and democratic governance models fit well with CI?
- How can these inclusive and democratic governance models be made to work effectively in a Collective Impact initiative?
- How can business and government be more deeply engaged without marginalizing, while ensuring meaningful participation, those individuals and groups most directly affected by the issue?

The swift and widespread uptake of the CI framework as well as the emergent concern for the place of equity, inclusivity, and community engagement creates a unique space and opportunity for the role of community development. It is not useful to wholly and uncritically adopt the Collective Impact five conditions without infusing the insights, principles, and practices of community development.

Neither, though, is it wise to ignore the CI framework given its widespread use by diverse social change efforts. The overall challenge is to animate the principles of community development in CI initiatives even as the CI framework informs and strengthens development efforts.

New Directions for Collective Impact within Community Development

Each key informant was asked: How does Collective Impact need to evolve over the next five to ten years to remain vital and relevant to social change, especially on the community level? While equity, inclusivity and community engagement were highlighted by several along with suggested new directions for CI, there was a diversity of responses. These included the need to: broaden ownership of CI beyond the originators (FSG); continue deepening, building, and sharing practice; reconsider and possibly upgrade the five conditions of CI; increase the evidence base for CI and its five conditions; understand how funders can effectively play a backbone role that is not distorted because of their role as funders; address the misunderstanding and misapplication of Collective Impact; improve evaluation at the system and population levels; make CI more about its practice rather than its language; and demonstrate it works by consistently generating measurable results that show a correlational, if not causal, relationship to CI.

The research for this chapter identified three recent and new directions for CI as it relates to community development: Collective Impact Principles of Practice (Brady & Splansky Juster 2016); the Tenacious Change Approach (Klaus & Saunders 2016); and Collective Impact 3.0 (Cabaj & Weaver 2016). Each builds upon, extends, and illuminates aspects of the original five conditions of Collective Impact but also recognizes that the original five conditions alone are not sufficient for the future.

Furthermore, each acknowledges that CI has had an immense and, likely, lasting effect on the field of community development. The widespread adoption of the term and implementation of the framework, even without complete fidelity to that framework, has sufficiently changed the landscape for practitioners, researchers, funders, and communities as to become a permanent part of the scenery. Each of these new directions focuses on looking ahead to improving the theory and practice of Collective Impact.

Collective Impact Principles of Practice (Brady & Splansky Juster 2016)

The eight Collective Impact Principles of Practice outlined in Brady & Splansky Juster (2016) are solidly anchored in, and are to be implemented within, the original five conditions framework described in the 2011 CI paper. The principles emerged from observations of practitioners in the field, many of whom participate in the Collective Impact Forum.

The Collective Impact Principles of Practice were created from a growing recognition by FSG and partners "that while the five conditions Kania and Kramer initially identified are necessary, they are not sufficient to achieve impact at the population level" (Brady & Splansky Juster 2016: p. 1). The eight principles are:

- Design and implement the initiative with a priority placed on equity.
- Include community members in the collaborative.
- Recruit and co-create with cross sector partners.
- Use data to continuously learn, adapt, and improve.
- Cultivate leaders with unique system leadership skills.
- Focus on program and system strategies.
- Build a culture that fosters relationships, trust, and respect across participants.
- Customize for local context.

It should be apparent, even from these eight short headings, that the Collective Impact Principles of Practice (CI PoP) attempt to address gaps in the original approach and its implementation. The focus on equity (1), inclusion of community members (2), collaborative leadership cultivation (5), establishing trusting and respectful relationships (6), and local customization (8) should be especially welcome improvements to those with experience and expertise in community development.

As early adopters of the Collective Impact framework, the authors understood these CI PoP were implicit in the framework from the outset. However, they observed the phenomenon of widespread adoption, even institutionalization, of the original five conditions framework but without the more nuanced awareness and understanding of these principles by many implementers. This situation contributed to the insight offered by one key informant: "In the U.S. there is as much misapplication of the language, misrepresentation of the work as there is actual Collective Impact work going on." The CI PoP make explicit what was implicit in the original framework.

Those devoted and committed to the original five conditions will find this new direction especially appealing. It will allow them to remain fully faithful to the CI framework while engaging in the work of CI in a way that is more consistent with the Principles of Good Practice in community development (Community Development Society 2016). The Collective Impact Principles of Practice can also be viewed as a governance tool that guides a group into integrating the Five Conditions into the actual work of doing collective impact. The danger of the Collective Impact Principles of Practice is that they will be treated as a checklist, in much the same way that the five conditions have been treated as a formula (Klaus 2016[11]). Nonetheless, these eight principles are a welcome addition to the evolutionary process of CI0.

Tenacious Change Approach (Klaus & Saunders, 2016)

Like the Collective Impact Principles of Practice, the Tenacious Change Approach (TCA), remains faithful to the original five conditions of CI. Unlike the Collective Impact Principles of Practice, TCA situates and animates the five conditions within an overall community development approach. TCA operationalizes Klaus and Saunders' *Roots to Fruit of Sustainable Community Change* (R2F) research-based model. R2F is grounded in the hypothesis that community engagement guided by a high-performing infrastructure leads to sustainable community change which progresses through a measurable sequence.

In TCA and R2F, the "roots" refer to the establishment of a high-performing infrastructure that emphasizes community readiness, community participation, collaborative change leadership (via CI or another collaboration framework which animates the five conditions of Collective Impact), and continuous learning and improvement of the infrastructure. The "fruit" refers to community change that occurs as the infrastructure engages in the change work of community engagement and mobilization to action.

Change occurs in four *stages of community transition*. It progresses through *awareness raising and education* via community engagement to *legitimization* of the change initiative and its leadership. This leads to broad *transformation* within the community by leveraging increasing community support to enlist late adopters. *Normalization* occurs as the changes are adopted and become part of the fabric of the community. The stages of community transition can be monitored and measured using the Tenacious Change Assessment and Monitoring tool (TCAM) developed and tested by Klaus and Saunders (2016). The Tenacious Change Approach focuses on developing leadership and group competencies and capacity needed to establish the "roots" infrastructure and implement the tasks related to producing the "fruit" of community change.

TCA and R2F integrates the CI framework (Kania & Kramer 2011; Hanleybrown, Kania & Kramer 2012; Turner, Merchant, Kania, & Martin 2012) with several other salient models and ideas. These approaches include: a psychosocial model of community readiness (Chilenski, Geenberg, & Feinberg 2007); inclusive approaches to decision-making and governance (Buck & Villines 2007; Guo & Saxton 2010); complexity theory (Begun, Zimmerman, & Dooley 2003); diffusion of innovation theory (Rogers 2003); and Klaus and Saunders' (2016) original description of the stages of community transition.

The Tenacious Change Approach will appeal to those devoted and committed to a community development approach yet embrace the original Collective Impact five conditions. Because TCA prioritizes community participation early in the process of community change, it may take longer for a community initiative to build infrastructure and momentum toward change. The developers claim, however, that time invested early in creating community participation is well-spent. By establishing solid community participation, it can take less time to move through the stages of community transition and can create longer lasting support (sustainability) for the initiative (Klaus & Saunders 2016).

Collective Impact 3.0 (Cabaj & Weaver 2016)

The Collective Impact 3.0 framework is based in the original five conditions of Collective Impact, but offers a reframe "of the basic ideas and practices due to the limitations of the original framework, the insights of other frameworks, our own experience, and FSG's own work" (Cabaj & Weaver 2016: p. 3). Likening the original CI five conditions framework to a computer "operating system," they claim it is time for an upgrade—to Collective Impact 3.0.

The upgrade proposed starts with a paradigm shift, from seeing CI as a managerial paradigm to a movement–building paradigm. They acknowledge that the management approach can generate results but "in a movement-building approach, by contrast, the emphasis is on reforming (even transforming) systems where improvements alone will not make a difference" (Cabaj & Weaver 2016: p. 4). They propose:

- Upgrading continuous communication to include authentic community engagement. Authentic community engagement means "to put community at the centre of the change process (Cabaj & Weaver 2016: p. 5).
- Upgrading common agenda to include shared aspiration. Shared aspiration is more than a common agenda, "it requires would be collaborators to find (or create) common ground despite their very different styles, interests, and positions" (Cabaj & Weaver 2016: p. 6).
- Upgrading shared measurement to include strategic learning. This upgrade is based on the insight "that CI participants have more success with shared measurements if they treat them as one part of a larger system of learning and evaluation" (Cabaj & Weaver 2016: p. 7).
- Upgrading mutually reinforcing activities to include a focus on high-leverage and loose/tight working relationships. The upgrade would mean that participants in a CI initiative would have permission to work as closely or loosely as required by the community context allowing them to focus more on strategies that have greater leverage to facilitate change.
- Upgrading backbone support to include a container for change. The authors argue that Collective Impact 3.0 will require a "strong container," rather than a backbone, "for change that support participants to dig deep when tackling stubborn social challenges" (Cabaj & Weaver 2016: p. 11).

Collective Impact 3.0 will appeal to those who have come to feel the original CI five conditions, in both their framing and operationalization, are inadequate for the future and need a major overhaul. Collective Impact 3.0 significantly extends the original CI framework intact. Like the Collective Impact Principles of Practice and Tenacious Change Approach, it is an effort to bring the lessons learned from Collective Impact 2.0 forward and to more explicitly prioritize equity, inclusivity, and community engagement.

The choice of these new directions for any community development effort is dependent upon many factors. Community context is always key, as is the implementer's knowledge and understanding of the framework relative to the context. The implementer's familiarity and comfort with the ideology of the framework is also a factor. The capacity and skill to operationalize any of the frameworks is important as well. Finally, the parameters set by resources and funders' interests will further inform the choice. Regardless of which new direction is chosen, each represents important progress toward the alignment of the Collective Impact framework with the Principles of Good Practice in community development.

A New View: Collective Impact as Disruptive Illumination

It is time to return to the question that opened this chapter: How are we to now make sense of Collective Impact within the field of community development? The authors' effort to answer this question began in an email debate about whether CI is a disruptive innovation or business-as-usual. Those discussions triggered an exploration that included deeper conversation about experiences with CI, an examination of the scarce but growing body of literature, and interviews with key informants closely tied to Collective Impact.

The theory of disruptive innovation in the business world was introduced by Bower and Christensen (1995). Christensen, Baumann, Ruggles, and Sadtler (2006) later applied the theory to social change. They argued that social-sector problems, such as infant mortality, life expectancy, and mathematical literacy among students, were not effectively addressed in the United States because of "misdirected investment" when "too much of the money available to address social needs is used to maintain the status quo, because it is given to organizations that are wedded to their current solutions, delivery models, and recipients" (Christensen et al. 2006: p. 93). Though they may do well at serving the needs of a well-defined constituency, they will not likely reach larger and broader populations that are in need.

This is true even when the needs of that broader population could be effectively satisfied with "simpler offerings" (Christensen, et al. 2006: p. 96), if those were available. What is needed, they proposed, are disruptive innovations focused on social change at a national scale. Disruptive innovations, in this case, would be those initiatives that offered simpler, "good enough solutions to inadequately addressed social problems" that exceeded the status quo (Christensen et al. 2006: p. 96).

Alternatively, "business as usual" refers to the maintenance of the status quo which is continuing to address social problems by analyzing current constituents' and stakeholders' needs with the services and products that are typically used (Christensen et al. 2006). Organizations attempting social change doing "business as usual" are those that try to do so using current methods, models, and solutions. For example, Collective Impact might be seen by some as an attempt to provide new, simpler, "good enough" solutions that affect broader social change, even as it changes the field of community development, while others may see it as just a group of well-known and widely-used strategies, models, and solutions under a new name.

The current authors put this question to the key informants interviewed: Is Collective Impact a disruptive innovation or business as usual? Here are some of their responses:

- "It is meant to be a disrupter and transcend business as usual. That said, it can often be misapplied to reinforce status quo."
- It may be "evolution more than a revolution" from other forms of community change.
- "I think it is both. I think it is ending up as business as usual."
- "I think it is a disruptive innovation but I think the problem is that sometimes people think it has to be new to be innovative . . . The main difference about Collective Impact. . .is the emphasis on holding a cross–sector group of leaders accountable to a set of results in a way that they are collaborating collectively."
- "If it isn't results oriented, it is business as usual . . . It is a disruptive innovation to the point that it challenges people to face how their intervention, their work, connects to a result."

Clearly, there was no consensus among the group of interview participants on the question: Is Collective Impact a disruptive innovation or business as usual? However, one response did resonate with the authors findings:

> I don't think it is either. Clearly it is not business as usual. This structured approach to collaboration does not happen naturally. At the same time, I'm not sure it is a disruptive innovation because it was already happening in some places and it builds on decades of previous experience in community work. I say it is neither.

If it is neither, what, then, is it?

Conclusion

It is a "disruptive illumination" that has grabbed attention like a beacon and focused it anew on the quest to more clearly understand and practice effective social change and community development. Collective Impact has triggered more thorough examinations of assumptions that have guided community change efforts. This examination has generated blogs, dissertations, popular articles, research, and peer reviewed articles, such as those in this volume. The examination has affirmed, for some, the validity of their assumptions and the knowledge and experience that undergird them. For others, it has triggered deeper questioning and renewed efforts to improve current social change practice.

Some practitioners have concluded, upon closer examination, that the framing and implementation of Collective Impact should be rejected as business as usual. Those working in social change and community development have been compelled to join the examination and conversation because CI has become so widespread as to be inescapable. It is, therefore, clear that Collective Impact has changed the conversation about social change and community development. Will it ultimately change and improve practice? That is yet another question which will be better answered in the future.

Notes

1 Accessed December 26, 2017 at www.proquest.com
2 Accessed December 31, 2017 at http://collectiveimpactforum.org/blogs/100061/ten-places-where-collective-impact-gets-it-wrong
3 Accessed December 31, 2017 at http://collectiveimpactforum.org/blogs/51306/advancing-practice-collective-impact
4 Accessed December 31, 2017 at http://collectiveimpactforum.org/blogs/51306/advancing-practice-collective-impact
5 Accessed December 31, 2017 at http://nonprofitgp.com/2015/02/24/beyond-the-comfort-of-what-we-think-we-know
6 Accessed December 31, 2017 at www.fsg.org/blog/developing-collective-impact-framework
7 Accessed December 31, 2017 at http://collectiveimpactforum.org/blogs/77371/why-communities-color-are-getting-frustrated-collective-impact
8 Accessed December 31, 2017 at http://ctb.ku.edu/en
9 Accessed December 31, 2017 at http://nonprofitgp.com/2013/04/04/when-collective-impact-isnt-part-2-2
10 Accessed December 31, 2017 at www.comm-dev.org/latest/item/86-principles-of-good-practice
11 Accessed December 31, 2017 at http://nonprofitgp.com/2016/05/09/how-is-your-collaborative-posture

References

Begun, J. W., Zimmerman, B. J., & Dooley, K. (2003) Health care organizations as complex adaptive systems. In S. S. Mick & M. E. Wyttenbach (Eds.), *Advances in health care organization theory*, 253–288. San Francisco, Jossey-Bass.

Born, P., Harwood, R., Savner, S., Stewart, S., & Zanghi, M. (2014, Fall) Roundtable on community engagement and collective impact. *Stanford Social Innovation Review.* [Online] 12–14. Available from: www.ssireview.org

Bower, J. L. & Christensen, C. M. (1995) Disruptive technologies: Catching the wave. *Harvard Business Review*, 73 (1), 43–53.

Brady, S. & Splansky Juster, J. (2016) Collective impact principles of practice. [Online] Available from-http://collectiveimpactforum.org/resources/collective-impact-principles-practice [Accessed September 21, 2016].

Buck, J., & Villines, S. (2007) *We the people: Consenting to a deeper democracy*. Washington, Sociocracy.info.

Butterfoss, F. D. (2013) Ignite: Getting your community coalition "fired up" for change. Bloomington, AuthorHouse.

Cabaj, M. & Weaver, L. (2016) Collective impact 3.0: An evolving framework for community change. Tamarack Institute. Community Change Series 2016.

Chilenski, S. M., Greenberg, M. T., & Feinberg, M.E. (2007) Community readiness as a multidimensional construct. *Journal of Community Psychology*, 35 (3), 347–365.

Christens, B. D. & Inzeo, P. T. (2015) Widening the view: Situating collective impact among frameworks for community-led change. Community Development, 46 (4), 420–435. Available from: doi: 10.1080/15575330.2015.1061680

Christensen, C. M., Baumann, H., Ruggles, R., & Sadtler, T. M. (2006) Disruptive innovation for social change. *Harvard Business Review*, 93–101.

Community Development Society. (2016) *Principles of good practice*. [Online] Available from www.comm-dev.org. [Accessed September 19, 2016].

Cullen-Lester, K. L. & Yammarino, F. J. (2016) Collective and network approaches to leadership: Special issue introduction. *Leadership Quarterly*. [Online] 27 (2), 173–180. Available from: doi: 10.1016/j.leaqua.2016.02.001

Flood, J., Minkler, M., Lavery, S. H., Estrada, J., & Falbe, J. (2015) The collective impact model and its potential for health promotion: Overview and case study of a healthy retail initiative in San Francisco. *Health, Education, & Behavior*. [Online] 42 (5), 654–668. Available from: doi: 10.1177/1090198115577372

FSG (2016, November 29) *Developing the collective impact framework*. [Online] Available from: www.fsg.org

Gopal, S. & Schorr, L. B. (2016, June 2) Getting "Moneyball" right in the social sector. *Stanford Social Innovation Review*. [Online]. Available from: www.ssir.org

Guo, C., & Saxton, G. D. (2010) Voice-in, voice-out: Constituent participation and nonprofit advocacy. *Nonprofit Policy Forum*, 1 (1).

Hanleybrown, F., Kania, J. V., & Kramer, M. R. (2012) Channeling change: Making collective impact work. *Stanford Social Innovation Review*. [Online] 1–8. Available from: www.ssireview.org

Kania, J. V., & Kramer, M. R. (2011) Collective impact. *Stanford Social Innovation Review*. [Online] 36–41. Available from: www.ssireview.org

Kania, J. V. & Kramer, M. (2016, May 4) *Advancing the practice of collective impact*. [Online] Available from: www.collectiveimpactforum.org

Kania, J. V., Hanleybrown, F., & Splansky Juster, J. (2014, Fall) Essential mindset shifts for collective impact. *Stanford Social Innovation Review*. [Online] 2–5. Available from: www.ssireview.org

Kemmis, S. & McTaggart, R. (2005) Participatory action research. In N. K. Denzin & Y. S. Lincoln (eds.), *The Sage handbook of qualitative research* (3rd ed.). Thousand Oaks, Sage Publications.

Klaus, T. (2013, April 4) When collective impact isn't (part 2). [Online] Available from: www.nonprofitgp.com

Klaus, T. (2015, February 25) Beyond the comfort of what we think we know. [Online] Available from: www.nonprofitgp.com

Klaus, T. (2016, July 15) How's your collaborative posture? [Online] Available from: www.collectiveimpactforum.org

Klaus, T. W. & Saunders, E. (2016) Using collective impact in support of communitywide teen pregnancy prevention initiatives. *Community Development*, [Online] 47 (2), 241–258. Available from: doi: 10.1080/15575330.2015.1131172

Le, Vu. (2015, December 1) Why communities of color are getting frustrated with collective impact. [Online] Available from: www.collectiveimpactforum.org

McAfee, M., Glover Blackwell, A., & Bell, J. (2015) *Equity: The soul of collective impact*. PolicyLink.

Oxford Living Dictionaries. (2016) [Online] Available from: https://en.oxforddictionaries.com/definition/equity [Accessed September 20, 2016].

Patton, M. Q. (2002) *Qualitative research & evaluation methods* (3rd ed.). Thousand Oaks, CA, Sage Publications.

Pyrczak, F. (2013) Evaluating research in academic journals: A practical guide to realistic evaluation (6th ed.). Glendale, Pyrczak Publishing.

Raderstrong, J. & Boyea-Robinson, T. (2016) The why and how of working with communities through collective impact. *Community Development*, 42 (2), 181–193. Available from: doi: 10.1080/15575330.2015.1130072

Rogers, E. M. (2003) *Diffusion of innovations* (5th ed.). New York, The Free Press.

Schorr, L. B. (2016, January 8) Reconsidering evidence: What it means and how we use it. *Stanford Social Innovation Review*. [Online] Available from www.ssir.org

Shier, H. (2001) Pathways to participation: Openings, opportunities, and obligations. *Children & Society*, 15, 107–117. Available from: doi: 10.1002/CHI.617

Turner, S., Merchant, K., Kania, J., & Martin, E. (2012) Understanding the value of backbone organizations in collective impact. *Stanford Social Innovation Review*. [Online] 1–12. Available from: www.ssireview.org

Walzer, N., Weaver, L., & McGuire, C. (eds). (2016, May) Special issue: Collective impact. *Community Development*, 47 (2), London, Routledge, Taylor & Francis Group.

Wolff, T. (2016, May 4) Ten places where collective impact gets it wrong. Available from: www.collectiveimpactforum

Wolff, T., Minkler, M., Wolfe, S. M., Berkowitz, B., Bowen, L., Christens, B. D. Butterfoss, F. D. (2017, January 9) Collaborating for equity and justice: Moving beyond collective impact. *Nonprofit Quarterly*. Available from: https://nonprofitquarterly.org

INDEX

Italic page numbers indicate tables; bold indicate figures.

accountability, backbone organizations 62, 63, 66, 70
Affordable Care Act 82
agenda development: ARCHI 85–86; Center for Public Partnerships and Research 61; systems tools 82–86
Agranoff, R. 41
Ahearn, L.M. 50
Alberta, Energy Futures Lab 111
aligned activities, backbone support 58
alternatives, to CI 153
Ambassador Group, The Hive 19–20
ambiguity, tolerance for 61
American Recovery and Reinvestment Act 138
Ansell, C. 42
Arab society: cultural competence/adaptation 160; families 160; position of women and girls 160; public spaces 161; residential patterns 161; social structure 13; value systems 13; volunteerism 161, 168–170
ARCHI Playbook 91
Asael-Eyal, V. 165
ASPEN Institute 2, 112
Atlanta Regional Collaborative for Health Improvement (ARCHI) 8–9, 82–84; agenda development 85–86; application of RTH model 85–86; *ARCHI Playbook* 91; Atlanta Transformation Scenario 86–89; attracting new partners 90; background to 82–84; collaborative working 83–84; community health needs assessment (CHNA) 85; evaluation 95; executive trio 83–84; organizational champions 84summary and conclusions 95; use of ReThink Health model 81–82; *see also* Atlanta Transformation Scenario; systems tools
Atlanta Transformation Scenario 86–89; pathways to advantage 89; *see also* Atlanta Regional Collaborative for Health Improvement (ARCHI)
Atlantic Philanthropies 107
Australia, Logan Together 27

backbone organizations: accountability 62, 63, 66, 70; activities 157–158; challenges 13; commitment 59–60; Commit! Partnership 59; functions 7; funding mobilization 60; healthTIDE 11–12; hope 73; importance of 12; as key 6–7; leadership 72–73; leave it better rule 63, 64, 70; likeability 58–59; literature review 57–60; mindset 71–72, 72; resilience 71; roles of 4–5, 10, 12, 27, 37, 58; Rules of Engagement 61–65ff; shared measurement 59; shared struggles 71; six common activities 58; staffing 60; strategy 58; success factors 158–159; supporting aligned activities

58; and supranational organizations 27;
and systems tools 94; transformation
see Center for Public Partnerships and
Research; vision 58; working with the
willing 62–63, *64*, 70; workloads 147;
see also Center for Public Partnerships
and Research; healthTIDE
backbone support 10; flexibility 151–152;
obesity prevention 144–145; roles of
backbone staff **144**; upgrading 109–112
Bandura, A. 51
Best Place to Raise a Child 105–106, 128,
132
Better Together 12–13, 156, 162–163;
see also Israel study
Bhargava, R. 59–60
Bill and Melinda Gates Foundation 105
Birchfield. V. 19
Born, P. 97
Boumgarden, P. 107
Bower, J.L. 189
Brady, S. 185–186
Branch, J. 107
Bryant, A. 43
Bryk, A.S. 41
Burnie Works 33–34, 38
Butler, B. 159

Cabaj, M. 99, 125–126, 127, 182, 188–189
Caledon Institute of Social Policy 26,
123–124, 125
campus-community partnerships 117–118
Canada: community of practice 123;
energy 111; homelessness 107; poverty
reduction 102–103; *see also* Community
First: Impacts of Community
Engagement (CFICE) research project;
Canadian Centre for Policy Alternatives
(CCPA) 120
Canadian Living Wage Framework 120
Carleton University 117
Center for Evaluation Innovation 107
Center for Public Partnerships and
Research 7–8; agenda development 61;
assessment 61; backbone role 56–57;
critical self-evaluation 57; descriptive
statistics *66*; discussion 70–74; feedback
57; improvement needs 57; linguistics
inquiry and word count (LIWC) 68–69,
74; methodology 65; mode of
functioning 61; Pearson correlations *67*;
qualitative results 68–70; quantitative
results 65–68; Rules of Engagement
61–65ff; study limitations 74; summary

and conclusions 74; themes 61;
transformation 60ff
Centers for Disease Control and
Prevention (CDC) 81, 83, 138
Charmaz, K. 43
Child Friendly Leeds 32
Christensen, C.M. 189
*Collaborating with Business for Social
Transformation* 121
collaboration 41–42; CI as starting point
36; costs and benefits 124; dealing with
complex problems 43
*Collaboration on Policy: A Manual Developed
by the Community–Government
Collaboration on Policy* (Caledon Institute
of Social Policy) 123–124
collaborative leaders 42
collaborative working, ARCHI 83–84
Collective Impact: alternatives 153;
evaluation 15; growth of interest 2–3,
17; starting assumption 78–79;
understanding of 177–178; weaknesses
153
Collective Impact 3.0 9–10, 182, 188–189;
adapting CI paradigm 100–103;
authentic community engagement
103–104; containers for change
109–112; context and overview 97–98;
development from 2.0 *101*; evolution
100; evolving vision 98–99; high-
leverage activities 107–109; overview
99–100; shared aspiration 104–106;
strategic learning initiative 106–107;
summary and conclusions 112
Collective Impact Forum 98–99, 176,
177–178
"Collective Impact or Collective
Blindness" (Boumgarden and Branch)
107
Collective Impact Principles of Practice
98–99, 185–186
Collective Impact Summit 182
Commit! Partnership 59
common agenda 9, 125; healthTIDE
139–140, 151; obesity prevention
146–147; Poverty Reduction Hub
(PRH) 118; upgrading 104–106
community-campus engagement (CCE)
118
Community Coalition Action Theory 153
community development: future of CI 15;
making sense of CI 182–185
Community Development Society,
Principles of Good Practice 183–184

community engagement 157, 183–184; structuring for 19; three stage process 20
community environments, importance of 12–13
Community First: Impacts of Community Engagement (CFICE) research project: co-leadership 118; context and overview 116; five hubs 116; funding 117; hub structure **117**; and poverty reduction hub 116–120; research question 117
community health needs assessment (CHNA) 82; Atlanta Regional Collaborative for Health Improvement (ARCHI) 85
community members, position in hierarchy 18
community of practice, Canada 123
complexity, institutional 34–37
complex problems, approaches to 79
conditions for success 2, 57–58; upgrading 9–10
confidence-building, Israel study 166–167
Connor, J. 97, 104
consensus, reaching 9–10
Constant Comparative Analysis 44
Constructivist Grounded Theory research 42, 43–44
containers for change 109–112
continuous communication, healthTIDE 149
Cornish, M. 121
Corporate Social Responsibility (CSR) model 121
credibility, backbone organizations 59
Crepaz, M.M.L. 19
Cullen-Lester, K.L. 175
cultural adaptation 158–159; to Arab society in Israel 160; Israel study 164–171
cultural competence 158; to Arab society in Israel 160

data, backbone organizations 59
Disrupting System Dynamics: A Framework for Understanding Systemic Changes (The MarketShare Associates) 36
disruptive illumination 189–190
Dream Big 33
DVF formula 79, 82
Dweck, C. 71–72

Edmondson, J. 59
Eggers, S. 137

elite socialization 5, 26
encourage the heart 73
End Poverty Edmonton 101–102
Energy Futures Lab, Alberta 111
engagement: authentic and inclusive 9; scaffolding 49; structuring for 19; in systematic framework 8
equity: access and justice 52; and inclusivity 183–185
Essentials for Childhood program 30
Etmanski, A. 101
European Integration, functional spill over 24–25
European Union 27
evidence-based solutions 178

Formula for Change 79
Foundation Strategy Group (FSG) 139
FSG Consulting 2, 98–99, 177

Gash, A. 42
Georgia Health Policy Center 81
governance: collaborative and multi-level approach 5; multilevel 29–30, 37–38
Graces, M.L. 121
Grounded Theory 43

Haas, E.B. 23, 28
Hamilton, Ontario 10–11; living wage employers (LWE) 131–132; *see also* poverty reduction
Hamilton (Ontario) Roundtable for Poverty Reduction 105–106; case study 127ff; formation and aims 128
Hanleybrown, F. 22
healthTIDE 11–12; alignment 148–149; backbone staff performance effectiveness **145**; challenges of CI 152; champions/advisors 139; roles of backbone staff **144**; shared measurement 150, 152–153; stakeholder engagement 146–147, 148; *see also* obesity prevention
Hecht, B. 59
Heifetz, R.A. 79
Hilltop Market Garden 33
Himmelman, A.T. 18
HIV 105
Hooker, D. 84
Housing First philosophy 107
Human Centered Design 20
Human Resources and Skills Development Canada (HRSDC) 26

Inner West CI 22–23
intergovernmentalism *see* liberal intergovernmentalism;
intermediary agencies *see* backbone organizations;
Israel study 12–13; families in Arab society 160; literature review 157; methodology 162; public spaces 170–171; recruiting men 165–166; recruiting teenage girls 165, 166–167; residential patterns and public spaces 161; volunteerism 161, 168–170
Ivanova, I. 120–122

JDC-Ashalim 162
justice, equity and access 52
Jutte, D.P. 95
J.W. McConnell Family Foundation 26

Kania, J. 1, 2, 5, 13, 14, 17, 18, 21, 22, 78, 93, 97, 103, 104, 109, 141, 157, 176, 177–178, 179, 186
Kemmis, S. 179
Klaus, T.W. 187
Klein, S. 120–122
Klenke, K. 43
Kouzes, J. 73
Kramer, M. 1, 2, 5, 13, 14, 17, 18, 21, 22, 78, 93, 97, 103, 104, 109, 141, 157, 176, 177–178, 179, 186

Langdale Industries 85
leadership: adaptive 159; backbone organizations 72–73; continuity 1
leadership paradigm 100
Lee, Y. 43
Le, V. 180, 183–184
liberal intergovernmentalism 5, 20–22, 38; applications 22; Inner West CI 22–23
Linsky, M. 79
Locke, J. 31
Loewen, G. 121
Logan Together 27

McChrystal, S. 71
McGuire, M. 41
McTaggart, R. 179
making sense of CI: action research 179–180; Collective Impact Principles of Practice 185–186; community development 182–185; disruptive illumination 189–190; equity and inclusivity 183–185; methods 175; new directions 185;

phases of CI 182; position of CI 180; progress of CI 181–182; progress towards understanding 180–182; purpose of CI 179–180; Tenacious Change Approach (TCA) 187;
management paradigm 100–102
mindset, backbone organizations 71–72, *72*
Mintzberg, H. 45
Modeling Expert Panel Meeting: A Collaborative Think Session 81
Moravcsik, A. 20
Mt Druitt 19–20
multiorganizational networks 41, 46
mutually reinforcing activities 91–95, 134; healthTIDE 147–149, 152; upgrading 107–109

Neofunctionalism 5, 23–24, 28, 38
Network Agreements (NA) 6, 41, 42–43, 44–45; co-designing 45–46; multiorganizational networks 46
networked individualism 47
network engagement lifecycle 48–49
Network Leaders (NL) 6, 42–43, 45; behavior modeling 49; fostering supportive environments 48; honest engagement 48–49; honoring expertise and experience 50; as informed connectors 47; one among many 52; skills 46
Network Members (NM) 42–43, 45; advisory role 46; expertise and experience 50; fostering supportive environments 48; honest engagement 48–49
networks: community-minded decisions 51–52; Constructivist Grounded Theory research 43–44; New Democratic Party (NDP) 130

organizational champions, ARCHI 84
Ostrom, E. 84
output legitimacy 32

Parkhurst, M. 11, 125–126, 132–133
Pathways for Change: Ten Theories to Inform Advocacy and Policy Change Efforts (Stachowiak) 122–123
Patton, M.Q. 179
Pea, R.D. 49
Pei, N. 122, 129
Pittman, K. 99
Popp, J. 42
Posner, B. 73

Poverty Matrix 118–119
poverty reduction 10–11; Canada
102–103; case study 128–135; case study
analysis 132–133, *133*; CI and policy
change 129–131; complexity 125;
Hamilton (Ontario) Roundtable for
Poverty Reduction 105–106, 127ff;
and ideology 125; key concepts 118;
methodology 127–128;
recommendations 134; summary and
conclusions 133–135; Waterloo
(Ontario) 108; *see also* Community First:
Impacts of Community Engagement
(CFICE) research project
Poverty Reduction Hub (PRH) 10–11,
116–120; calls for proposals 119–120;
common agenda 118; shared
measurement 118
Preskill, H. 11, 125–126, 132–133
Provan, K.G. 41
public spaces: Arab society 161; Israel study
170–171

Queensland 27

Raine, L. 47
Rasner, N. 166
Regional Economics Model (REMI)
79
residential patterns, Arab society 161
ReThink Health Initiative 84
ReThink Health model 79; application of
85–86; calibration 85; system dynamics
model 81–82
Richmond, B. 80
Roots to Fruit of Sustainable Community
Change (R2F) 187
Routhieaux, R.L. 51
Rowlands, J. 51
Rules of Engagement 57; backbone
organizations 61–65ff

Sanders, B. 130
Santo, R. 49
Saunders, E. 187
Schimmelfennig, F. 20
Schuchter, J. 95
Senge, P. 110
shared measurement 59, 118, 125–126;
backbone organizations 59; developing
system for **126**; healthTIDE 150,
152–153; practices 12; and systems tools
94–95; upgrading 10, 106
Shared Measurement (Cabaj) 99

Shemer, O. 165
Smismans, S. 31
social extrapreneurship 47
Social Network Analysis 27, 37
social structure, Arab society 13
Spectator 105
Splansky Juster, J. 185–186
Stachowiak, S. 122–123
staffing, backbone organizations 60
Stone, R. 159
Stott, N. 47
Strive Cincinnati 101
Struggle Street 19
success: four components for 28;
pre-conditions for 2; structures for
18–19
systems thinking: outcome evaluation 80;
principles 80–81
systems tools: agenda development 82–86;
application beyond shared agenda
90–91; attracting new partners 90;
and backbone organizations 94; and
continuous communication 93–94;
mutually reinforcing activities 91–95;
process framework 81; progress
evaluation 93–94; progress map **93**;
and shared measurement 94–95; value
and effort 80; *see also* Atlanta Regional
Collaborative for Health Improvement
(ARCHI)

Tamarack Institute 2, 26, 28, 99–100, 139,
182
Tasmania, Burnie Works 33–34
Team of Teams (McChrystal) 71
Tenacious Change Approach (TCA) 187
Tenderloin Healthy Corner Store
Coalition 151
The Hive 19–20
The MarketShare Associates 36
theoretical foundations 5–6; Burnie
Works 33–34, 38; Child Friendly Leeds
32; context and overview 17–18;
Dream Big 33; elite socialization 5,
26–27; Essentials for Childhood
program 30; Hilltop Market Garden 33;
The Hive Mt Druitt 19–20; Inner West
CI 22–23; institutional complexity
34–37; legitimacy 31–34, 38; liberal
intergovernmentalism 5, 20–22, 38;
multilevel governance 29–30, 37–38;
neofunctionalism 5, 23–24, 28, 38;
six-step framework 36; spill over
hypothesis 24–26, 28; structures for

success 18–19; Vibrant Communities Canada 10–11, 24, 25–26, 38
Three I's 59
Toyota 106
Tracey, P. 47
Turner, S. 58, 60, 157, 158

University of Kansas *see* Center for Public Partnerships and Research

Vibrant Communities Canada 10–11, 24, 25–26, 38, 117–118, 125–126; *see also* Community First: Impacts of Community Engagement (CFICE) research project
volunteerism, Arab society 13, 161, 168–170

Waterloo (Ontario), poverty reduction 108

Weaver, L. 125, 188–189
welfare dependence model 18–19
Wellman, B. 47
White, R.G. 121
Wisconsin 11–12; *see also* obesity prevention
Wisconsin Department of Health Services (DHS) 138
Wisconsin Obesity Prevention Initiative 139
Wisconsin Partnership Program 11–12
Wolff, T. 52, 98, 141, 153, 157, 176, 178, 180

Yammarino, F.J. 175
Young, A. 84
YoungStar 141

Zeira, A. 166
Zimmerman, B. 109